The MIT Press Series in Artificial Intelligence
Patrick Henry Winston and J. Michael Brady, founding editors. J. Michael Brady, Daniel G. Bobrow, and Randall Davis, current editors.

Artificial Intelligence: An MIT Perspective, Volume I: Expert Problem Solving, Natural Language Understanding, Intelligent Computer Coaches, Representation and Learning, edited by Patrick Henry Winston and Richard Henry Brown, 1979

Artificial Intelligence: An MIT Perspective, Volume II: Understanding Vision, Manipulation, Computer Design, Symbol Manipulation, edited by Patrick Henry Winston and Richard Henry Brown, 1979

NETL: A System for Representing and Using Real-World Knowledge, Scott Fahlman, 1979

The Interpretation of Visual Motion, by Shimon Ullman, 1979

A Theory of Syntactic Recognition for Natural Language, Mitchell P. Marcus, 1980

Turtle Geometry: The Computer as a Medium for Exploring Mathematics, Harold Abelson and Andrea di Sessa, 1981

From Images to Surfaces: A Computational Study of the Human Visual System, William Eric Leifur Grimson, 1981

Robot Manipulators: Mathematics, Programming, and Control, Richard P. Paul, 1981

Computational Models of Discourse, edited by Michael Brady and Robert C. Berwick, 1982

Robot Motion: Planning and Control, edited by Michael Brady, John M. Hollerbach, Timothy Johnson, Tomás Lozano-Pérez, and Matthew T. Mason, 1982

In-Depth Understanding: A Computer Model of Integrated Processing for Narrative Comprehension, Michael G. Dyer, 1983

Robotic Research: The First International Symposium, edited by Hideo Hanafusa and Hirochika Inoue, 1985

Robot Hands and the Mechanics of Manipulation, Matthew T. Mason and J. Kenneth Salisbury, Jr., 1985

The Acquisition of Syntactic Knowledge, Robert C. Berwick, 1985

The Connection Machine, W. Daniel Hillis, 1985

Legged Robots that Balance, Marc H. Raibert, 1986

Robotics Research: The Third International Symposium, edited by O.D. Faugeras and Georges Giralt, 1986

Machine Interpretation of Line Drawings, Kokichi Sugihara, 1986

ACTORS: A Model of Concurrent Computation in Distributed Systems, Gul A. Agha, 1986

Knowledge-Based Tutoring: The GUIDON Program, William Clancey, 1987

AI in the 1980s and Beyond: An MIT Survey, edited by W. Eric L. Grimson and Ramesh S. Patil, 1987

Visual Reconstruction, Andrew Blake and Andrew Zisserman, 1987

Reasoning about Change: Time and Causation from the Standpoint of Artificial Intelligence, Yoav Shoham, 1988

Model-Based Control of a Robot Manipulator, Chae H. An, Christopher G. Atkeson, and John M. Hollerbach, 1988

A Robot Ping-Pong Player: Experiment in Real-Time Intelligent Control, Russell L. Andersson, 1988

Robotics Research: The Fourth International Symposium, edited by Robert C. Bolles and Bernard Roth, 1988

The Paralation Model: Architecture-Independent Parallel Programming, Gary Sabot, 1988

Concurrent System for Knowledge Processing: An Actor Perspective, edited by Carl Hewitt and Gul Agha, 1989

Automated Deduction in Nonclassical Logics: Efficient Matrix Proof Methods for Modal and Intuitionistic Logics, Lincoln Wallen, 1989

3D Model Recognition from Stereoscopic Cues, edited by John E.W. Mayhew and John P. Frisby, 1989

Shape from Shading, edited by Berthold K.P. Horn and Michael J. Brooks, 1989

Ontic: A Knowledge Representation System for Mathematics, David A. McAllester, 1989

Solid Shape, Jan J. Koenderink, 1990

Expert Systems: Human Issues, edited by Dianne Berry and Anna Hart, 1990

Concurrent Systems for Artificial Intelligence: The Actor Perspective, edited by Gul Agha and Carl Hewitt, 1990

Artificial Intelligence: Concepts and Applications, edited by A.R. Mirzai, 1990

Robotics Research: The Fifth International Symposium, edited by Hirofumi Miura and Suguru Arimoto, 1990

Theories of Comparative Analysis, Daniel S. Weld, 1990

Artificial Intelligence at MIT: Expanding Frontiers, Patrick Henry Winston, 1990

EXPERT SYSTEMS: HUMAN ISSUES

edited by Dianne Berry
and Anna Hart

THE MIT PRESS

CAMBRIDGE, MASSACHUSETTS

First MIT Press edition, 1990

Printed and bound in Great Britain
First published in Great Britain 1990 by Chapman and Hall Ltd

Library of Congress Cataloguing-in-Publication Data
Expert systems: human issues/edited by Dianne Berry and Anna Hart.
—1st MIT Press ed.
    p.   cm.—(MIT Press series in artificial intelligence)
    Includes bibliographical references.
    ISBN 0-262-02307-5
        1. Expert systems (Computer science)   2. Human-computer interaction.
I. Berry, Dianne. II. Hart, Anna. III. Series.
QA76.76.E95E9764   1990   89-64289
006.3'3—dc20   CIP

Contents

Contents

Series Foreword

Artificial intelligence is the study of intelligence using the ideas and methods of computation. Unfortunately a definition of intelligence seems impossible at the moment because intelligence appears to be an amalgam of so many information-processing and information-representation abilities.

Of course psychology, philosophy, linguistics, and related disciplines offer various perspectives and methodologies for studying intelligence. For the most part, however, the theories proposed in these fields are too incomplete and too vague stated to be realized in computational terms. Something more is needed, even though valuable ideas, relationships, and constraints can be gleaned from traditional studies of what are, after all, impressive existence proofs that intelligence is in fact possible.

Artificial intelligence offers a new perspective and a new methodology. Its central goal is to make computers intelligent, both to make them more useful and to understand the principles that make intelligence possible. That intelligent computers will be extremely useful is obvious. The more profound point is that artificial intelligence aims to understand intelligence using the ideas and methods of computation, thus offering a radically new and different basis for theory formation. Most of the people doing work in artificial intelligence believe that these theories will apply to any intelligent information processor, whether biological or solid state.

There are side effects that deserve attention, too. Any program that will successfully model even a small part of intelligence will be inherently massive and complex. Consequently artificial intelligence continually confronts the limits of computer-science technology. The problems encountered have been hard enough and interesting enough to seduce artificial intelligence people into working on them with enthusiasm. It is natural, then, that there has been a steady flow of ideas from artificial intelligence to computer science, and the flow shows no sign of abating.

The purpose of this series in artificial intelligence is to provide people in many areas, both professional and students, with timely, detailed information about what is happening on the frontiers in research centers all over the world.

J. Michael Brady
Daniel G. Bobrow
Randall Davis

Preface

Despite almost two decades of intensive research and development there are still relatively few expert systems in working practice. Various different types of reasons have been put forward for this (e.g., Coombs, 1984), but the majority seem to be concerned with what could be loosely termed 'human issues'. The purpose of this book is to identify and address some of these key issues.

Early research in the expert systems area was very technology-oriented. It was largely concerned with formulating new knowledge representations, together with implementing more sophisticated reasoning strategies. In recent years, however, there has been a shift in emphasis. The failure of many purportedly working systems to gain acceptance has led a number of researchers and practitioners to question their current assumptions and practices. The result is that, in some areas at least, research is starting to become more people-oriented.

Although this can be considered to be a great advance, problems still remain. One of the foremost is that many people are uncertain how to proceed. They acknowledge the importance of crucial human issues but do not really know what to do about them. For example, many developers now realize the necessity of talking to users. Unfortunately, they are less clear about what questions they should be asking and how the information gained should be incorporated into the development process. The problem is even more serious when one wants to consider not only the direct effects of systems on individual users but also the indirect effects on other levels of personnel within a particular organization.

These concerns and others gave rise to a conference on the 'Human and Organizational Issues of Expert Systems' which was held in Stratford-upon-Avon in May 1988. At this conference several papers described common issues and there was a variety of proposed approaches and beliefs. It was felt that many of the recurring issues were important enough to warrant their being made available to a wider audience. Selected speakers from that conference were therefore asked to write chapters for this book. Their brief was to relate their experience and code of practice to key human issues in relation to expert systems. In line with the conference, the book is intended to be a forum for discussion, and many of the authors disagree as to how problems should be tackled. There is, however, a consistent theme of concern over the fundamental issues. The chapters are written from various different perspectives and the authors include computer scientists, psychologists, researchers, and practitioners.

The chapters have been grouped into four sections. Section One aims to identify some of the key issues by the use of case studies. Although all three chapters in this section describe projects in the medical domain, the majority of issues raised apply equally well to other domains. Medicine was chosen not only because it is familiar to most readers but because it actually highlights many of the significant issues.

A common misconception is that in order to address important human issues, both research and practice will inevitably become less rigorous. This does not necessarily have to be the case. One way to ensure rigor is the development of clear methodologies. A methodology provides a framework within which the development process can take place. It describes the stages that are required, prescribing what needs to be done and how. The three chapters in Section Two describe quite different approaches to the problem of deciding which methodology or method to apply. They are presented in this way so that the reader can compare and contrast the theories which have evolved out of practical experience of building systems and helping organizations to start knowledge-based system (KBS) development.

Section Three is concerned with the ways in which people and computers interact. Given that computers are not as yet able to understand people reliably and efficiently, it is necessary to develop appropriate forms of interaction that can be easily learned and used by people. The three chapters in this section provide different perspectives on the ways in which a mixture of text and graphics can provide an effective means of communication with users. They describe the relative merits of different representations and also identify possible ways forward for the development of effective interfaces.

The final section looks at some of the wider issues associated with the introduction of knowledge-based systems. It is concerned with the implications of systems for both individuals and organizations. The paucity of working systems and the consequent limited experience of the use of such systems mean that some of the issues are difficult to describe or predict. Few organizations have had long-term experience of the effects of using KBS, and the effects on society and the status of 'knowledge' are almost impossible to imagine. However, there are certain very clear issues associated with the role of a system and the responsibility of the people associated with it. Furthermore, some of the very large projects are now bringing to light issues which are fundamental and pervasive. This section therefore sets the scene for wider discussion of the implications of the technology being produced.

It should be noted that the allocation of chapters to sections involved a degree of arbitrariness: issues necessarily emerged in each of the chapters, as did proposed methods. However, the chapters have been ordered and grouped to provide a coherent book rather than a collection of individual papers. Although each chapter is self-contained, the introductions to the sections identify recurring themes and points of agreement and disagreement between authors.

This book would not have been possible without the efforts of many people. First of all we would like to thank the authors for their cooperation, hard work, and for incorporating our editorial comments. We are particularly grateful for the way in which they met the deadlines which were so necessary in this project. Thanks are also due to International Computers Limited (ICL) and the Ergonomics Society for sponsoring the original conference and to Sue Ottley for organizing it. We are grateful to Charlie Portman, Nigel Shadbolt, and Murray Sinclair for their thorough and professional refereeing. Finally, we owe a special thank you to Tony Gillie for helping to transform a collection of disks, in various formats, into a final coherent manuscript.

REFERENCES

Coombs, M. J. (ed.) (1984). *Developments in Expert Systems.* Academic Press, London.

Chapter 1

Expert Systems in Perspective

Anna Hart and Dianne Berry

INTRODUCTION

Since the early, almost euphoric, acclaim of expert systems there have been many changes in the approaches to system design. The objective of representing knowledge – in contrast to information – on a computer has proved to be a challenge. There has been severe criticism of some of the tenets of AI by those who claim that knowledge by its very nature is not amenable to representation on a computer (Winograd and Flores, 1986). Others have argued that expert systems can be no more than 'competent' (Dreyfus and Dreyfus, 1986). Thus early misconceptions about the ease with which powerful and knowledgeable systems could be built for use by relative novices have given way to concern about the real problems of knowledge elicitation, knowledge modelling and system design. People are now much more aware of the importance of getting users actively involved in specification, design and evaluation of systems, of the need to view expert systems as components of larger computer systems and of the crucial need to consider social and ethical issues. It is now being more generally recognized that knowledge engineering should be seen as a modelling and design activity within a system life cycle, rather than as the extraction and codification of 'bits of knowledge'. (Kidd, 1987; Hart, 1989).

It is interesting, and almost curious, to note the similarity between this development and that of information systems. Very similar mistakes were made with the latter, concerning the importance of user involvement, the relevance of effective interfaces, and the ways in which technology introduction was managed. Many expert-system projects have re-invented mistakes of the 1960s. There are also some new issues associated with expert systems owing to the crucial ways in which they differ from information systems. Software engineering has many good principles to offer knowledge engineering, but questions about the nature of knowledge and how it can best be shared or communicated pervade many other disciplines. Tackling such questions requires a merging of disciplines with technologists working together with social scientists and psychologists.

11

DIFFERENCES BETWEEN EXPERT SYSTEMS AND INFORMATION SYSTEMS

It is difficult, and not really helpful, to define an 'expert system'. We are moving into an era where complex decision-support systems are being built using a variety of techniques. Indeed within this text several authors allude to the fact that they refrained from describing their systems as 'expert' owing to the misconceptions this might engender. Nevertheless, in order to be able to distinguish between those methods from software engineering that are applicable to expert systems and those areas where new issues arise, it is beneficial to make some comparisons between expert systems and more traditional information systems.

Sometimes it is a 'new way of programming' which is the key factor. Problems have been solved which could in theory have been tackled by a more conventional method but which in practice would have proved intractable. In many other instances, however, it is the very problems and domains of application which are different. The nature of 'information' (or knowledge) processed by expert systems is qualitatively different. This is exemplified by the systems described in this book. Preece (Chapter 2) describes a system for use by nurses when discharging elderly patients from a hospital; Wyatt and Emerson (Chapter 4) are concerned with nurses screening patients for heart attacks; the objective of Jagodzinski, Holmes and Dennis (Chapter 3) is to assist social workers in the delicate job of detecting cases of child abuse; Hayball and Barlow (Chapter 5) address the problem of design in a manufacturing industry; and Taylor, Hardy and Weaver (Chapter 11) consider the problem of the administration of a complex system of legislation within an equally complex organization. In each of these cases much of the information is sensitive and impossible to define precisely.

Expert systems are in general less well defined than information systems, and their role is less precise. They are 'open' and need to be able to respond to changing environments, they handle incomplete and imprecise information, they cannot be fully tested and it is difficult to define exactly how they behave even after they have been built. In many instances the users of expert systems are professional people who are used to making important decisions on the basis of incomplete or imprecise information. The systems are often intended for judgmental tasks which are central to professional jobs.

INVOLVING THE USERS

Despite their apparent success in the laboratory, many early systems were not successful in practice. It seems likely that an insufficient awareness of user needs and requirements has contributed to this failure. As Kidd (1987) points out, the user is an active agent in the problem-solving process. She suggests that analysis of certain key aspects of prospective users should be a critical part of knowledge acquisition. It is clear that the knowledge-acquisition process should include identification of the different classes of users likely to use a system, an analysis of their requirements, and an analysis of the types of knowledge which they bring to bear on a problem.

There are various levels of involvement for users at different stages of development. During a feasibility study a large number of users can be consulted, whereas the number that can be involved in later stages is likely to be smaller. This does not mean that those who are involved will not need a strong commitment in terms of both effort and time. Such involvement can take various forms. Users might actually be part of the design team, working closely with knowledge engineers. They might be involved in knowledge-elicitation sessions with the experts, particularly if simulation exercises (Shpilberg, Graham and Schatz, 1986) or 'Wizard of Oz' techniques are used. They might be asked to comment on working versions of systems, or to comment on progress reports at strategic check points in the development. Involving users will not necessarily guarantee success since deciding which users to involve is far from trivial. One user is unlikely to be representative of a large group of users, and the user community may comprise several disparate groups. User involvement can also slow down the development process.

A fundamental problem inherent in any computer-system design process is that users seldom know what they want from a system. It is therefore almost impossible to get complete specifications at the start of projects. Users cannot assess the relative merits of system specifications from descriptions on paper; it is hard for them to evaluate the technology away from that technology. It is far easier to criticize a working version of a program than to describe how it should behave. All too frequently users realize what they actually need when they see, but do not like, the implementation of a specification which they had previously approved. This problem is exacerbated for expert systems. The operation of an expert system is almost impossible to describe on paper. Knowledge is used in a context to solve a problem, and it is in such a context that people can assess the merits of a system. Furthermore, developers cannot always predict how a particular knowledge representation or inference method will actually behave. For these reasons, the development of systems is often experimental. Designers try out models, users comment on them, and it is hoped that eventually an acceptable model will emerge.

Edmonds, Candy, Slatter and Lunn (Chapter 6) discuss such problems and advocate taking special note of the problems experienced by users. In common with many systems designers, they recommend that prototyping should be used as a method of eliciting user requirements; in particular, they advise that the interface should be prototyped first. That is, the designers and users should discuss requirements in the context of a prototype interface before the knowledge base is actually constructed. This may involve some simulation and talk-through by the designers, but the rationale is that the style of interaction has implications for the design of the knowledge base. It is well known that a knowledge base designed for one mode of consultation cannot easily be modified to cater for a different mode (Clancey, 1983).

METHODS OF SYSTEM DEVELOPMENT

Unfortunately an experimental approach to system design can result in coding which is badly structured and difficult to understand. Such coding is notoriously difficult to amend. Systems cannot be regarded as 'finished' even when they go into routine use: they will need to be maintained and modified. This is true for traditional systems, and given the changing nature of the domains in which expert systems are used, the need will certainly be no less significant. Prototyping in itself does not preclude the production of structured and maintainable systems, but an undisciplined approach to prototyping almost certainly will. There are different approaches to prototyping and people disagree about what to prototype and when. Some even dispute the need for prototyping and advocate a more conventional approach to system development.

Traditional software engineering relies on the production of a rigorous and complete system specification. Experience has shown that the earlier in the system life cycle a mistake is detected the easier it is to correct. The classical model is that of a waterfall as proposed by Somerville and outlined by Diaper in Chapter 12. The idea is that the design team concentrate their efforts on getting mistakes ironed out during the specification and design stages before coding starts. Diaper advocates that this ideal should also be sought in expert-system development. He believes that methods of analysis such as task analysis can be used to effect suitable system specifications which can be understood and agreed by the relevant parties.

The KADS methodology is less traditional than Diaper's proposed method, but still akin to software engineering. It specifically aims to build usability and maintainability into the design process, and to that end identifies a number of stages and techniques which can be used. It explicitly regards development as part of a system life cycle. There is a strong emphasis on analysis rather than implementation. Hayball and Barlow use the KADS methodology in their application.

A more general and theoretical analysis of methodologies for expert systems is given by Colbert, Long and Green (Chapter 7). They have worked on methods of developing expert systems for particular organizations, namely Research Associations. They provide a way of specifying methods by identifying features and values, and describe the effect of certain constraints and features in specific situations. Their work is of value to those who wish to specify their own method for system development.

There is a growing concern for quality assurance in expert-system development. As mentioned above an undisciplined approach to system using prototyping, or indeed any other method, can result in systems which are not open to auditing or to maintenance. Several companies and government bodies are establishing working parties to set up guidelines for assuring quality in expert-system development.(eg see Montgomery, 1989). Typically such guidelines attempt to constrain the development process by ensuring adequate documentation and control of change. They recommend the use of checklists for use in the various stages of development. They will, for example, encourage the design team to ask questions like 'have we checked this with the users?' or 'are the reasons for this change adequately documented?' These checks are explicitly built into the define-construct-evaluate cycle of prototyping.

DEFINING ACCEPTABILITY

Evaluation of a prototype or system requires a set of evaluation criteria. These are often not easy to draw up. They will include the functionality of the system – that is, what it actually does. Given a rigorous specification it is possible to use formal methods to produce a system which meets that specification. This does not, however, ensure the acceptability of the specification to the users, nor does it ensure that the system will be of benefit to the organization in which it functions. Preece identifies four types of acceptability criteria, namely technical, ergonomic, organizational and ethical. These recur throughout the chapters in this book.

In some respects the first of these categories is the easiest. It is possible to check for consistency in rules, for circular arguments, for redundancy or duplication and to trace a system as it runs. It is relatively easy to run a set of test cases through a system and check that the advice is 'adequate'. Experts can also validate the content of knowledge structures. In this context it is possible to use some of the metrics from software engineering which measure such features as efficiency, security and flexibility (Watts, 1987). It is, however, impossible to test complex systems completely. The number of possible routes through a program will generally be extremely large and not open to exhaustive testing. Furthermore systems can be sensitive to very small changes in parameters (Pearl, 1988).

15

Ergonomic issues are being addressed to an increasing extent. In recent years systems have progressed from the early rigid system-driven dialogues. Many designers now respect the part played by users and acknowledge the need for flexible interactions. There has also been a move away from textual input and output to graphical displays. The amount of information which can be conveyed graphically is generally far greater than that by words. The maxim 'a picture can speak a thousand words' is very pertinent here. At the same time, however, it is necessary to bear in mind a need for effective representation. A screen which is cluttered with messy diagrams is not easy to assimilate even if it contains important information.

The work on conceptual graphs by John Sowa (1984) has had a great influence on system development. For example, Kuczora and Ecklund (Chapter 10) have made use of such representations in two knowledge-engineering tools which they describe. Dodson (Chapter 8) is also very enthusiastic about the use of diagrams. He describes their use in various tools, and argues the case for research into the effectiveness of different techniques. Diagrams are not the sole means of communication. Natural language, or some subset of it, will almost certainly be used. Despite severe problems encountered in natural language research, there have been advances. Hanne and Hoepelman (Chapter 9) discuss several types of human–machine communication including natural language, and put forward the relative merits of the different methods. They are particularly interested in mixed modes of interaction, allowing users to point at objects on a screen.

An appreciation of the power of individual displays is not in itself sufficient. Designing an effective interaction requires an understanding of what information is needed, and how and when it should be displayed. Confining research to the more superficial aspects of the human–computer interface will mean that systems are likely to address the wrong problems in more and more sophisticated ways. In terms of explanation, for example, endless restructuring of rule-trace explanations will not result in improved human–computer interaction if the explanations do not actually provide answers to the types of questions that users would like to ask.

Organizational issues are rather more difficult to address. They are unlikely to be clear at the start of a project, but if they are not given due consideration the resulting system is likely to be unacceptable to the organization. It is not unusual for the designers to discover organizational issues well into a project. For example, in Chapter 11 Taylor *et al* relate how their initial ideas for the DHSS system were shown to be naive after they had gone into extensive analysis of the organization. Organizations are very complex entities made up of a number of individuals and departments. They are dynamic and changing, and therefore very difficult to model. It can take some time for a design team to gain an adequate understanding of such a complex organization and how the introduction of technology might affect it. Taylor *et al* point out that decision-making within an organization involves many agents and different types of knowledge. They warn that valuable lessons from the design of decision-support systems have not always been taken on board, and argue for a systemic approach.

Even given sophisticated modelling techniques it is improbable that the true effects of the use of an expert system can be anticipated before the system has been used for some time. This calls for field trials and system monitoring after systems have been put into routine operation. To date there have been few reports of formal trials within organizations.

Few ethical issues have been addressed. In sensitive domains the role of a system needs to be understood and approved by the appropriate ethical committees. Currently there is disagreement about the acceptability of some systems. Authors in this book describe adverse reactions from those who believe their domains to be inherently unsuitable for expert systems. Professional societies, including those for computer specialists, have been slow to incorporate relevant guidelines into their codes of practice.

Once systems have been approved and put into routine use, issues of responsibility become important. Systems are not perfect and they are likely to give poor advice at some time. Who is responsible for the consequences of users accepting this advice? The legal profession has a natural inertia and has not really tackled this question. We cannot evade the problem by ignoring the technology. It is conceivable that one could be negligent for not consulting a system if it were available. There is a need for professions to consider these issues and to produce appropriate guidelines.

In Chapter 13 Hollnagel argues that we cannot afford to wait until all these problems have been solved, and points out that we are ready to accept other types of technology which are also inherently untestable. We are growing accustomed to chemical plants and nuclear reactors. Hollnagel discusses responsibility issues and suggests that expert systems should carry a 'danger warning'. Unfortunately it is difficult to envisage how this could be done so that users would not simply disregard it. Clearly there is a general need for education about the capabilities and limitations of the technology.

CONCLUSION

We now have a very powerful technology. It is apparent, however, that technological advances must be accompanied by a consideration of human and organizational issues. There is a growing consensus about the nature of some of these issues, but there is less agreement about how they can best be tackled. The chapters which follow constitute a representative selection of genuine attempts to elucidate and tackle some of these issues.

17

REFERENCES

Clancey, W.J. (1983). The epistemology of a rule-based system – a framework for explanation. *Artificial Intelligence* 20, 215–51.

Dreyfus, H., and Dreyfus, S. (1986). *Mind over Machine*. Free Press, New York.

Hart, A. (1989). *Knowledge Acquisition for Expert Systems*. Kogan Page, London.

Kidd, A.L. (ed.) (1987). *Knowledge Acquisition for Expert Systems: A Practical Handbook*. Plenum Press, New York.

Montgomery, A.(1989). GEMINI: Government Expert Systems Methodology Initiative. In B. Kelly and A. Rector (eds). *Research and Development in Expert Systems* V. pp 14-24. Cambridge University Press.

Pearl, J. (1988). *Probabilistic Reasoning in Intelligent Systems*. Morgan Kaufman, San Mateo, California.

Shpilberg, D., Graham, L.E. and Schatz, H. (1986). EXPERTAX: an expert system for corporate tax planning. *Proc. 2nd International Conference on Expert Systems*, London, 1986. pp 99-123. Learned Information , Oxford.

Sowa, J.F. (1984). *Conceptual Structures Information Processing in Mind and Machine*. Addison Wesley, New York.

Watts, R. (1987). *Measuring Software Quality*. NCC Publications, Manchester, UK.

Winograd, T., and Flores, F. (1986). *Understanding Computers and Cognition: A New Foundation for Design*. Ablex Publishing Co., Norwood, New Jersey.

Dianne Berry
Department of Experimental Psychology
University of Oxford
South Parks Road
Oxford OX1 3UD, UK

Anna Hart
Faculty of Science
Lancashire Polytechnic
Preston
Lancashire PR1 2TQ, UK

Section I
Setting the Scene: Case Studies

Human decision making is not infallible. It frequently involves elements of judgement, uncertainty and risk. In recent years it has been assumed that knowledge based systems (KBSs) can play a useful role in the decision-making process. It is already becoming apparent, however, that the introduction of KBS into many domains will raise issues of acceptability beyond mere technical accuracy. Such issues include whether systems actually distort domain knowledge or the way people use it, whether they change the jobs of their users, either directly or indirectly, and whether they affect legal and professional responsibility. Each of these issues can be considered in both the short and long term.

The three case studies described in this section illustrate many of the critical issues that arise in non-trivial KBS projects. The first chapter by Preece, describes a project in the area of medical administration. The aim of the project is to develop a system for planning the discharge of elderly hospital patients. Preece considers the factors involved in making a system technically, ergonomically, organizationally and ethically acceptable.

A similar approach is taken in the following chapter by Jagodzinski, Holmes and Dennis. They describe a project being carried out with Devon County Council social workers to help manage cases of child abuse. It is difficult for social workers to be aware of all of the relevant knowledge. The aim of the system is therefore to provide a means of guiding people through this maze of knowledge. The sensitive nature of the problem requires a very careful design so that the information is presented to the users in a way which reduces the chances of making an unwise decision. Readers may disagree as to whether or not they believe that this domain is actually suitable for a KBS. It is instructive to try to formulate reasons why this domain is or is not suitable, and to consider the inherent risks and problems.

The final chapter in this section also stems from the medical domain. Wyatt and Emerson describe a project set up to develop a system to assist casualty staff in making rapid and accurate decisions about patients with chest pain. Many issues about the use of knowledge and the usability and evaluation of systems are highlighted in this study.

It is not simply a coincidence that all three studies come from the medical domain. Medicine was chosen not only because it is familiar to readers, but because it highlights many of the key issues involved. Most of the issues apply equally well in other domains however. Risk, for example, is an important factor in areas such as finance, marketing and retailing. Yet it is in domains such as medicine, where wrong decisions can have life-threatening consequences, that one really appreciates the nature of risk. This is clearly illustrated in all three case studies. In the area of chest pain, for example, one needs to consider the risks associated with both false-negative and false-positive diagnoses. Clearly it is necessary to completely avoid the former. Patients who are having, or who are about to have, a heart attack must be seen and treated urgently. Yet at the same time one does not want to be over cautious and admit everyone to the coronary care unit. This would use up limited and costly resources unnecessarily. The consequences of decisions are equally crucial in the domain of child abuse. Under-prediction leads to a risk of exposing children to continued abuse, whereas over-prediction leads to a risk of mistakenly separating children from their parents. Even when one considers discharge planning for elderly hospital patients, one can see that risk is an important issue. Sending a patient home too soon to an environment where there is insufficient support can have disastrous consequences. It should also be realized that the actual presence of the system influences the risk of the situation. In each of these three cases there is risk without the system and risk with the system. The risks are essentially different; without the system some poor decisions may be likely, whereas other poor decisions may result if a system is used. Risk analysis is therefore an important aspect of system design.

Related to risk is the question of responsibility. There are two aspects to this. First, who is responsible for the validity of the actual knowledge in the knowledge base and the inference methods used? If anyone is to be held responsible for this then it is unclear, professionally or legally, whether the relevant party is the knowledge engineer, programmer or one or more experts. Many systems carry disclaimers but it is likely that in the future this may be insufficient. The second issue here is the question of who is legally responsible for actions taken following use of the system? In the projects described by Preece and by Jagodzinski, Holmes and Dennis this latter issue was addressed by leaving the responsibility in the hands of the users and designing the system with this in mind. In the case of discharge planning, for example, any recommendation made by the system had to be either confirmed or rejected by users. The users would then take responsibility for the system's recommendation or for their alternative course of action.

Problems of responsibility are particularly acute where a system allows users to make decisions that would normally only be made by more senior or experienced personnel. Wyatt and Emerson describe an example of this in their chapter. The casualty nurses wanted a formally agreed, written policy to cover their referral of patients into the coronary care unit, an action that was previously only taken by doctors. Given that nurses have different skills from clinicians, and are not happy taking decisions outside of their field of responsibility, the project had to be approached sensitively. The resulting change in role had to be effective and not disruptive. It is interesting to note that the clinicians were keen for the nurses to make these new decisions. In other situations experts might not be so happy to allow less experienced personnel to assist, even with the use of a KBS. The question of responsibility is returned to in the final section of the book.

The introduction of KBSs can change jobs in significant ways, either at an individual or an organizational level. The chapters by Preece and by Jagodzinski, Holmes and Dennis look at the implications of systems for both immediate users and organizations. Preece suggests that it is necessary to define precisely at the outset the intended role for a system. This is clearly desirable, although as can be seen from the child abuse study the role of a system may be redefined once a project is underway. Defining the role of the system requires a thorough understanding of the problem, and this is not always there at the start of a project. The effects of systems on organizations are also discussed in the final section of the book.

The three projects described in this section all involve a considerable degree of complexity in terms of the number of factors that have to be taken into account in making decisions. In the domain of child abuse, for example, Jagodzinski, Holmes and Dennis state that there are over 30 factors which have been shown to predispose towards child abuse when present in various complex combinations. Similarly, the experts in the Wyatt and Emerson study came up with over 60 items which they believed to be relevant to heart attack screening. It is perhaps a weakness of this latter study that these factors were only considered in isolation, rather than in combinations. The study does demonstrate, however, the marked discrepancy between items that experts believe to be the most significant in terms of diagnosing potential heart attacks and items that are actually useful in the users' hands. Many indices which the experts believed to be very important were not useful predictors for the nurses; these typically included more subjective items, such as type and duration of chest pain. This is clearly a significant issue when the users of a system are very inexperienced, compared with the domain experts. The overall size of projects is also a very real issue. Problems do not 'scale up' and a technique which is adequate for a small system may be inappropriate for a larger one.

It is interesting to look at the origin of the three projects described in this section. The idea behind the discharge planning and chest pain screening systems came from the hospitals concerned. In the latter case the system was actually developed by the domain experts themselves. In contrast, the child abuse project was originally conceived by the academic team at Plymouth Polytechnic. They then had to convince Devon Social Services and the social workers concerned of the plausibility and value of the project. Clearly, this approach has drawbacks. If the need for a system is not obvious then the intended role might be somewhat misconceived. Moreover, it is often noted that for a project to be successful it is necessary to have an enthusiastic 'champion' at hand. However, it is sometimes easier for an 'outsider' to see a potential solution to a problem than for someone closely involved. In either case, the system must be developed within the constraints and values of the practical environment. The organization within which a system is to be used imposes constraints on the nature of the emerging system.

A final point concerns terminology; whether systems should be called expert systems, knowledge based systems or just systems. Jagodzinski, Holmes and Dennis avoid the term 'expert system' due to the nature of the child abuse domain. They say that the notion of expertise in child abuse decision making is decidedly suspect among practitioners. Preece also avoids using the term expert system in the discharge planning domain. He states that since the hospital did not as yet have medical information systems, there was little point in introducing the system as an expert system. It is sometimes better to avoid the use of jargon if it is likely to lead to misconceptions by the people involved, whether these be experts, users, or even the system developers. Potential users can have enough fears and problems, as outlined by Jagodzinski, Holmes and Dennis, without these being exacerbated by the use of misleading terminology. The notion of a system which is 'expert' can be very daunting. The similarities and differences between expert and conventional systems are discussed in the next section of the book.

Chapter 2

DISPLAN: Designing a Usable Medical Expert System

Alun D Preece

INTRODUCTION

Despite a promising start in the medical domain, expert systems have not been widely accepted in routine clinical use. We will argue that this is because designers have failed to address certain criteria which are essential for a usable system. By usable we mean simply that the system is acceptable to its users on the grounds of knowledge base soundness, system ergonomics, organizational integration, and ethics. The first part of this chapter will examine these criteria in detail. The remainder of the chapter will focus upon design strategies that can be adopted to meet the criteria, and assessment strategies to determine if a system is acceptable for use.

The criteria and strategies are illustrated in the context of a case study in medical administration: the DISPLAN system for planning the discharge of elderly hospital patients.

TOWARDS A USABLE MEDICAL EXPERT SYSTEM

Very few medical expert systems have actually found their way into routine clinical use, accounting in 1986 for only 4 per cent of operational expert systems in the USA (Spang-Robinson, 1986). This is in spite of the fact that many such systems have been extensively evaluated and show acceptable performance levels when compared with human experts, (eg Reggia, 1985; Politakis and Weiss, 1984). We argue that the problem goes beyond the validity of the knowledge base, which is just one of a set of issues that must be addressed for an expert system to be considered usable (that is, acceptable to health care professionals). We will identify four vital criteria for acceptability as follows:

Technically acceptable: The knowledge contained within the system must be sufficiently sound and complete for operational use. A formal definition of this condition will not be attempted here – the basic requirement is that the system's performance on tasks should be judged acceptable in comparison with the human beings already performing the tasks. This requirement has already been met in many projects and does not in isolation guarantee a usable system (Shortliffe and Clancey, 1985).

Ergonomically acceptable: Health care staff are becoming increasingly busy. Any expert system designed for their use must therefore be capable of being consulted efficiently and of presenting its conclusions and recommendations succinctly (Bischoff *et al.*, 1983). The user interface must be engineered to meet both the needs of the domain and the style of interaction appropriate to the users. This was a critical failing of the MYCIN system (Buchanan and Shortliffe, 1984).

Organizationally acceptable: The medical profession has existing procedures for advice and referral which are well-established and work satisfactorily most of the time (Rector, 1984). Any expert system designed to assist medical personnel must be carefully integrated into the clinical environment in order to be accepted. The system should be compatible with procedures within the organization, which may mean changing the system or changing the existing procedures.

Ethically acceptable: Many physicians and hospital managers are concerned about the ethical issues of responsibility for expert system-assisted decisions (Victoroff, 1985). It is crucial (particularly for legal reasons) to establish where responsibility lies for the system's recommendations being implemented. Until specific legislation exists to cover these issues, practical interim solutions are necessary for all operational expert systems.

In the DISPLAN discharge planning project we undertook to investigate design and assessment strategies that would result in each of the above criteria being fulfilled.

PROJECT BACKGROUND AND JUSTIFICATIONS

The DISPLAN Domain

The elderly use the health services heavily (Hunt, 1973). Discharge planning for the elderly patient needs to be performed successfully if the hospital and community services are to cope with a growing aged section of the population. To ensure a successful hand-over of care from hospital to home, a large number of factors usually have to be considered in planning discharges. Many professions and services may be involved in a particular case, including occupational therapy, physiotherapy, health visiting, community nursing, social service provision, general practitioners, the Department of Health and Social Security, voluntary bodies, and the patient's family and friends (Skeet, 1985).

Surveys have shown that discharge planning is one of the weakest aspects of hospital care (Moores, 1986; Skeet, 1974). Poor planning can result in anything from the GP not being informed of the patient's return home, to a patient being passed on a stretcher through a window because nobody arranged for the ambulance crew to have keys to the house! 'Good practice' guidelines to avoid such occurrences have recently been drawn up by a working group (Skeet, 1985). These are based on paper checklists which are lengthy and difficult to use due to the diversity of factors which must be considered in each case.

East Dyfed Health Authority has recently been taking steps to clarify nursing procedures using computer systems (Roberts and Taylor, 1987). As part of this work the unit general manager of Llanelli's Bryntirion Geriatric Hospital proposed that some kind of computerized information system could be employed to assist nurses in discharge planning procedures, without the need for volumes of extra paperwork.

Project Background and Objectives

The objectives of the DISPLAN system were defined as follows:

- to assist a team of medical, mental health, paramedical and social specialists in the formulation of discharge plans, ensuring that all relevant factors are considered;
- to assist nurses in the implementation of discharge plans, ensuring that all required procedures have been performed and that documentation has been produced;
- to improve communication and liaison between all staff concerned with the discharge process by compiling all the required patient data in one location;
- to formalize explicit procedures for discharge planning which would serve as valuable documentation and as a means of staff training and education. The nurses and other users would be made aware of the current 'good practice' approaches to discharge planning by the system recommending that plans are formulated and implemented according to the guidelines.

Why an Expert Systems Approach?

We decided to take an expert systems approach to developing DISPLAN for the following reasons:

- The domain involves a limited number of procedures, with a large number of special-case situations. An explicit representation of this knowledge using meta-rules, procedural rules and declarative rules therefore seemed entirely appropriate.

– Our aim to educate nurses in the 'good practices' of discharge planning indicated that the system would require some means of presenting its knowledge to users. Expert system explanation techniques appeared suitable for this.

– The importance of developing a usable system, according to the four criteria listed earlier, suggested a prototyping strategy (Alavi, 1984). This is a natural approach for expert system development and is well-supported by many expert system tools.

It is worth noting that we avoided the terminology of the expert systems field while developing DISPLAN. Since Bryntirion Hospital does not yet have any medical information systems, most of the clinical staff had nothing to compare DISPLAN with. The fact that it was developed using expert system techniques was irrelevant to them.

A FUNCTIONAL OVERVIEW OF THE DISPLAN SYSTEM

DISPLAN System Structure

The overall system structure follows the patient's progress from hospital admission to discharge, since discharge planning should begin on admission (see Figure 1). The knowledge base is partitioned into five main sections: the medical, paramedical, mental and social consultation modules, and the planning module. Each of the four consultation modules uses the patient assessment data to identify the needs of the individual in each area. These needs are compiled in the patient case notes (see Figure 1). The planning module uses the identified needs to assist the user in formulating the discharge plan, assisting in the selection of the most appropriate discharge destination, equipment and service support. (The details of this procedure differ between versions of DISPLAN and are fully discussed on pp. 37–38.) The planning module then ensures that nothing is left undone and that all required documentation is automatically produced. DISPLAN will never recommend that a patient should be discharged while any aspect of care is unknown.

DISPLAN is PC-based and is currently installed on a convalescent geriatric ward which discharges an average of 10 patients a week.

Use of DISPLAN

DISPLAN has two types of user:

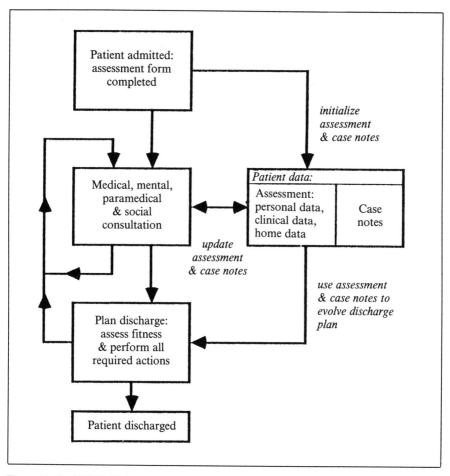

Figure 1. *The DISPLAN system structure*

Primary users: The nursing staff are responsible for keeping the patient records up to date, and for using DISPLAN to evolve and coordinate the discharge plans.

Secondary users: Medical, paramedical and social specialists need to consult and update the patient records according to their own needs.

A patient record is created on admission, normally by the ward clerk. Initially this contains only basic personal information (name, address, birth date, details of relatives and other contacts, etc). Later, the medical, paramedical and social/home assessments are made, and a nurse (or appropriate specialist) enters these details into the consultation system. DISPLAN is very flexible as to the order in which this data is entered.

A case conference is held weekly by the multidisciplinary planning team. This team is led by the consultant geriatrician, and includes at least one medical, paramedical and nursing representative. The hospital social worker and specialist health visitor are also normally present. All of these individuals are able to consult the system sufficiently well to be able to view and print out a current patient record. DISPLAN is normally operated by the attending nurse during the case conference, rather than being available on a 'free-for-all' basis. Once the discharge plan has been formulated a nurse implements the actions, such as mobilizing services. At these times DISPLAN acts as an 'intelligent checklist' and produces discharge documentation.

Since a patient's status will constantly change up to the time of discharge, for better or worse, DISPLAN has to frequently review current conclusions, using patient history stored with the case notes. It draws the user's attention to all known consequences of changed circumstances and automatically ensures that consistency is maintained. The re-consultations are shown in Figure 1 as the backward loops in the patient's progress.

Examples of DISPLAN Operations

The tasks performed by DISPLAN are diverse. During the patient assessment its primary function is to ensure that all relevant data are gathered. For example, if a patient has problems with activities of daily living (climbing stairs, washing, bathing, preparing meals, etc) and will be returning home after discharge, DISPLAN will recommend that a home assessment is performed. It will indicate the factors that should be checked in the assessment:

- access to home facilities (via stairs, ramp, etc);
- safety of facilities (especially heating and cooking arrangements);
- provision of basic facilities (adequate lighting, clothing, hot water, etc);
- attitudes of other occupants (a patient will never be discharged to a home where the family is hostile to their return);
- general comments (rising damp, rugs on polished floors, etc). Certain factors will be more significant if the patient has particular problems. For example, patients with partial sight will need a better lit home than fully-sighted patients.

During the discharge planning stage DISPLAN reminds the nurse of all the patient's requirements and will create specific checklists for each task. For example, if the patient requires an ambulance for the journey home DISPLAN will automatically print an ambulance request form and will remind the nurse to make sure that the crew can gain access to the patient's house. If the patient requires community services DISPLAN produces a referral form for each service, with a summary of the patient's needs. A letter is also produced to inform the GP of the patient's discharge.

OUTLINE OF IMPLEMENTATION STRATEGIES

Strategies for Design and Assessment

Our goal was to implement a usable system – one that met the criteria for acceptance established on pp. 25–26. We therefore needed both design and assessment strategies that would enable us to build a usable system and perform acceptance testing on it. The strategies we used will be outlined in this section before detailed discussion on pp. 34–38.

The overall approach we took was fairly standard. It was based upon the conventional software development cycle (Boehm, 1976) and the generic knowledge acquisition method (Welbank, 1983):

Stage 0 – establish specifications and objectives
Define the role of the expert system and the tasks it will perform
Determine who will use it and how it will affect their jobs
Determine who will take responsibility for the system's recommendations

Stage 1 – identify the domain structure
Determine what procedures the experts use to do the tasks
Determine the main concepts and interrelationships involved in the tasks
Determine what data the experts base their reasoning upon
Determine how this data will be captured by the system
Determine how the system's outputs will reach those who need them

Stage 2 – elicit the detailed knowledge
Obtain and organize the detailed knowledge, based on the Stage 1 structure
Design and implement the inference and control strategies
Design and implement the user interface

Stage 3 – test the system
Locate undesirable behaviour in the knowledge base, including contradictions, omissions, unnecessary rules and cyclic reasoning
Assess performance to requirements (acceptance testing).

Our criteria indicated that a closely cooperative strategy was needed for design and assessment, involving both experts and prospective users. To allow maximum involvement from these individuals we chose to operate the above model as a prototyping cycle, illustrated in Figure 2. Note that Stages 0–2 comprise design, whilst Stage 3 comprises assessment.

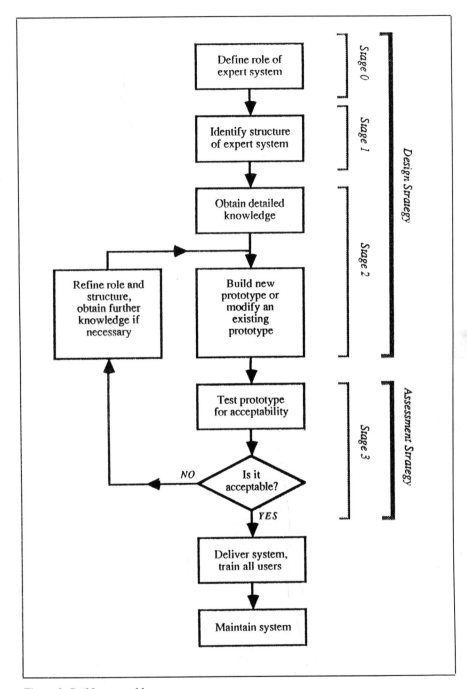

Figure 2. *Building a usable expert system*

Once the system has been passed as acceptable it can be put into operational use. Normally this will require thorough training of all users. Naturally, the operational system will need maintaining, which may involve minor design changes (corrections or enhancements to the system). These issues will not be addressed in this paper, primarily because the DISPLAN project has not yet reached the maintenance stage (we are currently involved in the user training course). However, we are confident that our rule-based approach will result in a more easily maintainable system than a conventional approach would have (some evidence supporting this belief is given on p. 39).

Addressing the Criteria for Acceptance

We will discuss how the above strategies address the four criteria of professional, ergonomic, organizational and ethical acceptability.

Technically acceptable: This is approached in a conventional expert system manner. Firstly, sources of knowledge must be identified (both documentary and human), and then knowledge is acquired from these sources via a combination of knowledge acquisition techniques (Kidd, 1987). A prototype knowledge base is then built and evaluated. The required content of the knowledge base can be determined by the tasks which the system needs to perform, which are in turn determined by the role of the system.

Ergonomically acceptable: Essentially the user interface and other physical aspects of the system are shaped by the system's tasks (and therefore by its role). The physical siting and hardware configuration will initially be determined from the Stage 0 and Stage 1 studies, although this may be revised when the system is assessed. Developing the detailed specification for the user interface needs a considerable amount of work in practice; this was done as part of our prototyping cycle (see Figure 2).

Organizationally acceptable: It is necessary to determine who will physically use the system and what effects the system will have on the users' job descriptions. New or modified procedures may be required to get data into the system and to distribute its recommendations to all the people who need them. The advantages afforded by the introduction of the system must outweigh any problems caused by such changes.

Ethically acceptable: Each distinct task that the expert system performs will normally involve it making a decision, offering a recommendation, or producing a justification for an action. Responsibility for each of these functions needs to be taken by a human being. Ideally this should be a member of the design team since they will be intimately familiar with the system, and will be most inclined to trust it.

DETAILED DESIGN STRATEGIES

Identifying a Design Team: Experts and Users

To meet the criteria for acceptance, our design team was selected to include both experts (knowledge sources) to ensure that the system's knowledge base was sound, and users (at all levels in the organization) to ensure that the system was ergonomically, organizationally and ethically acceptable.

The Experts: Multiple experts were required, since no individual had expertise in all the discharge planning operations, which include medical, paramedical, social, nursing and community services knowledge. Each of these 'sub-domains' had to be represented in our expert group. We obtained a list of the most articulate individuals in these fields from the hospital manager and carried out trial knowledge acquisition interviews with each of them in order to select a minimum group of the most suitable people for the design team (all useful knowledge acquired in these interviews was used for the first DISPLAN prototype). This final group comprised: the hospital consultant geriatrician (to cover medical knowledge, and to give an overall picture of the domain), two nursing sisters (nursing input), an occupational therapist (paramedical input), a social worker (social input), the hospital's specialist health visitor (community input) and a physiotherapist (paramedical input).

The Users: To represent DISPLAN's users in the design team we needed nurses (primary users) and various specialists (secondary users), the most articulate and clear-thinking of whom were already in the design team as experts. To this list we added the hospital's nursing officer, who, together with the consultant geriatrician would not be 'hands-on' users, but would nevertheless have a lot to say on the organizational and ethical issues of the system. In working within the hospital we found it essential to have highly-placed personnel committed to the project, to ensure that sufficient resources (primarily in staff time) were put into the development work, and that things were kept moving. Our 'champions' in this respect were the consultant geriatrician and the nursing officer.

Organizational Considerations

There were three types of ward: acute, convalescent and long-stay. Patients were discharged regularly only from the acute and convalescent wards. The acute ward tended to discharge only 'straightforward' cases directly home; that is, patients with few difficulties with daily living. Since complex cases were transferred to the convalescent ward first; DISPLAN was mainly targetted at the needs of the convalescent ward, although we did perform a trial of the system on the acute ward to assess its potential usefulness (see pp. 43–44).

We also had to address the issue of users' job descriptions and how they would be affected by the introduction of DISPLAN. The design team set out to minimize organizational change and effects on job descriptions:

– It was intended that the system should improve the nurses' skills, rather than take any away, since we wished to raise their awareness of 'good practice' in planning discharges.
– The system was originally designed to minimize the need for the nurses to acquire keyboard skills.
– We did not intend to redesign any forms already in use, although some forms would later be produced by the system automatically.
– DISPLAN was intended to take about as long to use as the existing manual procedures. There was no requirement to 'speed up' operations. As it turned out, unforeseen organizational changes resulted from implementing DISPLAN which we discuss later.

Ethical Considerations

Before work could commence on DISPLAN the project had to be passed by the Health Authority Ethical Committee. A proposal was submitted outlining the purpose of the system, the data it would contain, and an indication of how the patient's interests would be protected. A prime concern was who would take responsibility for the system's operations.

We opted for a simple solution to this: any recommendation made by DISPLAN would be considered by the users and either confirmed or rejected (and an alternative recommendation made). The user would then take responsibility for DISPLAN's recommendation or for their alternative course of action. The only sensitive area involved in such a situation is the offering of assistance or accommodation, and normally the discharge team would have to take the overall decision on such actions. Responsibility for such team decisions falls on the consultant geriatrician. The nurses are responsible for implementing the decisions and DISPLAN has a checklist mechanism to ensure that this is done. It will tag the action with the name of the person carrying it out so that a permanent record of responsibility is maintained. In this way we kept accountability exactly as it was before the introduction of DISPLAN.

The Ethical Committee was satisfied by these provisions. The hospital management had to ensure that we actually met them in practice, which was another practical reason to involve senior staff in the design team.

Task-Structuring the Knowledge Base

Discharge planning is a wide domain. It is an amalgam of knowledge from a set of fields: medicine, nursing, paramedicine, social work, etc. We took pains to limit our knowledge acquisition efforts to the operational knowledge required to do the tasks that DISPLAN was intended for. Even with this restriction, certain aspects of the DISPLAN domain involve very large numbers of factors to be considered, such as when assessing a patient's home with respect to his/her ability to cope with daily living activities. The rules for such cases tend to have large antecedents, and further expansion of each antecedent condition can result in combinatorial explosion, and an unmanageable rule set. For this reason, careful thought was required to structure the expanding DISPLAN knowledge base.

Two techniques were used. In the first place, some expansions could be pruned by reducing them simply to an 'ask the user' query, replacing complex rule antecedents by simple questions. For example, we reduced the assessment of patient's medical fitness for discharge to a yes/no query directed at the medical consultant, since internal medical conditions are too wide to be within the scope of the DISPLAN system. Furthermore a large number of alternative choices could sometimes be reduced by abstraction. For example, items of paramedical support equipment are too numerous for DISPLAN to cope with. We found that categorizing them carefully was often sufficient to make them manageable, providing that the user was allowed to add qualifying comments to indicate special requirements. For example, all the various different models and sizes of walking frame could be reduced to a single 'walking frame' item, with comment fields to specify type of frame and height.

Due to the scope and poorly-defined bounds of a wide domain, omissions, contradictions, unintentional cyclic reasoning and unnecessary rules are especially hard to detect. Our knowledge base has grown sufficiently large to make such tasks extremely difficult to do manually and work is underway to provide automated tools to assist with these operations.

Knowledge Acquisition Notes

Our knowledge had to be elicited from multiple, multidisciplinary experts, and this led to problems beyond the acknowledged difficulties of knowledge acquisition (Welbank, 1983). Our experiences of the three techniques we used (in addition to documentary sources of knowledge such as Skeet, 1985) are described below:

Interviewing: We found interviewing to be good for eliciting the structure and majority of the domain knowledge, but of little use for identifying omissions. This technique is very time consuming for the hospital staff and work pressure results in a bottleneck where development is hindered by the temporary unavailability of a key expert. In our experience, interview works best on a one-to-one basis, but in some cases where there is an overlap between the areas of expertise it becomes necessary to interview more than one subject in a session. This can be very unproductive since disagreements often arise over what constitutes correct practice.

Case Analysis: An important part of the discharge planning process is the case conference, where the multidisciplinary team considers all patient cases, discussing discharge fitness and planning proposed discharges. Observing these conferences and analysing later transcripts of the proceedings sheds considerable light on the actual strategies used by the team, particularly the way in which important problems are pinpointed by the team leader (normally the consultant geriatrician) and focused upon. These sessions have proved valuable for determining knowledge omissions, since the diversity of real cases provides many unusual combinations of circumstance. Highlighted cases can be followed up in structured interview sessions after the conference to rectify such omissions. Sample cases can also be used as part of the debugging process by running them through the prototypical system.

Model evaluation and criticism: Rapid prototyping to elicit feedback has proven a successful technique for acquiring knowledge and debugging the knowledge base. As test cases, real and hypothetical, are run through the system its behaviour can be studied, discussed and modified, usually with an appropriate subset of the design team. With a suitable tool we have been able to make immediate changes and elicit feedback on the results. It has proven a productive way to work, especially since the same team included prospective users, who could comment and propose modifications on the ergonomic aspects during the same sessions.

The Prototyping Strategy

DISPLAN evolved through four distinct prototypes, from a simple demonstrator to the current operational system. In this section we will examine the features of each in turn, how it was assessed, and why we built a new one. Note that we were prepared to continue prototyping until the system was judged sufficiently usable.

The first prototype was designed to demonstrate the feasibility of our intended approach to building DISPLAN, and illustrate the nature of an expert system to the team (as part of design Stages 0 and 1). It was based upon a review of the recent discharge planning literature (especially Skeet, 1985), preliminary interviews, and observational visits to the wards. It was initially built using the ESP Advisor expert system shell (Expert Systems International, 1985), but rewritten in Turbo PROLOG (Borland International, 1987) to allow more flexibility in experimenting with interface styles. This version maintained no patient records, did not allow backtracking and comprised about 35 rules. We demonstrated the system to the design team and they were most impressed with the explanation facilities which we used extensively to describe 'good practice' discharge planning guidelines to the user.

The second prototype was designed as a vehicle for detailed knowledge acquisition (Stage 2 of the design process). It was implemented in the CRYSTAL expert system shell (Intelligent Environments, 1986), since this offered a productive development environment for easy rule construction and modification. CRYSTAL also allowed file handling to be implemented, facilitating the construction of DISPLAN's patient record system. The 'educational' features from the first prototype were retained, but the knowledge base was restructured and expanded to 900 CRYSTAL rules, including the procedural rules handling the patient record maintenance. Testing of this version was done purely to elicit more detailed knowledge.

The third prototype was a largely expanded version of the second prototype; no rewrite was involved. It comprised the second prototype plus all the additional knowledge acquired after that version was demonstrated. By this stage the system had grown to about 1,500 unique CRYSTAL rules in seven different modules. Since this prototype was considered essentially complete we undertook a major ward trial with it, as described on pp. 39–41. There were two major deficiencies. Firstly, the user interface proved inadequate for routine use, and secondly, the manner in which the system presented its recommendations was considered inappropriate. We had taken the approach of letting DISPLAN evolve a detailed plan which the user could overrule. The team felt that it would be more efficient for DISPLAN to check the user's plan to see if *it* was deficient. This idea was based on the so-called 'critiquing' approach (eg Miller, 1983; Shortliffe, 1983).

The final prototype was another complete rewrite to allow us to address these deficiencies. We also took advantage of the additional facilities in a new version of the CRYSTAL shell. Considerable knowledge base reorganization, particularly with the increased use of meta-rules, reduced the actual rule count to just under 1,000 CRYSTAL rules in four modules. This version was acceptance-tested by all of the design team and judged suitable for operational use, and we are currently scheduling training for the staff of a selected ward so that the system can be tested in daily practice. The assessment of DISPLAN is discussed in the next two sections.

STRATEGIES FOR ASSESSMENT

There were two stages of assessment: design team assessment and ward trial. A prototype was only passed for ward trial if it was acceptable to the design team.

Design Team Assessments

Informal in nature, these involved presenting the prototype system to the team for evaluation. Real and hypothetical test cases were run and the team's comments noted. Further knowledge was often elicited in these sessions. The ergonomic aspects of the system were assessed by letting members of the team, especially the nurses, run the test cases through, watching them carefully and noting their comments. Awkwardness in DISPLAN's user interface could often be detected by observing a user attempting to do something perfectly reasonable and failing.

Our development tool enabled us to correct such problems very rapidly, often in a matter of minutes. We were able to test the modified interface immediately and continue refining it until the users were happy.

These sessions were usually relaxed and enjoyable, as well as very productive. They enabled assessment of basic ergonomic and technical soundness. Once the team was satisfied with these aspects of a prototype it was put on ward trial.

Ward Trials

DISPLAN underwent two such trials to assess the utility of the third and fourth prototypes. The first ward trial led to a major rethink and rewrite of the system, resulting in the current version which is currently on ward trial. The remainder of this section describes the conduct of the first ward trial, but most of the comments are equally applicable to the second.

We wished to test the performance of the system in the ward environment and assess the acceptability of DISPLAN to the primary users, the nurses. This was to serve three purposes:

- testing the system's practical utility (ergonomic and organizational factors);
- facilitating additional knowledge acquisition from the nurses and specialists;
- getting the staff used to having a computer on the ward.

DISPLAN was installed on-site for a month, spending half that time in an acute ward, and the other half in a convalescent ward. Twenty-two nurses and a number of other personnel (our secondary users) were exposed to the system during this time. Over 30 patients were run through DISPLAN during the trial, about two-thirds of whom were genuine cases. These proved of more value than the hypothetical cases since they focused the nurses' attention more clearly.

Feedback was elicited from the users via four methods:

– observation and comments during the training sessions;
– regular visiting and detailed observation of the system in use;
– written comments in a system log adjacent to the machine;
– formal questionnaires at the conclusion of the ward trial period.

Our experience of the usefulness of each of these assessment methods is as follows:

Observation and comments obtained during user training. As with the informal design team assessments, we found it valuable to listen to and observe nurses learning to use the system, especially those with prior computing experience (because we felt that any problems they encountered would most likely be due to a failing of system design rather than with their unfamiliarity with keyboards, etc). These sessions also offered a wealth of additional knowledge of unusual cases thrown up by the nurses' every-day experience. These sessions primarily contributed to the refinement of the technical and ergonomic aspects of DISPLAN.

Observation of DISPLAN in use. More than anything, this assessed the utility of the system. We were able to observe the nature and length of consultation durations, see in practice how information was presented to the system (from forms, directly by the specialists, etc), and determine the best site for the machine. That is, we were able to assess how effective DISPLAN would be in routine use on the sample wards.

Written comments in a record book adjacent to the machine. This method was designed to allow users to comment when an observer was not present. It was unsuccessful as the nurses proved reluctant to write their comments down. We believe that this was partly because their comments were difficult to describe on paper, and partly because they wished to devote their sessions with DISPLAN to exploring the system and did not wish to take time out to write lengthy descriptions of problems. It is therefore impossible to assess what information may have been lost.

Formal questionnaires at the conclusion of the trial period. Concerns addressed by the questionnaires were as follows:

Overall usefulness of the system:
    For operational use on the ward
    For training new staff
Operation of the system:
    Menus, keyboard, function key use
    Help and explanation information
    Moving around the system
The knowledge base:
    Omissions and level of detail
Structural organization:
    Using DISPLAN to do discharge planning
General considerations:
    Operating speed of the system
    Screen presentation
    Hard-copy provision (especially the discharge forms produced as output)

Responses were elicited from all staff with 'hands-on' experience of DISPLAN in the trial. This method was successful in assessing ergonomic and organizational factors, but ineffective for assessing the completeness and detail of the knowledge base.

Acceptance Testing of the Fourth Prototype

This was performed with the design team who represented all of the key staff groups. Demonstrations and tests were informal. The process took most of a month, during which all of the members of the team saw, and were satisfied with, the system. Following this, DISPLAN was released for a second full ward trial, which is still continuing.

DOES DISPLAN MEET THE CRITERIA FOR ACCEPTANCE?

This section examines the problems which caused greatest concern following the first ward trial. We discuss how each problem was solved in the final version of DISPLAN. The issues are discussed under our four criteria for acceptance.

Is DISPLAN Technically Acceptable?

A minority of users felt that there was insufficient detail in some areas of the knowledge base. These were mainly areas which we had specifically restricted in order to keep the system manageable (see p. 36). We compromised by allowing additional facilities for users to add detail by way of typing plain-text notes, which proved acceptable to them in the final testing even though it meant extra keyboard work. However, most nurses were happy with the perceived knowledge content of the system.

Following the first trial the knowledge base was restructured to change the philosophy of the system: the users are now given a freer hand in formulating the discharge plan. Much of the knowledge is brought to bear by the meta-rules in a 'critiquing' fashion. Additional control knowledge affords experienced users more flexibility, permitting many more ways of achieving basic tasks, and giving the users more 'initiative'.

A key use of a meta-rule strategy concerns patient assessment. In the third prototype this was done in a conventional backward-chaining fashion and the user had no control over the order in which data was gathered. The revised version leaves the user free to select any assessment category from an on-screen patient record facsimile and this invokes a meta-rule of the following form:

IF	User has selected value for assessment category
AND	Other category values have been inferred where possible
AND	Actions have been specified
AND	Actions have been checked
THEN	Patient assessment category has been considered.

Although this rule is invoked as part of a backward-chaining inference strategy, it is procedural and forces the data to be gathered and actions to be performed in a forward-chaining fashion. The first two antecedent conditions ask the user for an assessment (from a menu of alternative values), and try to infer other assessment values from it. For example, if the general mobility category of the patient is assessed as 'bedfast' then her ability to climb stairs is inferred as 'unable'. The third antecedent condition checks to see if the patient needs assistance in the particular category (for example, if she cannot carry out an activity of daily living), and if so it presents options for specifying assistance (family help, community services or support equipment). The fourth condition invokes a set of rules which try to determine if the actions specified by the users are appropriate and sufficient. For example, it might inform a user who indicated that the family would assist with the problem that family help was unavailable given hostile reaction to the patient's pending return home.

Use of such meta-rules have made the system more acceptable to the users, and demonstrate how rule-based systems can be made more flexible by the use of procedural knowledge and meta-rules. Empirical testing on over 50 real patients has suggested that DISPLAN is sufficiently complete for routine use. An open question remains as to whether the knowledge base can be formally verified, given the ill-structured nature of the knowledge.

Is DISPLAN Ergonomically Acceptable?

All users surveyed during the first ward trial said that DISPLAN's structural organization and prioritizing of tasks were realistic and usable, but problems were evident when the nurses attempted to use the system's components to evolve discharge plans. We found the main problem was that the users were having difficulty maintaining a clear idea of their goals in using the system. The main reasons for this seemed to be:

- Inexperience and insufficient training in the use of computer systems for problem-solving.
- Insufficient context-sensitive help and poor screen design (successions of similar screens gave rise to feelings of 'going round in circles', and there was not enough contextual information on some screens to let the nurses know exactly what level they were at in the system).
- Disk operations sometimes caused delays to occur at inconvenient times (often breaking the nurses' concentration).

These problems needed serious attention. Every screen layout was redesigned from scratch, using upgraded CRYSTAL screen-painting facilities. The succession of similar query screens was removed, replaced with large screen forms which the user could complete in any desired order. Additionally, every new screen featured a banner heading containing contextual information (what section/subsection the system was in, what patient was being worked on, etc). Our new version of the CRYSTAL software also afforded us faster file handling, removing most of the irritating delays.

These changes proved effective in the recent acceptance testing, and enabled users to achieve a greater degree of proficiency with DISPLAN than previously. Users of the latest version have also been noticeably more confident than users of the third prototype, and are clearly feeling more 'in control' of the system. Before DISPLAN becomes fully operational we will be providing a comprehensive instruction course for all users, to remove any problems that were due to lack of training.

Is DISPLAN Organizationally Acceptable?

All users surveyed were impressed by the potential of DISPLAN for training new staff, and welcomed its educational features. However, on the acute ward the majority of users said that they would have insufficient time to use the system operationally on the ward. We had previously suspected this might be the case, and therefore the design team decided that it would be most practical to implement DISPLAN solely on the convalescent ward.

A more difficult problem to solve was that 18 of the 22 nurses surveyed after the first trial said that a complete consultation for a patient took longer than 30 minutes. In practice, it was felt that between 15 and 30 minutes should be a typical consultation length. To reduce the consultation duration we eliminated some of the need for data capture. The patient assessment phase of the consultation involved DISPLAN inferring many intermediate conclusions that the users were themselves capable of inferring. So, instead of being asked (typically) three questions to establish an intermediate conclusion, the users were asked directly for the conclusion. This resulted in a saving of about five minutes on a typical session.

In effect, DISPLAN became 'less expert' while the users were allowed to be 'more expert'. Further savings were due to DISPLAN's more passive 'critiquing' role, and a wider variety of methods to achieve basic tasks. Recent tests in the second trial have suggested that users can now perform the whole of a patient discharge planning operation in 10-25 minutes, which is acceptable, especially since we would expect this to stabilize at around 15 minutes for an experienced user with a moderately complex case.

Finally, although our original intention was to minimize effects on hospital procedures and job descriptions a few significant changes occurred during development and trials. The medical, paramedical and social staff wanted parts of the patient medical notes to be maintained by DISPLAN, primarily for easy output on discharge referral forms. This meant that nurses had to acquire more advanced keyboard skills than originally intended (although the ward clerk would initially enter the bulk of these notes). Since this led to a high risk of information duplication we are currently in the process of removing from use certain written records, and having DISPLAN produce them as required. DISPLAN is therefore taking on more of the roles of a conventional information system.

Is DISPLAN Ethically Acceptable?

No objections were made to the responsibility arrangements determined by the design team, as described previously. The design modifications described above resulted in the system being accepted by the design team. We are currently organizing a training course for all nurses, appropriate specialists and support staff of the convalescent ward, to ensure the maximum effective use of the system.

CONCLUSIONS

On the whole we are satisfied that DISPLAN meets the criteria which we discussed at the start of this chapter. Our design strategies have ensured that we identified problems as they occurred and that all key personnel were kept informed, involved and enthusiastic. Confidence is high among the nurses and specialists that the system will now be naturally integrated into the daily routine of the hospital and will prove beneficial. Final confirmation of success will come only after an extensive period of routine use, and we will not be fully satisfied until it has been on-site for about 12 months. It will be monitored during this time by the hospital members of the design team, who will naturally be closely involved in its daily use.

The following list identifies the application-specific features that had most impact on our design strategy:

1. The application featured considerable procedural knowledge as well as declarative, and required non-monotonic reasoning, together with long-term record-keeping facilities.
2. The knowledge was multidisciplinary and needed to be compiled from multiple experts. We had to find articulate representatives of all disciplines and it was not always clear who was the best authority in each area. Frequent disagreements arose between the specialists where areas overlapped.
3. The domain was wide, and knowledge base expansion had to be carefully controlled and partitioned to keep the project manageable. This was difficult in practice.
4. Operation of the system was time-critical: ward efficiency could not be allowed to deteriorate as a result of introducing the system.

Finally, to anyone considering building a medical expert system, we offer the following advice:

1. Make sure you are building a system because one is needed, and not because somebody wants to build an expert system for its own sake. Expert system technology is seductive: don't get obsessed with it!
2. Find one or more on-site 'champions': it will be impossible to obtain the considerable resources needed for building an expert system (especially experts' time) unless you have key personnel firmly committed to the project.
3. Assemble a design team comprising an articulate expert in every area the system covers, plus similarly articulate and clear-thinking representatives of the would-be system users (at all levels – from high-level management to 'hands-on' operators).
4. Expert systems are still unfamiliar to most (and sound sinister to many). Build a small demonstrator as early as possible to clearly illustrate your approach to the problem, especially to the design team.
5. Establish what recommendations the system will make, and ensure that there are people willing to take responsibility for all recommendations that are carried out.

6. Use prototypes to expand the knowledge base, establish the interface requirements, and explore the organizational effects and needs. None of these can be fully specified in advance but, in our opinion, can be best determined by exploratory programming techniques.
7. Assessment of the basic knowledge base and interface aspects can be done informally with the design team, but large-scale, on-site trials will be needed to fully assess all aspects of the system. These will shed considerable light on the system in its entirety, but particularly on the knowledge base, the interface and the organizational effects.

ACKNOWLEDGEMENTS

The work described in this chapter forms part of a range of expert system-related projects being conducted by University College Swansea and East Dyfed Health Authority. The author is grateful to the SERC for funding and would like to thank Laurie Moseley, Ruth Roberts, Dr Peter Thomas and the staff of Bryntirion Hospital, Llanelli for their assistance and contributions.

REFERENCES

Alavi, M. (1984). An assessment of the prototyping approach to information systems development. *Communications of the ACM*, Vol 27, No 6, June 1984.

Bischoff, M.B., Shortliffe, E.H., Scott, A.C., Carlson, R.W. and Jacobs, C.D. (1983). Integration of a computer-based consultant into the clinical setting. *Proceedings of the 7th Annual Symposium on Computer Applications in Medical Care*, Baltimore, Maryland.

Boehm, B.W. (1976). Software engineering. *IEEE Transactions on Computers*, Vol C-25, No 12, December 1976.

Borland International, (1987). *Turbo Prolog Programmer's Guide*, (2nd Ed) Borland International Ltd, London.

Buchanan, B. and Shortliffe, E.H. (1984). *Rule-Based Expert Systems*. Addison-Wesley, Reading, Massachusetts.

Expert Systems International (1985). *The ESP Advisor Manual*. Expert Systems International Ltd, London.

Hunt, L.B. (1973). The elderly in hospital: recent trends in the use of medical resources. *British Medical Journal*, Vol 4, No 83.

Intelligent Environments (1986). *CRYSTAL Manual*. Intelligent Environments Ltd, London.

Kidd, A. (1987). *Knowledge Acquisition for Expert Systems*. Plenum Press, New York.

Miller, P.L. (1983). Medical plan analysis: the attending system. *Proceedings of the International Joint Conference on Artificial Intelligence*, pp. 239–41.

Moores, B. (1986). What 1,357 patients think about aspects of their stay in British Acute Hospitals. *Journal of Advanced Nursing*, Vol 11, pp. 87–102.

Politakis, P.G. and Weiss, S.M. (1984). Using empirical analysis to refine expert system knowledge bases. *Artificial Intelligence*, Vol 22, No 1, pp. 23–48.

Rector, A.L. (1984). Knowledge-based systems in medicine: a review. In J. Fox (ed.) *Expert Systems*. Infotech state-of-the-art report. Pergamon-Infotech, Maidenhead.

Reggia, J.A. (1985). Evaluation of medical expert systems: a case study in performance assessment. *Proceedings of the 9th Annual Symposium on Computer Applications in Medical Care*, Baltimore, Maryland.

Roberts, R. and Taylor, J.A. (1987). A Computerised Clinical Nursing Information System. In *Current Perspectives in Health Computing*. Royal College of Nursing, London.

Shortliffe, E.H. (1983). Adapting a consultation system to critique user plans. *International Journal of Man Machine Studies*, Vol 15, pp.479–96.

Shortliffe, E.H. and Clancey, W.J. (1985). Anticipating the Second Decade. In W.J. Clancey and E.H. Shortliffe (eds) *Readings in Medical Artificial Intelligence – The First Decade*. Addison-Wesley, Reading, Massachusetts.

Skeet, M. (1974). *Home from Hospital*. Dan Mason Nursing Committee of the National Florence Nightingale Memorial Committee. Macmillan Press, London.

Skeet, M. (1985). *Home from Hospital: Providing Continuing Care for Elderly People – Some Key Issues and Learning Experiences from the Field*. (Rev. ed), Kings Fund Centre, London.

Spang-Robinson Report (1986). Vol 2, No 10, October 1986, Spang-Robinson, Palo Alto, California.

Victoroff, M.S. (1985). Ethical expert systems. *Proceedings of the 9th Annual Symposium on Computer Applications in Medical Care*, Baltimore, Maryland.

Welbank, M.A. (1983). *A Review of Knowledge Acquisition Techniques for Expert Systems*. Martlesham Consultancy Services Report, British Telecom Research Laboratories, Martlesham Heath, Ipswich. December 1983.

Alun D. Preece
Artificial Intelligence and Expert Systems Research Group
Department of Computer Science
University College Swansea
Swansea,
Wales, UK.

Chapter 3

User-Acceptance of a Knowledge-Based System for the Management of Child Abuse Cases

Peter Jagodzinski, Steve Holmes and Ian Dennis

INTRODUCTION

The introduction of KBSs into a practical working environment raises issues of acceptability beyond mere technical credibility. This is particularly true when their potential users are largely computer-naive and entirely KBS naive. This chapter identifies issues and approaches which have emerged during the design phase of a pilot KBS project being carried out with Devon County Council social workers to help them manage cases of child abuse.

The project has practical and academic aims. At a practical level the aim is to take advantage of KBS techniques in order to guide social workers through the maze of decisions involved in the assessment and long-term management of child abuse cases. At an academic level the aim is to explore the acceptability issues involved in the implementation of KBS for complex decision support in a real working environment, and to develop techniques which take account of them.

Considerable time and effort has been spent in establishing effective working relationships with the Department of Social Services. These were seen as a vital prequisite for the elicitation of practical knowledge, and effective participative design and implementation with field workers. While this was taking place the team undertook a thorough investigation of relevant background material. The project has now reached the stage where extensive practical knowledge elicitation has taken place and prototype systems are being developed.

Progress to this point has revealed that, as anticipated, there have been several instances where issues of acceptability to users have had a major effect on the design and implementation of the KBS. Some issues and techniques have been carried forward from the methodology of conventional computer systems design and implementation, while others emerge as being specific to KBS. They will be described in the following sections.

PROBLEM DOMAIN

Child abuse is defined by the Department of Health and Social Security (DHSS) criteria for registration and categorization. Briefly, these cover:

- physical injury (suspected as non-accidental and inflicted by persons having care of the child);
- physical neglect (eg exposure to cold and starvation);
- failure to thrive (non-organic) and emotional abuse;
- children in the same household as a person previously involved in child abuse;
- sexual abuse.

(Devon Social Services, 1986). Cases of child abuse usually run through three phases, as shown in Figure 1. Each case has a designated 'key worker', usually a social worker, who is responsible for co-ordinating the various agencies' contributions.

Once the key worker has made the decision either for a Place of Safety Order or a co-ordination meeting the case will be scrutinized in great detail by all of the agencies involved (Social Services, NSPCC, Police, GP, School, Hospital). It is the making of this initial decision which is crucial to the detection of child abuse. Furthermore, it is at this point where the failure to make a decision, or making the decision to take no action, can have disastrous consequences. Task analysis of social work teams has shown that the individual social worker at this point relies heavily on the support and advice of the whole team, including the social work supervisor. However, detection is just the beginning of any case, and most are likely to remain active for up to several years while the social worker and other agencies follow a long-term plan for the assessment and rehabilitation of the family, or take other measures such as fostering to provide a permanent, secure home for the victim. The key worker must act as a focal point for communication between agencies and must ensure that an inter-agency, long-term plan of action is developed, implemented and regularly reviewed on a multi-disciplinary basis.

Detailed examples of some of the many problems are found in the cases of Jasmine Beckford (Beal *et al*, 1985) and Maria Colwell (HMSO, 1974). Under-prediction leads to a risk of exposing children to continued abuse, whereas over-prediction leads to a risk of mistakenly separating children from their parents. For this reason social workers are likely to be particularly sensitive to the quality of the advice which they are given.

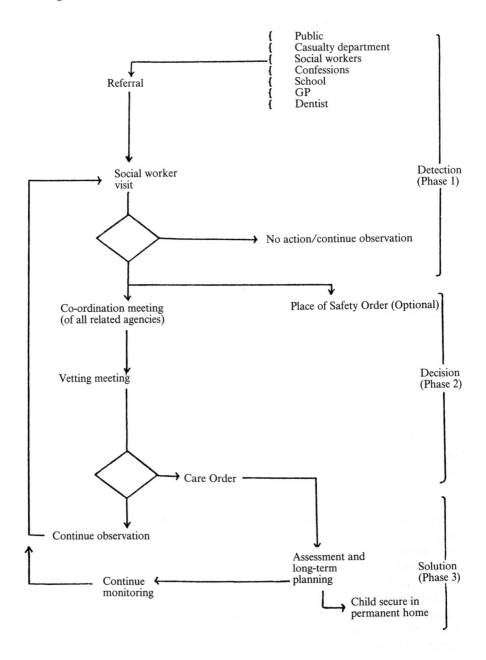

Figure 1. *A summary of procedures in cases of child abuse showing the three phases of social workers' involvement*

THE NEED FOR A KNOWLEDGE-BASED SYSTEM

It is acknowledged that the management of child abuse cases is very difficult because of the wide variety of forms which the abuse can take and the enormous range of background circumstances which can contribute to its perpetration. In practical terms this means that while child abuse cases constitute about 5 per cent of West Devon's total number of cases, they consume up to 80 per cent of social workers' effort in some districts. Inevitably resources become very tightly stretched, which sometimes results in social work teams only being able to deal with the most urgent of the competing pressures.

A nationally-based report by the Social Services Inspectorate (SSI, 1986) identifies some specific shortfalls in the management of child abuse cases in the UK:

> comprehensive assessments for the purposes of long-term planning were conspicuous by their absence in seven out of nine authorities.
> ... information useful for assessment was on file but it was incomplete and uncoordinated and therefore could not provide a good basis for long term planning.
> In several authorities isolated examples of assessments were seen which were of a quality far above the usual. These were assessments which have been undertaken for a specific purpose related to legal action such as preparing an affidavit for court. This demonstrated that social workers have the ability to compile systematic assessments when there is a clear purpose and structure requiring them to do so.
> The main resource needed for comprehensive assessment – social workers' time – was not found to be lacking but needed to be re- directed and focused on the tasks required.
>
> (pp. 42,43)

The need for greater focus, direction and structure in the long-term planning of child abuse cases cannot be met by simple guidelines or checklists because of the diversity of complex factors which may be present. The knowledge required for case management often exists in the collective expertise of social work teams but is not necessarily easily available when it is needed for individual cases. It is envisaged that a KBS could provide the social worker with a clearer route through the vast array of possibilities while at the same time be able to ensure that the necessary information has been collected and the correct checks and procedures have been implemented.

In addition the KBS could provide access to knowledge which is not normally available to 'coal-face' social workers. This is the knowledge derived from academic research and the national statistical records of the

National Society for the Prevention of Cruelty to Children (NSPCC) (Creighton, 1984). It identifies over 30 factors which have been shown to predispose towards child abuse when present in various complex combinations. For example, stress factors such as early parenthood or alcohol/drug abuse are present in a disproportionately high percentage of abusing parents. In addition there are factors which tend to protect children from abuse, for example the presence of a close grandmother. Table 1 shows further examples. None of these factors, even in combination with others, is sufficiently significant to determine absolutely the threat of abuse. However, particular combinations should ring alarm bells.

The manual processing of case notes to evaluate these factors is virtually an impossible task given the wide variations in the way the data are described, the complex criteria which must be applied and the shortage of time of skilled staff. A further aim of the project is to enable the social worker to bring this expert knowledge to bear when assessing child abuse cases.

To summarize, the KBS will be able to help social workers in two ways:

1. Providing an organized, structured set of procedures and checklists of the

Child factors

current age
sex
birthweight
change in weight
legitimacy
order of siblings
handicap behavioural problems
(bedwetting, hyperactivity)

Family Factors

employment character
unemployed
violent criminal record
family size
extended family
accommodation (tenure, amenities)
income

Stress Factors

family discord
low self-esteem
alcohol/drug abuse
unrealistic expectations
psychiatric history
early parenthood
high mobility
services/separation
close spacing of children's ages

Table 1. *Some factors which ought to be considered in identifying cases of child abuse* (extracted from Creighton, 1984)

questions which the social worker should be considering, based on the evidence which is available.
2. Providing additional information about the likely relevance of some aspects of the evidence (see Table 1) derived from national statistics and academic research. Knowledge in this second category cannot be used predictively, even on a probabilistic basis. It merely helps to alert the social worker to possible problems.

ACCEPTABILITY – A MULTIDIMENSIONAL TARGET

In addition to the technical difficulties of implementing a KBS in this domain, many potential difficulties exist in the form of issues of acceptability both to the end users (social workers) and to their host organization, the Department of Social Services. On closer examination these issues of acceptability can be seen to operate in related but distinctly different dimensions, discussed below.

Responsibility and Support

When the KBS mediates in decisions about child welfare, who is then responsible for the decision? In the existing system responsibility for the actions of individual social workers is officially inherited through the management hierarchy from social work supervisors upwards. In practical terms much of the crucial decision making is shared by the social work team. Both forms of responsibility-sharing are seen by social workers as a vital part of the job.

Credibility and validity

Is the relevant knowledge presented in a valid and appropriate way? For example, the notion of 'expertise' in child abuse decision making is decidedly suspect among practitioners. It is not thought to be possible to design a system which identifies cases of child abuse with any degree of certainty. Nevertheless, it does seem practicable to design a system which rationalizes the way in which data are collected and stored and then provides a structured route through the planning and management of the case.

Organizational

Will the KBS affect the existing roles, lines of communication and authority? For example, the traditional style of 'case conference' which brings together all of the agencies involved (social workers, police, school, general practitioner, NSPCC), may be supplemented by an on-line dialogue with the

KBS. In effect this introduces a new participant into the forum, bringing facets of expertise which have not previously been available at this level.

The traditional participants may well react to the introduction of the system in ways which do not benefit the decision-making process. For a second example, pilot interviews have shown that social workers may be suspicious of additional management scrutiny of their case-loads. They fear that the prioritization of cases may be linked to the allocation of resources.

User-comprehension

Will the user understand both how to use the KBS as a computer system and the nature of the advice given by that system? It has been demonstrated by many authors (eg Jagodzinski and Clarke, 1988) that the acceptability of any computer system to its users is heavily dependent on their understanding of how to use the system. KBSs have the additional requirement of producing their advice and explanation in a comprehensible way, well matched to the domain knowledge of the user.

THE PARTICIPANTS AND THEIR CONCERNS

The four facets of acceptability described above emerged strongly during the systems analysis and knowledge elicitation phases of the project. They affect different participants in different ways:

The domain experts: senior social workers and NSPCC personnel are clearly aware of the tenuous nature of some of the specialist knowledge which the KBS is designed to contribute. They are anxious that it should not be misrepresented, for example, as being strongly predictive. At the same time they believe that it can make an important contribution to child care decisions.

Managers: managers in the field are highly sensitive to the organizational implications, particularly where they affect resources.

Social workers in the field: a particular concern within the social work teams at District level is the amount of support provided by the team for the individual social worker. During our knowledge elicitation with field workers it became apparent just how stressful it is for them to take responsibility for a case of child abuse, with all the potential for wrong decisions and the full range of awful consequences. All four of the teams with which we are working cope with the stress by having within the team a high level of discussion of each child abuse case in its early stages, and a good deal of formal contact and case planning with the social work supervisor. This practical and emotional support is clearly a vital requirement for the social workers and, as can be seen in the next section, it led to a redefinition of the role of the KBS.

The social workers are also concerned with comprehension issues. Through informal contact they have displayed the full range of computer-naive users' concerns which are found in conventional computer system implementations (eg Mumford and Weir, 1979; Jagodzinski and Clarke, 1986). They have also began to be aware of the more complex difficulties involved in understanding the role of the KBS in the decision-making process, for example, in justifying advice or attributing responsibility for decisions. It is likely that most of these issues would be present in any KBS implementation, although their exact nature and priority would vary a great deal.

APPROACHES TO THE ISSUE OF RESPONSIBILITY AND SUPPORT

At the start of the project, when the general principles were discussed, it was appreciated that the issue of responsibility would be important. The issue was seen then as defining who should take responsibility for decisions made following use of the KBS. This aspect of responsibility was soon resolved and it became clear that the KBS should act only as an advisor, leaving the responsibility for decisions with the social workers and their managers. However, once observation and knowledge elicitation got down to the level of the 'coal-face' social work teams it became clear that responsibility for decision making was, in practice, much more involved. The responsibility and support priorities of social workers at this level has been described in the previous section. These were made clear by observation of working styles and, in some cases, by the explicit comments of social workers who feared that the KBS might be used to supplant the support given by the team.

This discovery led to an important shift in the intended role of the KBS. It had initially been seen as a diagnostic aid to help social workers in the detection of cases of child abuse from available evidence; that is for use in the first phase. It became apparent, however, that in practice these diagnoses were usually made urgently out of discussions within the team or a subset of it, including the teamleader or social work supervisor. In many cases other members would contribute additional information from their own knowledge of the family concerned and from their own working experience. The quality of the decision and the burden of responsibility for it were inseparable from this team approach. The original idea that a social worker would sit alone at a computer terminal and resolve the problem in a generalized dialogue was clearly misconceived.

More appropriate use of a KBS is to help in the third phase of cases, that is assessment and long-term planning. While the detection phase might in practice last only a few hours following a referral, assessment and long-term planning usually go on for months or years. The objective of this phase is to establish a permanent, secure home for a child, preferably with its natural parents. The data, rules and procedures remain the same, but there is usually less urgency than in detection. Effective assessment and long-term planning are crucial to the repair of the victim's life, and yet they are probably the areas of case management which are most in need of improvement. Social workers and social work supervisors are far more enthusiastic about the use of a KBS in this role than in detection. They welcome the idea of access to comprehensive, structured guidance in the preparation and maintenance of a considered long-term plan, for presentation to the multi-disciplinary case team.

APPROACHES TO KNOWLEDGE REPRESENTATION

The credibility and validity of our KBS depend ultimately on its ability to represent faithfully a range of different types of knowledge, and to combine these knowledge sources to produce useful inferences. On examination, the main areas of domain knowledge match reasonably well with one of three styles of representation:

Child and case knowledge: this comprises a collection of static data (date of birth, name, birthweight etc), data which also changes over time (weight, address etc) and the procedures which maintain and manipulate this data. A frame-based style of representation is well suited to intrinsically hierarchical knowledge of this type. The static and time-changing data items are shared by most of the children considered. This is also true of many of the procedures, for example those which calculate weight trends and compare them with normal development curves. Frames allow these generic characteristics to be inherited by each case. In many cases, further selective inheritance of data values will be possible, such as between siblings.

Family knowledge: this is largely declarative and is easily represented, for obvious reasons, as a series of relationships. Semantic nets provide a natural medium.

Inference rules: these are needed to evaluate the known facts of a particular case in order to produce advice on, for example, the specialists required to assess a particular problem with the child's parents.

A Development Environment – SMALLTALK 5

The diversity of knowledge types, and the importance of being able to represent all of them with the minimum of compromise, required some method of combining the techniques outlined above. The diversity of styles ruled out the use of expert system shells, and the requirement for a reasonably cheap delivery environment (among other factors) ruled out the high-powered development environments such as ART and KEE. SMALLTALK 5, running on an IBM PS2/50 was chosen for its ability to accommodate all of the knowledge representation styles required. The technical advantages of this object-oriented environment are described fully by Holmes (1987), and Cox (1986). For our purposes it also provided the major benefits of good screen-handling facilities and the ability to create prototype systems rapidly, both important in developing a system comprehensible to users.

A Blackboard Architecture

When using a range of different knowledge sources, each represented differently, it is important that they should communicate effectively. Ni (1986) suggests the blackboard architecture as a solution. The blackboard model of problem solving is a highly structured case of opportunistic problem solving. It is based around an object-oriented approach in which objects communicate by means of a large global database, known as the blackboard. The domain knowledge needed to solve a problem is partitioned into 'knowledge sources' which are kept separate and independent, in much the same way as are SMALLTALK objects. The objective of each knowledge source is to contribute information that will aid the solution of the problem. A knowledge source takes a current set of information on the blackboard and if it is able to contribute anything to the current state, updates it according to its own specialized definition of behaviour (similar to methods in SMALLTALK). The knowledge sources are represented as procedures, set of rules or logic assertions. All of these are possible within SMALLTALK. The only things which are allowed to modify the blackboard structure are the objects which contribute to the solution; that is, the knowledge sources. The definition of each knowledge source object contains information regarding the circumstances in which it can contribute to the solution.

The purpose of the blackboard data structure is to hold computational and solution-state data which are needed as input to, and produced as output by, the knowledge source objects. The knowledge sources use the blackboard data to interact with each other indirectly. (SMALLTALK has an automatic facility, the process-frame stack, which achieves the same effect.) The blackboard consists of objects which make up the definition of a solution; they can be partial results, input data, sets of alternatives, and final solutions. They are arranged in a hierarchical manner which gives varying levels of analysis. Information associated with the properties of objects on one level is the input to knowledge sources which can place new information on the blackboard at either the same level, or different levels. As a solution is built up on the blackboard, the solution itself can be arranged hierarchically, if necessary, as a series of alternatives. In order to allow the knowledge source objects to access the blackboard without causing problems of concurrency, such as deadlocking, there is a blackboard control module. This monitors the changes on the blackboard and decides what actions need to be taken next. It communicates with each of the knowledge sources as this becomes necessary.

This kind of problem solving can be easily implemented within object-oriented programming languages (OOPS), and in particular SMALLTALK. Most of the facilities which comprise a blackboard architecture already exist in one form or another. For the purposes of building a knowledge-based system, for example, the blackboard can be used as a convenient database for different forms of representation, eg rules, frames, nets.

APPROACHES TO ORGANIZATIONAL ISSUES

The equilibrium of an organization is almost always changed by major innovation, such as the introduction of a computer system involving a large proportion of staff. The problems caused by such changes have been recognized by the methodology of conventional computer system implementation. Briefly, they can be summarized as:

- task design issues such as task size, de-skilling, task scheduling, error detection and correction;
- job design issues such as levels of supervision, lines of authority, status, span of control. These issues have been described in practical contexts by Mumford and Weir (1979). The adverse attitudes and preconceptions caused by these issues have frequently led to computer systems being effectively rejected by users employing a range of strategies such as pseudo co-operation, sabotage and absenteeism. The mechanisms by which such attitudes arise are described by Jagodzinski and Clarke (1986).

In order to avoid such problems in this project we are borrowing a group of techniques from Mumford and Weir and Jagodzinski and Clarke:

1. Inform potential end-users (managers and social workers) of the nature

of the proposed KBS early in the analysis and design phases. Informal discussion, presentations and circulars have been used. In the event this process has necessarily been long drawn-out. The project was originally conceived by the academic team at Plymouth Polytechnic. It has been necessary to sell the idea to successive levels of Devon Social Services from County Hall down to the individual social workers. Staff at each level have, quite properly, been concerned to ensure that the scheme is viable in terms of their own priorities. For example, at County Hall the concern was for the general principles of a KBS in this domain and for its possible integration with the county-wide, client database computer system. At area level the concern was for possible impact on staff resources:
– would the design process consume valuable staff time?
– would the finished product alleviate the pressure of caseloads?
At the 'coal-face' the concerns were mainly about support and responsibility, as described previously.
2. Identify, by discussion and informal pilot interviews with the users, aspects of the innovation which are causing concern. These revealed, for example, that there was concern in the social-work teams about the way in which computer systems had been implemented in the past. The feeling was prevalent that the client database system was there only for the benefit of administrators and did nothing to help social workers.
3. Elicit the attitudes and preconceptions of all potential end-users by a questionnaire. An example of its questions and style is shown in Figure 2. The design of the questionnaire is described in general by Oppenheim (1966) and in particular by Jagodzinski and Clarke (1988). The questionnaire has been distributed to staff but not yet collected in.
4. Analyse responses (Jagodzinski and Clarke, 1988) to identify users' fears, preconceptions and expectations with regard to the KBS and its implementation.
5. Concentrate in the design and implementation of the KBS on eliminating or avoiding features which may create problems, for example:
– allow users to learn to use the system in private so they are not exposed to criticism at this stage;
– ensure as far as possible that the KBS does detract from task features such as levels of skill and the ability of users to schedule their working day;
– protect existing job features such as the extent to which individual social workers retain control of their own cases;
– integrate KBS with existing client database system to avoid the need for additional data inputs, such as case details;
– design the user-interface to be as comprehensible as possible (see below) and;

2. If a knowledge-based system was used as part of your work would it provide you with more guidance and structured help?

I'd worry that it would reduce any guidance and structured help			It wouldn't make any difference			I'd look forward to more guidance and structured help

13. Do you think that the use of a knowledge-base system in your work would affect your opportunities to consult with colleagues?

Would lead to very much less opportunity to consult with colleagues			I wouldn't expect any significant change			Would lead to very many more opportunities to consult with colleagues

28. If a knowledge-based system was introduced into your work would you be at all worried that it might require the use of special skills or aptitudes that you may not have?

Yes. I would be very worried						No. I wouldn't be at all worried

33. Do you sometimes feel that your decisions and understanding of child abuse cases might be helped by more knowledge of the national statistics on child abuse and contributory factors?

More knowledge of national statistics would be a great help						More knowledge of national statistics wouldn't help at all

45. Would you be suspicious that a knowledge-based system may, in some way, be used to further the objectives of administration rather than to support social workers?

It would be used to further the objectives of administration						It would be used to help social workers

Figure 2. *Examples of questions designed to elicit users' attitudes and preconceptions to the introduction of a KBS*

– involve the users as far as possible in all stages of the design and implementation (the participative approach).

APPROACHES TO USER COMPREHENSION OF THE KBS

Once knowledge is represented adequately, user comprehension is the next most important link in the acceptability of the KBS. The design of the system is as yet at an early stage so that no details have become fixed. However, some principles and ideas have emerged. Some of these arise from the methodology of conventional computer system design and some from the methodology of expert systems. For example, the system will use menus and direct manipulation (Shneiderman, 1987; Norman, 1986). It will have pictorial maps showing overall system functions and routes between them (Jagodzinski, 1983). By these measures it is hoped that the users will be able to operate the system easily and navigate around it as they wish.

A more difficult and crucial aspect of user comprehension concerns the knowledge which the system is trying to convey. The intention here is to create a number of alternative prototype interfaces to the KBS to find a form which is both easily understood and capable of imparting the shades of inference needed to make effective decisions. The styles of interface which may be developed include:

– the traditional expert system approach as used in the classic systems such as MYCIN, in which the system asks questions of the user and produces diagnoses. Explanation consists of statements of the chains of rules which have been followed (Shortliffe, 1976);
– the consultative style proposed by Kidd (1985), particularly the idea that the KBS does not suggest or prescribe a conclusion but simply leads the user through the problem space, acquainting her with the issues as they are relevant to the case in question;
– as an extension of the above, a form of graphical display of the problem space – for example one which positions the data items of the case in question in a two-dimensional plot comparing the pattern of the same characteristics in the population in general.

The use of SMALLTALK has proved to be particularly useful for this prototyping approach to interface development. OOPS are unusually suitable for the kind of programming, required to build user interfaces. By making use of inheritance a generalized interface can be produced which can serve as a basis for any user interface. An interface can be implemented as a subclass of the generalized one, allowing all of its structure and behaviour to be inherited. The principles of Cox's (1986) three-layered architecture have been followed to separate interface from application and display issues.

Application level: this level implements the functionality of the application, without concern for how the functionality will be interfaced to the user. The components of the application level are called models because the functionality of most applications is to model some aspect of reality. Models are slaves of the user interface. They never hold any information about the user interface because the presentation layer may be detached and replaced at any time. Models are always referenced from views – never the inverse.

Presentation level: this level interfaces a specific application to a specific class of user. The components in the presentation level are views, each of which implements a user interface to a specific model in the application level. A given model may well have many different kinds of users, so there will in general be many different views to serve their diverse needs ...

Virtual terminal level: this level implements a device-independent interface between the presentation layer and some class of hardware graphics devices ...' This permits a variety of alternative presentation level interfaces to be constructed without the need to affect application or virtual terminal layers.

CONCLUSIONS

It has been confirmed that acceptability issues in this problem domain are crucial in the design and implementation of a KBS. The particular difficulties associated with child abuse have raised the sensitivity of everybody involved, especially on the issues of credibility, validity, responsibility and support. The approach adopted by the development team has been consciously user-centred and has tried as far as is practicable to take account of all the perceived dimensions of acceptability. It is still too early to assess the contribution of this approach as a whole, although the feeling of the team is that it is worthwhile and effective. Relations with end-users have improved rather than declined during the course of the project.

One major success for a user-centred approach has been the shift in role of the KBS. Task analysis and knowledge elicitation at theoretical and management levels had not revealed the responsibility and support requirements of the end-users. The system would certainly have been unacceptable to social workers in the field in the role which was originally envisaged for it. Credit must go to a user-centred philosophy for the fact that the design was not set in stone before the needs of the end-users had been elicited.

The corollary of the approach is that the systems design must remain fluid right up to, and perhaps after, 'going live'. In practical terms this means using an incremental, prototyping style of system development in which each function of the system is refined by user testing before being included.

REFERENCES

Beal, J., Blom-Cooper, L., Brown, B., Marshall, P. and Mason, M. (1985). *A Child in Trust: the report of the Panel of Inquiry into the circumstances surrounding the death of Jasmine Beckford*. London Borough of Brent.

Cox, B.J. (1986). *Object-oriented programming: an evolutionary approach.* Addison-Wesley, Reading, Massachusetts.

Creighton, S.J. (1984). *Trends in child abuse 1977-82.* NSPCC, London.

Devon Social Services. (1986). Child Abuse (guidelines). Devon County Council, Exeter.

HMSO (1974). *Report of a Committee of Inquiry into the case and supervision provided in relation to Maria Colwell.* HMSO, London.

Holmes, S. H. (1987). SMALLTALK: the only truly object-oriented programming environment. In R. Hawley (ed.) *AI programming environments.* Ellis Horwood, Chichester.

Jagodzinski, A.P. (1983). A theoretical basis for the representation of on-line computer systems to naive users. *International Journal of Man-Machine Studies*, **18**, 215–52.

Jagodzinski, A.P. and Clarke, D. (1986). A review of methods for measuring and describing users' attitudes as an essential constituent of systems analysis design. *Computer Journal*, **29, 2**, 97–102.

Jagodzinski, A.P. and Clarke, D. (1988). A multi-dimensional approach to the measurement of human-computer performance. *Ibid.*, **31, 5**, 409–19.

Kidd, A.L. (1985). The consultative role of an expert system. In P. Johnson, and S. Cook (eds) *People and Computers: Designing the Interface.* Cambridge University Press.

Mumford, E. and Weir, M. (1979). *Computer systems in Work-Design.* Associated Business Press, London.

Ni, H.P. (1986). The blackboard model of problem-solving and the evolution of blackboard architectures. *AI Magazine*, Summer 1986; 38–53.

Norman, D.A. (1986). Cognitive engineering in user-centred system design. In D. Norman and S.W. Draper (eds). *User-Centred Design.* Erlbaum, New Jersey.

Oppenheim, A.N. (1966). *Questionnaire Design and Attitude Measurement.* Heinemann, London.

Shneiderman, B. (1987). *Designing the User Interface.* Addison-Wesley, Reading, Massachusetts.

Shortliffe, E.H. (1976). *Computer-based Medical Consultations: MYCIN.* North Holland, Amsterdam.

SSI (1986). *Inspection of the supervision of social workers in the assessment and monitoring of cases of child abuse when children, subject to a court order, have been returned home.* DHSS, Social Services Inspectorate, March 1986.

Peter Jagodzinski,
Steve Holmes and
Ian Dennis
Polytechnic South West
Drake Circus
Plymouth, UK

Chapter 4

A Pragmatic Approach to Knowledge Engineering with Examples of Use in a Difficult Domain

Jeremy Wyatt and Peter Emerson

INTRODUCTION

The aim of many expert system projects is to encapsulate knowledge about a circumscribed task so that, instead of junior staff bothering their seniors by asking them to solve routine problems, the juniors can do it for themselves with the aid of the system. This enhances their sense of responsibility, allows the experts to apply themselves to more interesting problems, and may result in a more thorough and more consistent approach to the problem than the frustrated experts ever provided. Engineering such a system requires two distinct stages: knowledge acquisition and representation in a computable form, and a cycle of testing and refinement of the resulting prototype.

Knowledge acquisition frequently poses difficulties and has earned its reputation as a bottleneck. A variety of techniques are available which seem to fall at two ends of a spectrum. At one end are knowledge elicitation techniques such as structured interviewing and the building of repertory grids, either by hand or by machine (Shaw and Gaines, 1986; Boose and Bradshaw, 1987). These rely on the expert declaring which are the key variables needed for solving the problem and how they are related to the solution. The usual procedure is then for a computer scientist or knowledge engineer to translate the knowledge harvested from the experts into a representation which can be used for problem solving by the chosen inference engine. At the other end are machine learning techniques which rely on the automated discovery of patterns in sample data, using statistical algorithms such as ID3 (Quinlan, 1979) and others (eg Carbonell *et al*, 1985; Adlassnig and Kolarz, 1986; White, 1987). Here, the experts are usually involved solely in selecting the sample cases and in deciding which are the key variables.

Less attention has been focused upon the other component of the knowledge engineering process, the testing and refinement of prototype systems. There is some guidance about how suitable parameters may be identified and measured (Gaschnig *et al*, 1983; Miller, 1986; Wyatt, 1987a), but the testing process often adopted is *ad hoc*, and may not result in a system which matches expectations. The blame may then be placed on the problem's complexity, or on an inappropriate method of knowledge representation. This chapter describes some of the problems with knowledge acquisition, system building and testing, and the pragmatic solutions we have adopted for our medical domain.

THE BACKGROUND TO OUR PROBLEM

Hospitals are notorious places for keeping patients waiting, and it is unfortunately common to wait for up to two hours in out-patient departments. However, it has recently emerged that, despite our casualty department being run by highly motivated and experienced doctors and nurses, patients with heart attacks were also waiting for undue periods before being admitted to the cardiac care unit (Wyatt *et al*, 1988). Delays in the out-patient department may mean that patients miss their bus home: delays in admitting patients with heart attacks can mean that they miss their chance of receiving a special streptokinase treatment that is now used to unblock the damaged coronary arteries (ISIS-2, 1988). We therefore decided to build an expert system, to assist the staff in our casualty department to make rapid, accurate decisions about patients attending with chest pain.

It was clear from a previous study that the system would need to be operated by nurses, not doctors, as it is they who see arriving patients first. This meant designing a system which could cope with less experienced users, collecting only a subset of all the data that an expert doctor might have access to. As the central issue facing casualty staff about a specific patient is whether to Admit to the CCU OR Not, the name ACORN was chosen for the system.

PROBLEMS WITH CONVENTIONAL KNOWLEDGE ACQUISITION

We were disappointed during and after knowledge acquisition sessions to discover that there were three major difficulties with the experts' insights. Firstly, our experts disagreed with one another. Secondly, their insights about the symptoms and signs of patients with chest pain did not always match 'reality', as judged by data collected by our prospective system users. Finally, the data items suggested by the experts were not always those that could be elicited reliably by our users.

Experts' disagreements

It is common knowledge that experts differ in their opinions (Yu *et al*, 1979; Fox *et al*, 1985), and only a naive system developer would set out to build a system using a single domain expert as the source of knowledge. However, as soon as a committee of experts is formed, contradictions arise and the range of data items considered relevant to the solution escalates. Sometimes only a unilateral decision allows the first working prototype to be built.

In our case, when a panel of three senior doctors was asked which data should be collected by the nurses for input into ACORN, they disagreed and the total number became unmanageable. Our doubts were confirmed when we surveyed 75 doctors about their opinions on the value of various data items in chest pain: the percentage who subscribed to the 'commonest opinion' (mode) of the value of each item varied from 32 to 88 per cent, with a mean of 51 per cent. This clearly reflected a wide spread of opinion about chest pain and the significance of symptoms. If an attempt had been made to build a system from the collected personal constructs of this group of experts, the resulting repertory grid would have defied all known methods of analysis.

With disagreements between experts, the interests of one important group, the future system users, may be neglected. An example of this is when an expert misses out a vital condition in a rule because he is so familiar with the problem and assumes that the user will be too. In a system to aid car mechanics to diagnose starting problems, few experts would include the condition that there must be petrol in the tank; but if the system is used by a non-mechanical driver he might omit this check unless reminded. Careful definition of the users and their level of competence is clearly important before building an expert system.

An alternative, perhaps cynical view, is that experts miss out vital stages in the reasoning process, either because they themselves are unaware of certain tricks of the trade, or because they deliberately withold certain information to preserve their position. Either way, the conventional knowledge acquisition technique can miss out important chunks of expertise, which need to be traced before the system is exposed to real users.

Mismatch between experts' insights and users' reality

A further problem is that it is unusual for experts to understand the difficulties that users will have collecting the data considered necessary for the system to work. By definition, experts are highly competent at eliciting the information required to solve the problem. The new decision makers, however, may not have the necessary skills to collect this data as accurately and as reliably as the experts (eg Ellam and Maisey, 1987). Unless the domain allows a close definition of every data item, problems may result.

To distinguish between data items that appeared to have large discriminatory power and those which were essentially neutral with respect to the outcome, we asked the prospective users of our expert system, casualty nurses, to interview all patients arriving at the casualty department with chest pain, using a form containing 64 questions suggested by the three experts. Then each patient was followed-up, further tests were done, and the 'real' reason for their pain identified. Patients were then classified as having a 'high risk cardiac' (HRC) condition, requiring urgent admission to a cardiac care unit, or 'other'.

Figure 1 shows the extent of the mismatch between the values our panel of 75 doctors placed on a representative subset of 20 of the data items for the diagnosis of chest pain, and the actual value of these data when collected by the casualty nurses. The shaded bars show the doctors' opinions of the relative power of the various data items to discriminate patients having a high risk cardiac (HRC) condition from 'others', and are taken from the

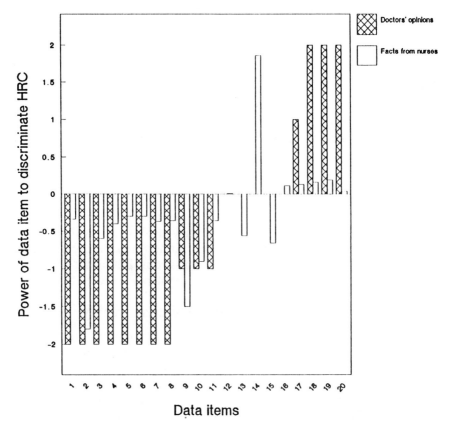

Figure 1. *Comparison of doctors' opinions with data obtained by nurses*

doctors' survey. The open bars show the actual power of the same items taken from the data collected by the nurses.

In the case of the doctors' opinions, the length and direction of each bar is proportional to the commonest opinion expressed by the doctors on the value of this data item, on a scale extending from 'strongly in favour of HRC' (at minus 2), via 'irrelevant' (at 0) to 'strongly against HRC' (at plus 2). In the case of the data collected by nurses, the length and direction of each bar is proportional to the likelihood ratio of this data item. This is a measure of the relative probability of a feature being present in patients with and without a disease (Wulff, 1976). High negative values (-1 to -2) indicate that the data item has the necessary power to identify HRC cases, values close to zero indicate that the feature is just as likely to occur in the 'others' as in the HRC cases, and positive values show that the data item strongly supports 'others'.

It is clear that, although generally there was good agreement as to the direction of the items' value, in most cases the doctors overestimated the size of the item's contribution. In three cases (items 13, 14 and 15), the doctors claimed that the data item was of no value while, in the nurses' hands, it proved quite a valuable determinant of the outcome. In general, the features which matched closest were those which could be measured objectively such as pulse rate and blood pressure, while those which showed a mismatch were more subjective, such as the type and the duration of the patient's chest pain.

It is tempting to conclude that this overturns conventional views about the value of certain symptoms in patients with chest pain, but it would be dangerous to do so. The technique described only allows us to determine the value of these data items in the hands of this particular group of users; if it emphasizes different items than are described in medical textbooks, this is not surprising. It simply confirms our earlier claim that naive users obtain data in a different way from experts, and that expert systems should be tuned to the users' most powerful data items, not to the experts'.

Reliability of data for input

Expert systems can only perform well if the intended users are able to collect and input reliable data. Even if certain data items have a reasonable power to discriminate in the users' hands, a further problem may arise which can adversely affect the system's accuracy: intra- and inter- observer variation. This is especially likely with the more subjective data items. To determine the amount of variation, a repeatability study (Wulff, 1976) should be performed. This consists of a comparison of the same data input to the system on two occasions separated by 2-3 days, preferably by different users on the second occasion.

We conducted a study to compare the answers given by the same patients

69

to questions read out from a printed questionnaire, firstly by a nurse in the accident and emergency department, then by a doctor in the follow-up clinic two to seven days later. For each question, the mean percentage agreement between the first and second answers was calculated. This varied for questions with a Yes/No answer, from 98 per cent for 'Have you ever coughed up blood ?' to 66 per cent for the question 'Is the pain sharp in nature ?', with a mean repeatability of 81 per cent. Since a 50 per cent agreement would be expected by chance for such a question, this suggests that the patients were unsure of at least some of their answers. We consider that any question with a repeatability below 70 per cent is not worth incorporating in a decision-aid.

When building our chest pain advisor we were therefore able to reduce the total number of input data items from the 64 suggested by the experts to 24, by studying the power and repeatability of each proposed data item in the users' hands.

POTENTIAL PROBLEMS WITH KNOWLEDGE ACQUISITION BY RULE-INDUCTION

It might be argued that a machine-learning approach should be adopted to avoid the problems of experts' disagreements, their difficulty in tailoring their knowledge to the users' data, and the effort of harvesting their knowledge. Some would even claim that the knowledge base resulting from rule-induction on sample cases simply cannot escape being correct. However, great care must be used in the selection of the example set and the parameters that are used for induction (Fox, 1984). A simple example (Spiegelhalter, 1983), illustrates the problem. Say that we are trying to classify patients into disease categories, and have access to a database of patients with known diseases. It is quite possible that a rule-induction program will conclude that the patient's name (or their age, if that is unique) is the best predictor of the diagnosis. Although we can instantly recognize the absurdity of this, the machine has no conception of the problem; it is using a classification algorithm and has found an excellent indicator of the disease class. The expert clearly must be very careful to exclude from consideration any parameter that could give rise to such spurious conclusions.

The next potential difficulty lies in the selection of the example cases. Should they be real examples, perhaps common cases covering only a small part of the overall range, or should they consist of invented, somehow 'instructive' cases? It is easy to see how, unless great care is taken here, unintentional bias may be built-in to the resulting, automatically generated rulebase.

A final comment about rule-induction techniques is that they go against the tide of building expert systems using knowledge-rich representations, incorporating deep knowledge about causal, temporal and spatial relationships in the domain. Experts use this knowledge to adapt their reasoning to rare or atypical cases and to give plausible explanations. Many hope that incorporating this deep knowledge into expert systems (eg Szolovits *et al*, 1988) will allow them to display the same robustness and ability to account for their reasoning that human experts enjoy. Machine learning, by contrast, relies on the discovery of associations at the heuristic level, and on the building of deterministic decision-trees; it has no capacity for generating deep knowledge (Fox, 1984).

PROBLEMS WITH THE CONVENTIONAL APPROACH TO BUILDING THE PROTOTYPE

Typically, the prototype is built by a computer scientist with experience of knowledge-based systems, using the knowledge obtained from one or more experts. This knowledge engineer selects a suitable representation for the knowledge and then the appropriate tools. He usually builds a small prototype to demonstrate to the expert, as a check on the correctness of his chosen methods, and this prototype is then revised and extended incrementally.

The problems with this approach in medicine stem from the difficulty some experts may have in communicating with the knowledge engineer, and the complexity of the domain. It is not surprising that, since it takes a student five years to learn to practise medicine, a knowledge engineer will need to spend several weeks or even months learning basic medical principles and some vocabulary. For this reason, as well as to make the resulting system easier to validate and to allow it to provide more adequate explanations, the ideal knowledge engineer for a medical system may well be one of the experts. In the ACORN project, this approach has provided a much more direct line of communication between other experts and the knowledge base than if a knowledge engineer had been involved. This has meant that the refinement of the knowledge base is under the control of those who understand the domain, and could therefore continue indefinitely.

We have already mentioned that the preliminary to building our system was to screen the experts' suggested data items using measures of their actual power and repeatability in the users' hands. Only then did our domain experts start work on building the knowledge base, using the shortlist of data items to solve the problem. This constraint appeared to be quite acceptable, and may even have allowed them to clarify their thoughts more easily than if they had been given free rein over the full range of available input data.

PROBLEMS WITH THE CONVENTIONAL TEST AND REFINE CYCLE

Whatever technique is used to construct a prototype expert system, it is usual to check its performance against a library of sample cases with known correct answers. This helps in debugging and to focus attention on problem areas. The 'training' cases used are often quite unrepresentative of those which will be encountered outside of the testing laboratory: they may have been collected by the experts some time before, perhaps as part of a special study or because of certain unusual features, or be completely synthetic cases designed to explore certain troublesome parts of the system. Frequently the system's performance on these cases approaches 100 per cent after successive test and refine cycles, and the developers are sufficiently encouraged by their ability to match the domain expert's accuracy that they release the system for general use.

However, if this training set is the only standard against which performance is judged, there may be a marked drop in performance when the system is used in the field. The first reason for this is that the training cases may be unrepresentative of those encountered in the field by the system's users, with the result that the more effort that is put into tuning the system to the training set, the lower will be its performance on cases to which it has never been exposed. The second reason is that, while the data from the training cases may have been gathered painstakingly by experts, the data now being input is gathered routinely by their inexperienced juniors. Finally, factors such as poor human-computer interface and lack of understanding of the intended role of the system may degrade the system's performance in the users' hands. To avoid this, we have extended the conventional cycle of testing to include not only a laboratory-based 'test set' analysis (Wyatt, 1987a), but also a preliminary field trial.

The test set analysis of ACORN's performance was conducted after construction of the prototype and the usual debugging on a training set of data. It consisted of a comparison of the system's conclusions about a new set of real data collected by the users, with the correct conclusions. It was performed with a fresh set of unseen data each time there was a substantial change to the knowledge base – an incremental build-test-modify cycle (Alvey and Greaves, 1987). In this way we ensured that ACORN's development was performance-led, rather than an undirected meandering down the blind alleys of certain knowledge engineering styles.

After several man-years of development involving the collection of data from over 600 patients, the point was reached when a predefined level of performance on the test was passed, and it was decided to carry out a preliminary field trial of the system in the actual casualty environment. The purpose of this trial was to ensure that the potential problems such as the human-computer interface, speed of operation and so on were explored before moving on to a full field trial. This trial was conducted by asking the nurses to input the data into ACORN from each patient with chest pain as they saw them, and then to act on its advice. We checked to see if ACORN's advice was appropriate and whether it affected the time taken to admit patients to the coronary care unit.

We were disappointed to find that neither the speed nor the accuracy of decision making was improved during this preliminary field trial, but discovered that there were three main reasons for this. The first was that the accuracy of ACORN's advice when used by the accident and emergency nurses dropped by 7 per cent compared to that obtained when it had been used in the laboratory. This was due to two factors. Firstly, each patient's electrocardiogram (ECG) was interpreted by a doctor before the results were input to ACORN and the doctors' ECG interpretation was not always accurate. Secondly, some nurses reported that the system was 'answering questions for them' – we traced this to their slow keystrokes and the keyboard auto-repeat.

The second problem was that instead of using ACORN as soon as a patient arrived at the accident and emergency department, the nurses often did not input the data they had collected on questionnaires until later. This was again due to a combination of factors. The major problem was that the computer was slow and each consultation took about four minutes. This was exacerbated by the fact that the only place where the computer could be accommodated was out of sight of the main accident and emergency area. The trained nurses were reluctant to leave the department in the hands of juniors and spend four minutes feeding the computer with data. A further delay that occurred was that the mean time for a doctor to interpret an ECG was 20 minutes.

The third problem was that ACORN's advice was inappropriate for the nurses. It consisted of one of 13 possible conclusions about the diagnosis and further tests to perform which did not fit in with the nurses' 'triage' system, which emphasizes the selection of one of only three courses of action. In addition, nurses do not usually admit patients to a CCU without a doctor's agreement, and although we had obtained informal agreement for them to do this from the relevant authorities, the nurses complained that they were not formally covered to follow ACORN's advice without a written document.

Following this field trial we adapted ACORN to overcome these difficulties. A special automated ECG interpreting machine, producing more accurate ECG reports within seconds, was purchased and has eliminated both the delay and most of the inaccuracies of the doctors' ECG reports. To improve both ACORN's speed of operation and its ease of use for the nurses, an improved version has been installed on a fast laptop PC fixed to a trolley which can be wheeled to the patient's bedside. This allows the nurse to ask the patient questions and to enter their answers directly into the keyboard without the need for a paper questionnaire. The keyboard type-ahead buffer has been disabled to ensure that the nurses can only answer a question when it is displayed on the screen.

Finally, the advice given by ACORN was reduced to three triage options: 'Admit urgently', 'See the doctor soon', and 'Wait in the queue to see the doctor'. This, combined with a formally agreed, written, policy about CCU admission without the intervention of doctors, now allows the nurses to make more effective use of ACORN's advice (see Emerson *et al*, 1988 for further details).

THE PRAGMATIC APPROACH SUMMARIZED

Our pragmatic approach to knowledge engineering therefore consists of modifications to the three major components of the expert system development cycle (see Figure 2): the knowledge acquisition process, the building of the prototype, and the evaluation of the system.

The modified knowledge acquisition process resembles in some ways the techniques of rule-induction, and in others the construction of rules by 'guided discovery' (Blum, 1982). Our conviction is, however, that we are producing by this means not a decision tree, nor a statistical formula, but a marriage of the relevant facts with the experts' insights. This reflects the experts' overall strategy and, perhaps more importantly, incorporates the characteristics of the prospective users and their abilities at data collection in a more rigorous way than systems built using conventional methods. This said, there are difficulties; for example in the derivation of the 'facts' in the first place and in the need for large quantities of test data. Clearly there are areas where the conventional style of knowledge acquisition is more appropriate – such as in the construction of a system which is to advise in a pure classification problem or on some aspect of policy, where the distinctions are man-made. However, a predictive type of decision-aid, that is designed to solve problems in the real world where some element of subjectivity or 'star-gazing' is involved, is likely to benefit from our approach.

The second part of our approach involves a minor modification to the process of building the prototype and subsequent versions of the system. This consists of eliminating the knowledge engineer and allowing the experts to build the system, and may improve both system performance and the acceptability of explanations as well as allowing easier maintenance of the knowledge base.

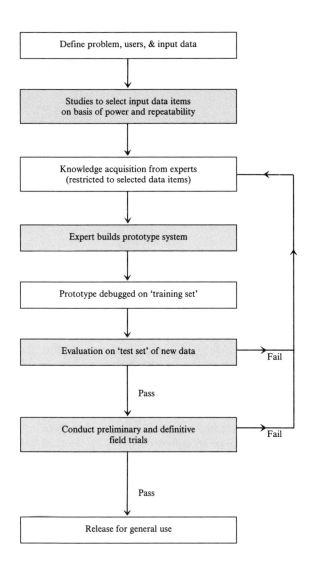

The shaded boxes represent additions or modifications to the conventional methods

Figure 2. *Proposed 'pragmatic' knowledge engineering cycle*

The third component of our pragmatic methodology, the rigorous evaluation of the prototype in both laboratory test set analyses and in field trials, is most appropriate to those domains where failure could be life-threatening, such as medicine and air-traffic control. However, if we are to enhance our understanding of those factors which influence system usability [Wyatt 1987b] and improve the value of our systems to their users, we must develop effective methods for evaluation of decision aids.

ACKNOWLEDGEMENTS

Thanks to Drs Charles Pantin, Nicola Crichton and Nicholas Russell and to Lucy Dillistone for their contributions to data collection and to the ideas and techniques discussed in this paper. This work was supported by the BUPA Medical Foundation and Westminster Medical School Research Trust.

REFERENCES

Adlassnig, K.P. and Kolarz, G. (1986). Representation and semi-automatic acquisition of medical knowledge in CADIAG-1 and CADIAG-2. *Computers in Biomedical Research,* Vol 19, pp. 63–79.

Alvey, P. and Greaves, M. (1987). Observations on the development of a high performance system for leukaemia diagnosis. In M. Bramer (ed.) *Research and Development in Expert Systems III*, Cambridge University Press.

Blum, R.L. (1982). Discovery, confirmation and incorporation of causal relationships from a time-oriented clinical database: the RX project. *Computers in Biomedical Research*, Vol 15, pp. 164–87.

Boose, J.H. and Bradshaw, J.M. (1987). Expertise transfer and complex problems: using AQUINAS as a knowledge acquisition workbench. *International Journal of Man-Machine Studies*, Vol 26, pp. 3–28.

Carbonell, J.G., Evans, D.A., Scott, D.S. and Thomason, R.H. (1985). *The MEDSORT project: final report on the automated classification and retrieval project*. Technical report; Department of Philosophy and Computer Science, Carnegie-Mellon University, December 1985.

Ellam, S.V. and Maisey, M.N. (1987). A knowledge-based system to assist in medical image interpretation: design and evaluation methodology. In M. Bramer (ed.) op. cit.

Emerson, P.A., Wyatt, J.C., Dillistone, L., Crichton, N. and Russell, N.J. (1988). The development of ACORN, an expert system enabling nurses to make admission decisions about patients with chest pain in an accident and emergency department. In *Proceedings of Medical Informatics: Computers in Clinical Medicine*, Nottingham, British Medical Informatics Society, September 1988.

Fox, J. (1984). Doubts about induction. *Bulletin of SPL Insight*, Vol 2, pp. 32–6.

Fox, J., Myers, C.D., Greaves, M.F. and Pegram, S. (1985). Knowledge acquisition for expert systems: experience in leukaemia diagnosis. *Methods of Information in Medicine*, Vol 24, pp. 65–72.

Gaschnig, J., Klahr, P., Pople, H., Shortliffe, E. and Terry, A. (1983). Evaluation of expert systems: issues and case studies. In F. Hayes-Roth and D. A. Waterman (eds), *Building Expert Systems*, Addison Wesley, Reading, Massachusetts.

ISIS-2 Collaboration Group (1988). Randomized Trial of Intravenous Streptokinase, Oral Aspirin, Both or Neither Among 17187 Cases of Suspected Acute Myocardial Infarction. *The Lancet*, 13 August 1988, pp. 349–60.

Miller, P.L. (1986). The evaluation of AI systems in medicine. *Computer Methods & Programs in Biomedicine*, Vol 22, pp. 5–11.

Quinlan, J.R. (1979). Discovering rules by induction from large collections of examples. In D. Michie (ed.) *Introductory Readings in Expert Systems*, Gordon & Breach, London.

Shaw, M.L. and Gaines, B.R. (1986). Interactive elicitation of knowledge from experts. *Future Computing Systems*, Vol 1, pp. 152–90.

Spiegelhalter, D.J. (1983). Evaluation of clinical decision-aids, with an application to a system for dyspepsia. *Statistics in Medicine*, Vol 2, pp. 207–16.

Szolovits, P., Patil, R.S. and Schwartz, W. B. (1988). Artificial intelligence in medical diagnosis. *Annals of Internal Medicine*, Vol 108, pp. 80–7.

White, A.P. (1987). Probabilistic induction by dynamic path generation in virtual trees. In M. Bramer (ed.) op. cit.

Wulff, H.R. (1976). *Rational Diagnosis and Treatment*. Blackwell Scientific Publications, Oxford.

Wyatt, J.C. (1987a). The evaluation of medical decision support systems: a discussion of the methodology used in the ACORN project. *Lecture Notes in Medical Informatics*, Vol 33, pp. 15–24. (*Proceedings of European Conference on Artificial Intelligence in Medicine*, 1987.)

Wyatt, J.C. (1987b). Improving the usability of knowledge-based medical decision-aids. Paper presented at *IKBS in Medicine*, EEC, Brussels, November 1987.

Wyatt, J.C., Dillistone, L. and Emerson, P.A. (1988). Thrombolysis in acute MI: why the delay? *British Heart Journal*, Vol 59, p. 618.

Yu, V.L. Fagan, L.M. and Wraith, S.M. (1979). Antimicrobial selection by computer: a blinded evaluation by infectious disease experts. *Journal of the American Medical Association*, Vol 242, pp. 1279–82.

Jeremy Wyatt
National Heart and Lung Institute
Brompton Hospital
London SW3 6HP, UK

Peter Emerson
Westminster Hospital
London SW1P 2AP, UK

Section II
Methods For System Development

Design is a creative process and it is impossible to prescribe how effective design can be achieved. It requires a degree of inventiveness as well as a thorough understanding of what is technically feasible. However , for any system there will be a number of requirements and constraints within which the design process must take place. These include the requirements of the users and organization, and the facilities and expertise which are available. In a practical situation quality is a key issue; systems should be built with quality and maintainability in mind. A methodology provides a framework within which the creative process can take place. It cannot provide the conceptualization of 'the problem' which is fundamentally important, and it cannot generate the ideas which drive the process, but it can impose a methodical, consistent and self-checking approach to system design. A methodology therefore describes the stages that are required, prescribing what needs to be done and how. It identifies the various steps and checks which are to be carried out, and often provides a standard system of documentation for recording the elements, processes and relationships which are identified.

There are a number of methodologies for information systems design. Many of them work on the assumption that implementation should only take place after a thorough analysis of the problem, and that it should be possible to provide a complete and correct specification of the required system before technical design or implementation take place. However, some designers maintain that this is impractical, and that users can only comment on a real(as opposed to paper) system. They advocate that a prototype system should be built in order to verify the principles of the design before a full system is constructed (Boar, 1984). These contrasting philosophies are exemplified by the various methods employed by expert system designers, and the chapters in this section illustrate the different views which exist.

Unfortunately, the term 'prototyping' is used in different ways and so it is worthwhile to distinguish between them. A common failure is misunderstanding within an organization, or even within a design team, about the purpose of a prototype system. Essentially a prototype is a system which has some of the essential elements of the final system, but not all. Sometimes the prototype is never intended to form the actual basis of the final system; that is, it is built with the intention of being thrown away when it has served its purpose during design. On other occasions it can be constructed with the express intention of its evolving, by a process of successive refinement, into the final system. Rapid prototyping is usually used to describe a 'throw-it-away' approach, whereas evolutionary prototyping, or incremental prototyping refer to different approaches. In incremental prototyping the system is sub-divided into parts each of which is prototyped, developed and then added to the whole. Evolutionary prototyping is the process whereby the system is successively refined until it is adequate for use.

An expert system is likely to be very large with many constituent parts. It is a question of some debate as to what should be prototyped and when. For example, it would be possible to prototype the knowledge base and leave the user interface in a relatively crude form. Alternatively one could prototype the user interface before implementing a detailed knowledge base. These questions are directly related to the issue of user involvement. The basic issue is 'What should you take to the users, when should you take it, and what do you expect them to do with it?' A related question which is often posed by people new to prototyping is 'When should I build my first prototype?'

In this section the chapter by Edmonds, Candy, Slatter and Lunn (Chapter 6) argues that prototyping should be used as a method for eliciting users' requirements and views of the system, and that this should be done before the knowledge base is constructed. This is based on the belief that it is actually necessary to see complex systems at work in order to evaluate them. However, many projects have resulted in a number of 'throw-away' prototypes, and designers have concluded that they rushed into prototyping too soon and that they would have been better spending the time understanding the problem rather than constructing a possible solution for a poorly-understood situation. Certainly, an undisciplined approach to prototyping can result in hacking and in poor quality systems. The aim is to get the balance right: it is important to have a thorough understanding of the problem and what is possible, together with an appreciation of how the users will react. The problem is knowing what to implement and when. Those who are not in favour of rapid prototyping advocate the use of intermediate representations; that is, complete models away from the computer, which can be checked for adequacy (in terms of correctness and completeness) before implementation (eg Diaper; Chapter 12). Such approaches may use new notations and different techniques from those of systems analysis, but they are in essence more like the traditional information system life cycle and methodologies.

A well-known method which is based on the system life cycle is called KADS. This is used and described by Hayball and Barlow in Chapter 5. The methodology identifies three stages in system development, these being orientation, problem identification and problem analysis. During orientation, a vocabulary of the domain is identified together with an analysis of the types of problem, characteristics of the domain, and the tasks which are performed. During problem identification the tasks are analysed and classified, and the concepts of the domain are structured. After this the feasibility is assessed, the knowedge base is specified, the processes are defined, and the user and environment are analysed. The methodology specifies which technique of knowledge elicitation can be used during which stage, and attempts to provide a classification of different types of knowledge which can be elicited during the different stages by the various methods. The methodology therefore has a set of terms which the designer maps on to the problem in hand, and then uses the appropriate documentation method to record and communicate the findings and analysis.

This is, of course, in direct contrast to the approach advocated by Edmonds *et al* (Chapter 6). Note also the contrast with the approach by Wyatt and Emerson in Chapter 4. In their 'pragmatic' approach a key stage is establishing which elements can be used effectively by the users of the system. In their project this required a careful analysis of the symptoms which the experts (the clinicians) found useful, and then an analysis of which of those could be used by the users (ie the nurses). This involved the use of questionnaires and statistics. Only when this was complete could a system be constructed. This match between the knowledge of the experts and the problem situation of the users was done away from a computer.

The chapter by Colbert, Long and Green (Chapter 7) adds yet another perspective to the problem. There are a number of methods available for system development, but in a practical situation one is often severely constrained by , for example, resources and time. This chapter provides a method for deciding which technique can be used given the actual constraints. It is no good aiming for perfection if that requires infinite time and resources where a system is required quickly with limited expertise. This chapter, while philosophical in nature, is a sharp reminder that the method for development must be determined in the context of the organization's resources.

At present there is no universal methodology for expert system development. This is hardly surprising as there is none for information systems, and it is still difficult to get effective user co-operation in conventional system design. Expert systems are often an order of magnitude more complicated, and also less well defined, than information systems and so a universal methodology is unlikely to emerge. Methodologies should also take account of the fact that expert systems are often for different users than those of information systems. They tend to be professional people with skills and status. They are accustomed to thinking about what they are doing and evaluating their results. They are likely to be talkative , with analytical and critical skills . Certainly a careful consideration should be given to the types of user involved: one can no longer assume that they are like 'clerks' of data processing systems. This is part of Edmonds *et al*'s (Chapter 6) argument for prototyping the interface – it was necessary for Wyatt and Emerson (Chapter 4) in order to carry out their analysis, and it must be a 'feature' of Colbert *et al*'s (Chapter 7) method. The selection of a method is therefore non-trivial. What is very important is for the designer to appreciate the potential pitfalls in the process, to be aware of the principles of good practice, and to impose a disciplined method of thorough investigation, recording and cross-checking on the design process. It may well be that a taxonomy of knowledge elements for that domain will emerge as part of this discipline. The chapters in this section illustrate the arguments and methods used by other people, and form a good basis for deciding on a suitable approach to be taken for a specific project.

REFERENCES

Boar, B.H. (1984). *Application prototyping: a requirements definition strategy for the 80s*. Wiley Interscience.

Chapter 5

Skills Support in the ICL (Kidsgrove) Bonding Shop – A Case Study in the Application of the KADS Methodology

Clive Hayball and Dave Barlow

INTRODUCTION

Many past attempts to develop installable and usable expert systems have failed due to inadequate consideration being given to environmental and user considerations. This paper describes the successful use of a knowledge engineering methodology to develop and install an expert system called Bond-Aid for the bonding shop at ICL Manufacturing Operations, Kidsgrove. It outlines the issues related to the provision of an expert system in this particular environment and shows how the use of a methodology can assist in many aspects of expert system conceptualization and construction. Special consideration is given to human issues since these often distinguish successful instances of installed expert systems from the many failures which progress no further than the stage of exploratory prototyping.

THE KADS METHODOLOGY

The development of the Bond-Aid expert system was undertaken as an experimental activity under ESPRIT project 1098. The objective of this project is to produce a sound methodology (now known as KADS – knowledge acquisition and design structured methodology) to support the commercial development of knowledge based systems (KBSs). The ESPRIT work was undertaken following the realization that, in the past, KBSs of any complexity have largely been developed in research environments using *ad-hoc* techniques of rapid prototyping which engender the likelihood of unconstrained iteration. In order for KBSs to become commercially viable, developers of KBSs must come to terms with constraints which are likely to be imposed by real-life environments, such as performance, reliability, security, integration with other systems, etc. In addition they must be able to develop these systems within clearly defined budgets and timescales.

The KADS methodology seeks to fuse elements of good conventional software engineering practice with the special techniques which are applicable for the development of KBSs. KADS has been successfully applied to a variety of tasks and domains, including:

- Assessment: bank loans, social security, credit guarantees;
- Configuration: research portfolios, oceanographic acoustics, plastic mould layouts;
- Scheduling: master production scheduling;
- Diagnosis: information retrieval, machine tools, PCB bonding equipment;
- Decision support: strategic marketing, computer network management.

A discussion of the needs for a KBS methodology and the way in which they are met by KADS may be found in Stratil and Hayball (1987). They provide a pragmatic overview of the current 'state of the art' within commercially available KBSs. They illustrate KBS requirements by two examples from opposite extremes of the scale, to illustrate the breadth of applications that a KBS methodology must accommodate.

The KADS methodology is directed towards commercializing the development of KBSs which are potentially more complex than most currently installed examples. KADS seeks to provide a distinction between 'first' and 'second' generation expert systems and places an emphasis on how to build the latter. A comprehensive distinction between these two expert system types is provided by Luc Steels (1987). Briefly, a second generation expert system is one which exhibits most or all of the following distinguishing features:

- Differing levels of knowledge (eg shallow, deep, support knowledge);
- Multiple forms of knowledge representation (frames, rules, nets etc);
- Several reasoning techniques (forward, backward, depth/breadth first etc);
- Flexible interaction (mixed initiative as opposed to system controlled dialogue);
- Explanations at several levels (user-oriented, not rule traces);
- Self-knowledge and user-knowledge to support functional flexibility and/ or learning.

In order to achieve these objectives, the KADS methodology places a strong emphasis on bridging the chasm between expert and system problem solving by providing structured methodological as well as practical support for aspects of problem understanding, requirements specification and system design. The overall methodological framework is based on a life cycle model (LCM), which details the activities which should be carried out in order to achieve well-defined checkpoints on the road to system solution. The top level of the LCM shows a breakdown of the total development activity into phases concerned with:

- requirements analysis
- knowledge refinement
- system design
- implementation
- installation
- use
- maintenance.

The practice of each of these activities for the bonding shop expert system is described on pp. 89–95. Most activities in the KADS LCM are supported by tools and/or techniques. A more detailed description of the LCM may be found in Barthemely *et al* (1987).

Figure 1 outlines the LCM for the requirements analysis phase of the methodology. The bulk of requirements analysis consists of two streams of activity which are performed in parallel – the internal and external streams. The external stream is mainly concerned with conventional aspects of requirements capture, such as organizational objectives, problems, constraints on system solutions, functional and user requirements etc. The internal stream is concerned with capture and description of the expertise which will form the basis of the system problem-solving component. These two streams of activity are subject to overlap and cross-feeds, since it is recognized that requirements analysis is, in the main, a process of negotiation across diverse and potentially conflicting viewpoints.

KADS also places great emphasis on modality issues – that is, the impact on the system of its having to interact with a human user who has unique characteristics which affect his or her ability to use the system in an effective manner. In particular, we note that 'mimicking' the expert problem-solving behaviour is not always the best system solution because (amongst other things):

- the user may not wish to establish the same relationship with the system as with the expert;
- the expert will undoubtedly display a flexibility in problem solving which a system will be unable to emulate;
- the introduction of a KBS will effect subtle changes in the organization which will lead to new perceptions of problem-solving roles and responsibilities;
- the system may be forced into certain modes of operation which are imposed by technical or cultural constraints.

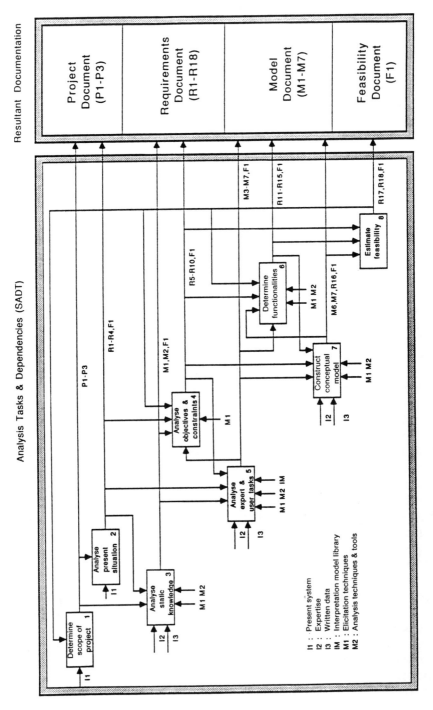

Figure 1. *The KADS requirement analysis life-cycle*

THE ICL BONDING PROBLEM

The factory at ICL Manufacturing Operations, Kidsgrove is involved in the production of printed circuit board assemblies (PBA) for inclusion in ICL computer equipment. A crucial stage in the production of PBAs takes place in the bonding shop, where the various layers of a multi-layer board are fused together under vacuum using a cycle of high temperature and pressure.

STC Technology Ltd were approached by ICL Manufacturing Operations early in 1987 and asked to develop an expert system to assist in solving problems in the bonding shop. The introduction of high technology process control equipment into the bonding shop had engendered a serious skills shortage. Operators were unfamiliar with many aspects of the new process and were often unable themselves to diagnose problems as and when they occurred.

Problems in the bonding area are potentially very expensive because thousands of pounds worth of boards are processed in a single cycle. Some problems may also involve hazard to human life (eg escape of nitrogen from the bonding press into the immediate environment). Although a process engineer is generally available during the working day, his time and expertise are needed in other areas of the factory. The night shift involves a more serious lack of support. In the past the operators have had to resort to calling the engineer out of bed, often for quite minor incidents.

This complex production environment was selected as a suitable size industrial problem which would benefit from the installation of an expert system. It was decided to develop the expert system as a controlled study within the ESPRIT KBSM project in order to test the effectiveness of using the KADS methodology and to feed back results into ongoing research. The human issues were of particular importance in this development because the process operators (the eventual users of the system) were, to a large extent, inexperienced in the use of computers and so required a readily understandable facility coupled with an interface style conforming to that used by other hardware and software within the factory environment.

THE BOND-AID DEVELOPMENT

Requirements Specification

The study commenced with an analysis of the project parameters. The initial meeting with the client brought to light a variey of human and environmental constraints which had to be taken into consideration when developing a system solution. The most important of these were as follows:

1. The development timescale was extremely tight – ICL were due for a

factory shut-down six months on from project inception and wished to have a proven expert system by then.

2. The system had to be developed on an ICL PC using standard screen layouts because the prospective expert system users were untrained in the use of computers and needed to have a system which looked and behaved in a familiar way (the ICL PC Quattro is the standard computer equipment in use in the factory).

3. ICL wanted the system to have some kind of knowledge editor so that they could extend the system themselves; in particular they wanted the system to be extendible later on to other areas of the factory where similar classes of problem were envisaged.

4. The expert system was to be de-coupled from the process control computer by placing it at a distance; the client felt that this was the only way to alleviate the fear which the operators felt when dealing with a computer which offered the possibility of ruining a batch of boards with a misplaced command.

5. The total cost of the system to the customer should not exceed £5,000, being the approximate cost of an ICL PC Quattro (the experimental software development was helped by funding under the ESPRIT project).

The second of the above constraints was found to present an almost insuperable problem. An investigation of the software packages available for the ICL PC Quattro highlighted the lack of any support for AI programming. The only possibility that was unearthed was an unsupported, three year-old version of Micro-PROLOG. This restricted the programmer to working within a 128K program space as well as restricting the Quattro system to single-user operation (the Quattro normally supports up to four simultaneous users). Fortunately, the manager of the newly formed AI centre within the factory viewed the bonding shop development as a high profile project and agreed to loan the bonding shop a bottom-of-the-range SUN workstation for an indefinite period. This was provided on the basis that it could be used to run the expert system inference engine, with a Quattro screen and keyboard providing the friendly user interface.

The main requirements analysis phase was carried out by allocating tasks amongst the four team members. Responsibilities were allocated for interviews with client, expert and prospective users, as well as for the production of four documents as defined by KADS (the project, require-ments, model and feasibility documents). Each person with the responsibil-ity for the production of a document had to ensure that the relevant information was available with which to populate that document, if necessary by placing a request for that information with the appropriate interviewer.

Interviews with Users

The KADS documentation structure forces a development team to consider a problem from a user-centred viewpoint. The requirements documentation includes:

- functioning objectives of the user organization;
- functioning problems of the user organization;
- objectives of the prospective system;
- man-machine interface;
- operational environment;
- control and security constraints;
- consequences (of system introduction).

The user-centred view was obtained by conducting interviews with five of the prospective bonding shop expert system users. Questions raised included:

- length of service in the bonding shop, time of shift, level of experience and responsibility;
- familiarity with the various alarm systems;
- real problems experienced in the past;
- opinion of the process control equipment;
- level of computer experience;
- suggestions for improvements to the existing equipment;
- attitude and suggestions concerning the introduction of an expert system.

These interviews showed up a variety of interesting results. The operators who were interviewed represented a broad spectrum in terms of length of service, type of shift and responsibility. They were generally familiar with the process controller alarms but unsure of some of the other alarm systems in the immediate environment. They could generally recognize but not diagnose alarms. They had dealt with a variety of problems in the past, but vacuum problems were a common type experienced by most.

With one exception, the new bonding process controller was the first computer system used by the operators. They found it generally easy to use, but complained that the system was fragile and insecure and needed a more visual or audible indication when raising an alarm. Most of the operators thought that they would make good use of an expert system, especially to become familiar with the procedures for dealing with environmental alarms such as the fire and evacuation alarms. General opinion was that the expert system should sit along-side the process controller in order to facilitate the transfer of data from one computer to the other – a view which was in conflict with that of the client.

The level of correspondence of opinion amongst the operators was encouraging. The operator interviews supported the opinion that an expert system solution was appropriate and provided valuable insight into the man-machine interface requirements. The client accepted that the users were probably correct in suggesting that the expert system should be positioned adjacent to the process controller.

Knowledge Acquisition and Refinement

The KADS methodology facilitates a structured and efficient acquisition of expert knowledge via a modelling approach. KADS provides a library of generic task descriptions called interpretation models. Once an expert task type has been identified from an initial analysis, a suitable model is selected from this library. Each model presents an idealized view of task performance at a level of abstraction which renders it domain independent. The model must be shaped and adapted for use in a particular domain by mapping it onto the expert's approach to problem solving. The concept, construction and use of interpretation models is presented in Wielinga and Breuker (1986); a library of models can be found in Wielinga *et al* (1987).

The diagnostic knowledge for the bonding shop system was obtained through interviews with the responsible process engineer. A model for systematic diagnosis was rapidly selected and moulded to reflect the real-life task characteristics. These included the ability to use several types of process model and to cope with multiple concurrent problems. Figure 2 depicts the resultant model for mixed-mode diagnosis.

Once the interpretation model had been formulated, knowledge refinement proceeded in an efficient top-down manner. The benefit of having a model was that it prescribed the types of knowledge and forms of deductive process to look for, so that interviews with the expert were structured and directed.

System Design and Implementation

The expert system was designed by focusing on the important constraints and then decomposing the functions in a way that effected a separation of concerns. The resultant system software architecture is depicted in Figure 3. It exhibits a close correspondence between elements of the conceptual model which resulted from knowledge acquisition and the resultant design modules. Each module was specified in detail in terms of its interfaces and internal functions and then passed to a programmer for implementation in Quintus PROLOG. Although some functional changes were specified during implementation and integration, the basic architecture remained unchanged with modifications limited to a small number of modules.

An important feature of the system architecture is that it results in a

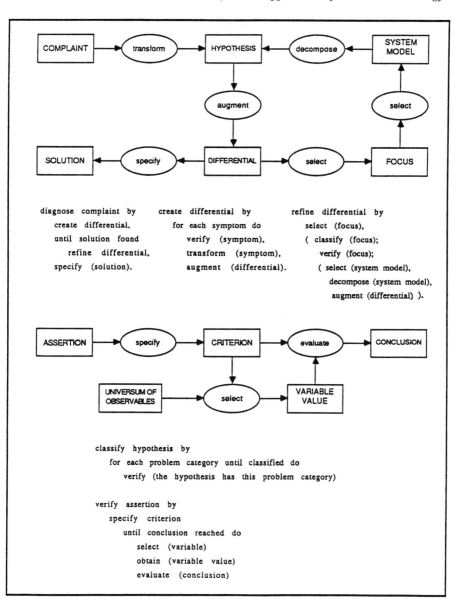

Figure 2. *Mixed-mode diagnosis interpretation model*

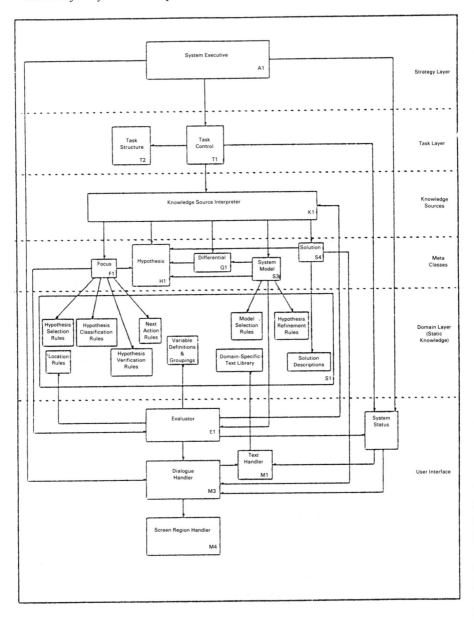

Figure 3. *Bonding shop expert system design architecture*

careful separation of the generic diagnostic problem expertise, the supporting knowledge and the human-computer interface, the last two of which are tailored for the Kidsgrove bonding shop. The system can therefore be viewed as a specialized industrial shell which can be re-used if a similar problem arises in another domain, provided that this also involves similar human issues.

System Installation, Use and Maintenance

The expert system was delivered to the AI centre at ICL Kidsgrove who had agreed to become the official first line of support in case of problems or difficulties with use. Despite the original urgency to see the system installed and in use, the client now agreed to a controlled programme of gradual introduction. This involved:

- validation of the knowledge base by the expert (production engineer);
- demonstration to the production manager and to a couple of the prospective users;
- installation in the bonding progress area for training purposes;
- final installation in the bonding process area for diagnostic and advisory purposes.

The first impressions of the prospective users were very favourable. Since then a number of comments have been raised which have led mainly to textual changes. None of the comments made so far has necessitated a major design change. The system was installed in a position in the process area some distance away from the bonding process control computer, as stipulated initially by the client.

RESULTS OF THE STUDY

The ESPRIT study of the development of a bonding shop industrial expert system application has resulted in a valuable feedback into the KADS methodology. Firstly, the study has shown that it is possible to develop, deliver and install a commercial expert system under the same constraints, and within the same timescales, as those normally associated with a conventional computer system. The approach of rapid prototyping fails to achieve this result because a lot of the costly effort is wasted and discarded during the subsequent iteration(s). The bonding shop expert system resulted from a sequential, not an iterative, development phase and yet is a fully developed industrial system, not a prototype. It utilizes a SUN-3 workstation with an ICL Quattro screen and keyboard providing a familiar interface vehicle. The software was written primarily in Quintus PROLOG, with a small interface program in 'C' used to emulate the Quattro screen-handling house style.

Secondly, the study has shown the benefits which resulted from a thorough understanding of the problem prior to system design and implementation. The external stream of requirements analysis in KADS ensures that the developers understand the constraints under which the system must be constructed, especially with regard to user needs. The internal modelling framework provides the basis for efficient knowledge acquisition, the result of which is an implementation-independent model of expertise. This model is structured so as to effect a clear separation between the static description of the support knowledge of the task concerned and the dynamic description of how that knowledge is to be used in problem solving. Although not demonstrated within this study, it is clear that this kind of separation provides the basis for portability of the problem-solving component across domains and for the static knowledge to be utilized in a variety of different tasks.

Finally, the bonding shop expert system exhibits most of the distinguishing features of a second generation expert system:

1. The bonding shop knowledge is expressed at several levels of depth, ranging from simple heuristic matches between symptoms and faults to complex models of a variety of aspects of the bonding shop environment.
2. The extendable syntax of PROLOG is used to ensure that each category of bonding shop knowledge is expressed in a specific and natural way.
3. The bonding shop system employs several reasoning techniques – forward chaining breadth first search through successive hypotheses, backward chaining lazy evaluation for verification of hypotheses, focused depth first search on high priority factors etc.
4. Graphical explanation is provided in the development environment to assist an understanding of the various threads through the software; this form of explanation is expressed at the level of the expert task, in terms of successive hypothesis refinement, and not at the level of individual rule invocation.
5. The system provides a fixed mode of interaction and does not support self-knowledge or user-knowledge. These features are not required because the level of dialogue between user and system was fixed by the need to conform to standard user interfaces in the factory environment.

In conclusion, the KADS methodology has been shown to work in practice. The wider project experience indicates that it can support a variety of problem-solving tasks in diverse domains.

ACKNOWLEDGEMENTS

The work on which this paper is based was carried out by Tim Mulhall and Lise Land (Knowledge-Based Systems Centre – KBSC) together with Ian Wright and Mike Knul (STC Technology Ltd). Thanks are expressed to Marie Stratil (STC) who provided invaluable comments during the editing process.

This work was funded under the ESPRIT programme as part of project 1098. The partners in this project are STC plc, SD-Scicon, NTE, Cap Sogeti Innovation, Universiteit van Amsterdam and Touche-Ross. For phase 2 of P1098, NTE replace SCS GmbH from phase 1 and Touche-Ross replace the KBSC at the Polytechnic of the South Bank.

REFERENCES

Barthemely, S., Edin, G., Toutain, E. and Becker, S. (1987). Requirements Analysis in KBS Development. ESPRIT P1098 deliverable D3.

Steels, L. (1987). Second Generation Expert Systems. In *Research and Development in Expert Systems III*. Cambridge University Press, Cambridge.

Stratil, M. and Hayball, C. (1987). Emerging Methodology in Knowledge Engineering. *Proceedings of KBS '87*.

Wielinga, B.J. and Breuker, J.A. (1986). Models of Expertise. *Proceedings of ECAI 1986*.

Wielinga, B. *et al* (1987). Model-Driven Knowledge Acquisition – Interpretation Models. *ESPRIT report P1098* deliverable D1.

Clive Hayball
STC Technology Ltd
Harlow, UK

Dave Barlow
ICL Manufacturing and Logistics
Kidsgrove, UK

Chapter 6

Issues in the Design of Expert Systems for Business

Ernest Edmonds, Linda Candy, Philip Slatter and Steven Lunn

INTRODUCTION

This chapter is concerned with critical issues which have emerged from experience in the design and implementation of expert systems in a commercial application. The key elements of the design process which are vital to the success of the system are identified and discussed with reference to a recent collaborative project. Some current approaches to system design, which arise from differing perspectives, are surveyed briefly. It is suggested that, in the context of expert system applications, the conventional phased, incremental approach has significant limitations. There are a number of reasons for this. Three significant factors which can affect the running progress and the ultimate success or failure to meet expert system project objectives are:

– the difficult nature of the requirements analysis process and its relationship to the knowledge acquisition activity;
– the requirements of different groups of users within the particular business environment and the way these impinge upon the system design and its evaluation;
– the impact that different perceptions of the design process within the development team can have on both the nature of the design concept and the way it is carried out.

These issues are thrown into sharp relief when the development team is faced with the problem of how to reconcile corporate aims, different departmental and user management objectives and end-user needs. A design and development model is described which provides a framework that places user involvement and the establishment of system acceptability in a prime position. It also addresses the organization of collaborative team work in a complex and dynamic situation. In particular, a view of the role of prototyping, and its relationship to system evaluation by users within the whole process, is discussed. It is recognized that there is no ideal generally applicable method for expert system development because the organizational context imposes its own imperatives within which priorities, resource allocation and deployment of personnel are decided. An expert system development team which comes from outside that environment faces considerable demand on professional abilities, from communication and interpersonal skills to sheer ingenuity and resilience.

The Case Study

The ideas put forward in this chapter arise from recent experiences in the development of an expert system for an Estimating Office within a UK manufacturing company. The context of the application was the estimation of machining costs prior to tender. The expert system was intended to be used by experienced cost estimators whose job it is to produce the estimates, usually to very tight timescales. In the existing manual system, the estimates appear as hand-written 'operation layouts'; that is, sets of machining actions required for a particular part, in this case aircraft landing gear, which are then conveyed to management for further action. The application development group consisted of the lead partner, a software company, and two academic partners. This group was funded both to deliver a demonstrator application and to produce longer term research results in the design and implementation of knowledge bases and their user interfaces. The overall project objective was to demonstrate the value of logic programming in the design of mainframe-based expert systems integrated with conventional DP systems.

DESIGN AND DEVELOPMENT METHODS

Design is a complex activity encompassing the decisions which finally determine the characteristics of a product. The process of achieving successful products is understood only in a limited way. In the case of software products, the emphasis at this time is on the identification of explicit, often formal, strategies that can be employed. There is, however, considerable debate and disquiet about design strategies or, more accurately, an agreed standard strategy for the development of computer systems. A rapid expansion in applications, particularly of expert system technology, is currently taking place against a background of evidence that the majority of software systems developed commercially are 'poorly specified, poorly designed, poorly documented, (and) difficult to use' (Wilkinson and Winterflood, 1987, p. xv).

Various design and development methods have evolved to meet the increasing complexity of applications in the business world. Some embody elements of traditional phased development, whilst others such as structured analysis stress the role of logical models that focus on *what* must be done rather than *how* it is done. More recently, the structured systems analysis and design methodology (SSADM), developed as a standard for government applications, attempts to widen the scope of structured analysis and offers a prescription for a more rigorous conduct of system development (Downs *et al*, 1988). For a useful summary of the design methodologies for constructing software systems from structured approaches such as top-down functional decomposition, data structure and object-oriented methods, stepwise refinement, graphical notations etc, see Wilkinson and Winterflood (op. cit.).

Depending on the application or research goal, the methods may focus on one or other point in the design and development life cycle. There are many divergent views as to efficacy and appropriateness. The legacy of traditional systems analysis, based as it is on developing successively tighter definitions of the proposed application until the final series of programs is obtained, affects the way people approach current applications. In the minds of many, the analysis and design are separate and consecutive processes: 'Analysis specifies what the system should do. Design states how to accomplish the objectives' (Senn, 1985). But, the concept of what design is, which underpins the basic philosophy of the arguments put forward here, challenges that definition and draws from the discipline of design in the broader sense. Design is, in reality, a co-ordinating activity which encompasses task analysis, requirements definition and development. It is particularly important to understand in relation to expert systems that requirements definition cannot be dealt with as a discrete stage prior to development. We will discuss this more fully later on.

There has been a considerable history of ideas relevant to the understanding and development of systems. It has not always been clear, however, that computer science has fully taken account of that history. Checkland (1984) reviews the background to the development of systems thinking in the 1950s and 1960s and to the attempt to apply these ideas to complex human activity systems in the late 1970s. He also reviews the subsequent 'soft systems methodology' which he characterizes as 'a formal way of moving from finding out about a real-world situation, which some actors regard as problematical, to taking action in the situation'. The approach assumes the need for continuous debate where the conceptual model is seen not as a model of the situation, but one relevant to it and to be used as a means of comparing alternative perceptions with a view to change. He is, of course, referring to information systems development but the recognition of the existence of uncertainty and the dynamic environment applies even more to expert system development where the territory is entirely new and where the end-users are often professional and expert.

Approaches such as 'Multi-view' for information systems definition, attempt to encompass the human dimensions of system design (Wood-Harper *et al*, 1985). The Multi-view method is distinguished by the attempt to take account of the different points of view of everyone involved in the analysis and design of information systems. It does this by combining an analysis of human activity, socio-technical systems, data analysis and structural analysis. Similarly, Shackel (1986) puts forward the ergonomic approach to design as an iterative process involving systems analysis, workstation (or task) analysis and evaluation. Usability is defined in terms of the effectiveness with which a system allows a task to be carried out, its learnability, flexibility and the attitudes it engenders in users. Design in this sense involves both human factors and software engineering. The notion of usability must be defined in the context of the total design methodology: the criteria for usability are determined by the specific user and task requirements. It must also satisfy the objectives of the corporate body, user management and, perhaps, the computing department of the business.

It is apparent from the range and diversity of these methodologies that there is no one agreed way. It could be argued that attempts to find one best way to deal with a wide variety of applications are misguided and lead to 'elaborate and bureaucratic methodologies' (Benyon and Skidmore, 1987). They propose a solution based upon toolkits. However, solutions which centre on particular toolkits are inadequate (Avison *et al*, 1988). There is a need to provide a flexible framework within which a variety of tools can be applied where and when appropriate. In addition, it is clear that system design must take account of the impact of the system on the organization and, in a sense, become an aspect of the management of change. The guiding design principles must be clear and carefully implemented in order that the coherent philosophy is understood and carried through by all participants (Long, 1986). This is easier said than done and the tendency to adopt 'reductionist' approaches for applications reflects the difficulty of addressing all aspects, from technical and resource considerations to the broad socio-political issues such as organizational and user requirements. The problems are accentuated in the expert system field where the prospective users are more often people with specialized, professional skills. However, where specific methods have been devised, the focus has been on the problems of knowledge acquisition and the structuring and representation of the knowledge acquired : the concomitant issues of user requirements) and design for usability and acceptability have received considerably less attention.

Experience shows that the exclusion of the users from the design of a system has serious implications for loss of time, due to lack of acceptance and resistance to change. The lack of consideration of the end-users in particular has played a part in the poor performance of some IT systems developments to date (AHIC report, July 1987). It is all too easy to overlook the complexity of the user requirements. In particular, the professional practitioner's requirements are not easily defined and, in relation to the impact of support systems, are ever-changing (Schon, 1971, 1983). Edmonds (1987) argues that the notion of a 'total design' concept contributes to understanding the extent of that complexity. Not only is it impossible for the designer to master all the specialized skills of the system builder; it is also impossible to master all the specializations from which factors contribute to design decisions. The designer must co-ordinate a variety of specialists in a process of 'synthetic production' and integrate their work into its wider context.

The integration aspect and the introduction of such a system into a live business environment make the issue of how to bring about user involvement a more difficult matter. The wide variation in users and the evident complexity of addressing their requirements deter many developers from tackling the problem. There are a number of different ways in which users can be brought into the design process or excluded from it as the case may be (Damodaran and Eason, 1981). User representatives, for example, provide controllable user expertise and are, inevitably, influenced by the design team. Participative design where users are involved in selecting the form of work organization, but not the technical design or programming, is known to be successful in engaging users' commitment (Mumford, 1983). However, user-centred design in which users design and experts advise, is a practice which is rarely seen. The critical issue is not 'Who does the work?' but 'Who has the power to influence the design?' All sections of users need to be represented and this is particularly important where there might be more than one user group with varying requirements of the system. The main problem is that there is no reason to suppose that corporate management, user department management, the data processing department and groups of end-users, will agree on where to strike this balance. Where the end-users are experts or professional people in their own right, it may be that the only way to design an acceptable system is to centre the process on them, their task scope and operational conditions. However, it must be remembered that the product of a user-driven development can be quite different from that of a knowledge based system/expert system driven process.

One might note that the development of methods in this area has come from general work in information systems rather than from the expert systems field itself. However, expert systems pose particular problems that may not be fully catered for in the more general methods. These problems relate to the much stronger emphasis on flexible systems for professional users that we have mentioned above when discussing the work of Checkland and others. It seems that we may well be able to draw upon research in general systems theory, but such actions will imply different approaches to new and changing human-system environments. Most of what follows should be viewed in the light of these comments.

EXPERT SYSTEMS DESIGN

In expert system development, much attention has been given to the problems of knowledge acquisition and representation. The effort is directed towards identifying and interpreting expert knowledge from interviews with experts (or textbooks) followed by mapping directly from verbal data to a chosen form of representation (eg rules). Knowledge acquisition is carried out at the very beginning because of the need to understand how to structure the knowledge and the inferencing mechanism. The nature of the knowledge required is important to define. In this complex process, there is much scope for misrepresentation (Hayward *et al*, 1987). More seriously, attention to these difficult areas usually takes precedence over how and by whom the system is to be used. In the KADS project, which aims to tackle knowledge-based system development methodology on a broad front, recognizing that 'partial advice is worse than useless to the system developer', it is acknowledged that their analysis techniques concentrate on the modelling of expertise, and that the modelling of user-system interaction requirements is left ill-defined (Hayward, 1987). Since that paper was written, attention has been given to modelling in other areas, notably what in KADS is known as architectural design and modality analysis. The latter addresses the issue of how the co-operative problem solver can interact in a variety of modes. This theoretical work is to be incorporated into KADS and validated through experimental system developments (Mulhall, 1989).

There are factors such as the initial focus of attention and overall goals which predetermine the knowledge engineer's view and, thereby, the system design concept itself. In the present case study the knowledge acquisition activity concentrated on determining and categorizing knowledge manifest in the final stage of the user's task process that is, the writing out of the operation layout (Slatter *et al*, 1988). The resulting analysis led to both an expansion of that component and a significant change in its implementation. When requirements analysis for the user interface was carried out later, doubts about the concentration of system support for this aspect arose. This was because the requirements analysis included consideration of task operational features, such as the relative time spent on different stages in the estimating process, as well as the information needed at various times.

An important consideration was that the system in the example under discussion was intended to be a co-operative one. Co-operative expert systems aim to provide assistance or support in a way which broadly conforms to a user's existing methods, and normally allows the expert to make decisions during the consultation process which may affect subsequent advice. The user's methods in carrying out a given task must be taken account of in the overall design of the operational aspects of the user-system relationship. Thus, the process of co-operation is significant in itself, as well as the functions made available and the accuracy of the advice given. In the present state of computer systems it is probably more appropriate to talk about human co-operation and system response. The ideal of the 'co-operating' computer is still to be attained.

Nevertheless, it must not be assumed that a user-centred design approach will result in a co-operative expert system. It is sometimes more attractive to users to operate in a simple well-defined manner that could not be called co-operative in the strict sense. However, both approaches represent a shift away from a fixation on the autonomous expert in expert system research, towards a greater emphasis on user involvement. In the case of co-operative problem-solving systems, this relates to the involvement of users in the reasoning processes of expert systems (Pollack *et al*, 1982). But equally important in practice is the way the expert knowledge appears to the user. If the representation of the knowledge is carried out separately and prior to the total system design , there may well be irreconcilable conflict. Where the two are in conflict our experience suggests that the user-centred design approach should take precedence. In user-centred design, the designer would need to 'advise' the users about the available co-operative problem-solving options but not to impose particular solutions based on a functional analysis of the situation.

Thus, a co-operative problem solving approach is only likely to facilitate user acceptance if:

– it is closely modelled on how users and experts actually co-operate in a particular task domain; and
– the users actually want a computer system that models this form of co-operative assistance.

This last point is of special relevance to experts who are likely to be very reluctant to see the interesting elements of their work subsumed within a system but who, by contrast, may welcome the provision of simple on-line information support, as was clear in this case. On the other hand, user management may be keen to see some of the expertise available in this form because it could provide them with a degree of standardization and could also be useful in training new recruits. We can clearly see that there are issues that expert system designers must resolve.

KEY ELEMENTS OF THE DESIGN PROCESS

The attention paid to the different aspects of system development varies according to the circumstances and the objectives of the power agents in any given project. Very often a key individual with enthusiasm and drive is to be found behind the successful scheme. If a system is to become more than someone's pet project and instead perform a productive commercial function, it goes without saying that it should be used. All too often, the importance of end-users in the measurement of success or otherwise is notional. To ensure sufficient attention to user requirements analysis and specification, and to place it correctly in relation to other activities such as knowledge acquisition, it must be included explicitly in the project plan. It is not an easy task to ensure that users are taken account of, let alone directly involved, in design. However, some activities lend themselves more readily than others to enabling the user-voice to be heard. The approach to evaluation and prototyping as vehicles for increasing user involvement and helping re-design the system is an important part of any strategy (Candy and Edmonds, 1988). In combination, user evaluation and the deployment of the user interface prototype as a vehicle for clarifying user requirements, provide practical mechanisms for assessing the appropriateness of the whole system design. A deeper exploration of the operational and functional aspects of the proposed system in relation to the total user task scope must then follow. In this section certain key elements in the process are considered.

Requirements Analysis

The specification of user requirements is a difficult problem. Requirements that arise from the early task analysis work may well contain errors or misconceptions on the part of the developers. A failure to apprehend the degree of complexity of user requirements is often the root of the problem (Edmonds, 1987). It is doubtful whether methodologies which are mainly directed at the computer core of the application, such as Structured Systems Analysis and Design Methodology (SSADM), address the area of requirements analysis adequately. Indeed, there is evidence that the most successful systems analysts pay attention to the socio-political aspects (Vitalari, 1984).

It is also worth bearing in mind that the word 'requirement' implies uncovering something which is already there in the minds of prospective users and management. This assumption can be mistaken on two counts. Firstly, where a 'requirement' is discovered, it may not be very clearly articulated or, indeed, may be expressed in vague terms, such as 'the output must exhibit 5–10 per cent accuracy, because that is the current figure for human performance', stated without the provision of a method for measuring accuracy. Secondly, and commonly in the case of people with no previous experience of computer use, there is a difficulty in imagining what support a computer system could offer, particularly in the case of highly complex work; in other words, there is in fact no requirement. Another important factor is that requirements are constantly changing. The very act of introducing a computer system into the thinking of the users creates an impetus to perceive tasks and relationships in a more dynamic manner. This will be increased with the first and ensuing contact with any early versions of the system. Chasing the changes in user requirements is traditionally one of the nightmares of system designers. How much of the well recognized high cost of maintenance arises from this factor?

There are a number of misconceptions about identifying user requirements – in particular, the notion that users can visualize the proposed system from documentation or a few screen designs. Another misconception, that a user can evaluate a system without a user interface, is evident in the guidelines on expert systems for the British Civil Service. The development phases identified reflect the traditional system development approach and preclude early user evaluation of prototypes by specifically excluding the user interface until after phase two (HM Treasury – CCTA, 1985).

Design strategies which take full account of the complete business environment are needed (Stow *et al*, 1986). In particular, there is a need to see requirements specification involving prospective end-users as an integral part of the design process. This is particularly important in relation to the early stages. The key point is that end-user considerations in those early stages are vital to getting the initial design concept right, as distinct from the nature of the domain knowledge or details of the system functionality. Another important issue to be determined at that stage is where boundaries of the human and machine are drawn. It is necessary to determine the place of the system within the total task and user scope which includes understanding how manual and computerized activities relate. The complexities involved in the provision of co-operative expert systems to professional workers are such that the requirements specification can only be completed after the users have experienced prototype systems. Indeed, considerable development progress may be needed before requirements can be completely finalized.

The User Interface as a Requirements Elicitation Tool

As we have seen above, when a new computer system is to be designed it is often difficult to gather the requirements accurately. In modern computer systems the user interface is often a separable module that can actually be run, in some sense, on its own. The user interface goes deeper into the system than the screen and keyboard (Edmonds, 1982; Green, 1985). This fact can offer an opportunity to assist with the problem discussed above. It is possible to prototype the user interface module and to allow users to operate it. Discussions with them, concerning their actual requirements around this prototype, may yield quite different results from studies based purely upon a paper exercise. Such a prototype can represent most of the operational aspects of a system even though its functional responses may be limited, by example only or not available. The evaluator can, without major problems, explain such limitations to the user.

Hekmatpour and Ince (1987) describe a project where a working version of a system was provided throughout all stages of the project. This is an example of evolutionary prototyping rather than a phase-oriented paradigm. During each iteration, re-specification, re-design, re-implementation and re-evaluation take place. In the present case study the intention was to treat the first prototype as a means of clarifying requirements and then discard it. When an acceptable design is achieved, the team then moves into the evolutionary development stage. Detailed functional and architectural design, and specification of the presentation aspects and operational behaviour of the user interface, form part of a rigorous software engineering exercise where the emphasis is on design for flexibility. Knowledge acquisition continues within the structures elaborated and proven in the exploratory phase and now embedded in the engineered system architecture. The first version should be sufficiently advanced to put into operational use. In the traditional life cycle this is the end of development and the beginning of maintenance. In the exploratory design cycle, described in the section on the design and development model, this is the first evaluation and design review point in the process. Changes and tuning will be followed by a series of such iterations until the evaluative role diminishes into a watching brief.

In the application of expert systems in general, it has been the knowledge base that has been the subject of the prototyping emphasis in order to refine its accuracy. There is an earlier need for prototyping in projects such as this one – using the user interface as the prototyping focus in order to elicit requirements from users. Prototyping in this way is, of course, distinct in kind from prototyping to refine the design. It is, therefore, important that there is a common understanding of *which* approach to prototyping is to be used within the development team and that this is conveyed to the users from the outset. Initial perceptions of the system (that of an early limited function version of the final system) can lead to confusion about what to expect and will prove to be difficult to change in later stages. Where there are high expectations, any signs of poor performance of the prototype leads to a lack of confidence in the development.

Definition of user interface requirements definition typically takes place within the design context established by the knowledge base analysis and, because of this, the end-users may be asked to define their requirements basically in terms of screen layouts. The user interface design is seen as a front end to functions already determined. However, users can have a limited awareness of the intended functions (Buckley, Candy and Edmonds, 1988). There is a common view in computing that the user interface component is the 'icing on the cake' and this view of the interface, the surface level of the design concept, was clearly shown to be untenable by the evaluation exercise in this case. It had become apparent that the original task analysis and knowledge elicitation, oriented as they were towards the domain knowledge rather than the users' task processes, and towards management views rather than those of end-users, had resulted in a proposed design which did not provide the kind of support to estimating that was originally envisaged.

Several reasons are given by Ince and Hekmatpour for the necessity of prototyping the user interface design. These are as follows:

- user interface formal specification can be very difficult (eg a written document does not enable users to visualize the system in use);
- there is a variation in the types and styles of users for any system;
- the complexity of requirements often leads to conflicting design goals which cannot be detected or resolved by written documentation;
- properties such as user-friendliness and ease of use are highly subjective; the 'look and feel' is revealed only when the system is 'live'.

The prototyping approach deals with these difficulties by allowing the design to iterate and involve end-users. In the early stages it is argued that the emphasis of the prototyping should be on the user interface. The reasons for prototyping the user interface relate directly to the dynamic and multiple nature of user requirements. Firstly, it is argued that the establishment of the users' operational requirements can be best explored and evaluated through the prototyping of the user interface, both at the beginning of requirements analysis and throughout the design process. In addition, it is important to recognize that operational requirements can differ from functional requirements. The latter are usually comparatively easily obtained, but it may only be by allowing end-users to experiment with the system that they can articulate the operational requirements. In practice, we know that several iterations are needed due, to a significant extent, to the dynamic nature of the requirements process.

Secondly, if this kind of development process is to be used, the prototype user interface must be deliverable in the field and it must be a reasonable view of the proposed system in order to allow the end-users to evaluate it in the light of their experiences. It is an important consideration at this point to remember that the requirements may belong to different groups, and that these requirements may be very different, or even opposed, in their natures

(Candy and Lunn, 1988). This may be due to different perceptions of what a particular system is for. Requirements which initially agree with the management and which include new disciplines such as standardized terminology, are likely to make the system restrictive from the point of view of the end-user. Installation of the prototype user interface will enable sufficient understanding of the proposed system for such issues to become explicit, be challenged and, it is hoped, resolved.

Since requirements analysis in a complex task domain can clearly be thought of as a particular example of knowledge elicitation, it is interesting to note that experiments, for example, by Berry and Broadbent (1984), show that verbalization may not accurately reflect the most significant aspects of a task. There are, in any case, problems associated with knowledge elicitation which cause difficulties:

- experts may not tell the individual who elicits the knowledge all the relevant details;
- they may assume that certain facts are 'obvious';
- their subject of expertise may be too complex for them to tell the implementors all the details except by asserting or refuting specific examples.

Given that verbalization alone can be misleading or incomplete, the user interface can provide a concrete object to facilitate both discussion and observation relevant to the knowledge that stems from requirements analysis. It can also provide a means of refining this knowledge, and, in a realistic way, give end users something to complain about! In this way, general requirements can be refined into specific ones in a series of iterations. While a good user interface is desirable, the real value in using the user interface in this manner is to enable the end-users to talk about what they want the system to do, and to detect problems before the main system is built. Prototyping to define requirements in this way is not a new idea, but, from the experience of this project, prototyping the user interface alone *will* facilitate a majority of the requirements definition. A similar view is taken from the software engineering position in the USE methodology (Wasserman *et al*, 1986). If the knowledge base is built first, the user interface must simply reflect its functionality and can therefore only be designed at a presentation level, which is well understood to be an incomplete view.

Knowledge Acquisition

Knowledge-based systems methodologies such as KADS (Hayward *et al*, 1987) have tended to focus on knowledge acquisition as the major development task. In KADS the objective is to construct a conceptual model of the expertise in some task domain. Requirements analysis, including establishing the appropriate role of the system, have tended to be regarded as separate and secondary activities. This is precisely the contrast that we have discussed above in relation to approaches to co-operative systems.

The KADS view may be compared with a design strategy where knowledge acquisition is directed to obtaining just that knowledge required to fulfil a system's intended role. Such an approach was adopted in the prototype of this case study, where an early decision was made to develop a co-operative problem-solving system – supplying prompts, suggestions and explanations as required, and critiquing user inputs. The subsequent knowledge acquisition activity was targeted at supporting these forms of assistance. This is reflected in the acquisition techniques employed. Informal interviews helped to establish an initial 'map' of the domain, including the main domain entities (machines, operations, parts and material) and the relations between them. In particular, this technique provided information about the main determinants of operation layout such as material type and form, part type and configuration machine technology. An analysis of estimate forms enabled the examination of the operation layouts for complex components, which deepened the understanding about the relationship of the estimate/part/materials parameters to certain operational sequences. These provided a basis which could be verified in interview sessions with experts. 'Talking through' estimates provided an informal version of protocol analysis. While completing an operation layout from an engineering drawing, the estimator was asked to report on his decision processes. The knowledge engineers took notes and intervened for clarification. In retrospect, this technique may have been overused – the quality and quantity of knowledge elicited was limited given its time-consuming nature. Finally, standard forms such as matrices drawn up to capture all possible permutations of machines against actions, stage of manufacture against actions, and so forth were completed. This knowledge was used in the generation of the dynamic action menus and in the interactive checking of operations.

As indicated previously, however, these techniques on their own were insufficient to ensure that the prospective end-user requirements were established in the early stages of the design process. In particular, the relative importance placed upon different stages in the estimating process and the importance of information derived directly from drawings within that, was not fully understood.

The knowledge needed to understand the requirements of the users performing the task is much broader than the knowledge required to understand adequately the functional answers that must be provided to the problems posed. This point is, of course, particularly significant in the case of a co-operative expert system. A concern for requirements must clearly figure highly in the early stages of a project. But it must be borne in mind that this is only the start of ensuring the design is satisfactory. The emphasis on 'getting the requirements right' from the outset is misguided (Nosek and Sherr, 1984) and, by implication, the knowledge acquisition process is more complex than is sometimes proposed.

EVALUATION: THE CASE STUDY

The evaluation exercise within a user-centred design process is important in two particular respects. Firstly, it is an aid to arriving at the most satisfactory design in a basic sense and hence, getting it right in a complete sense; and secondly, it is a means to facilitating user involvement. The two elements are, of course, interrelated. It cannot be assumed that even where experts are brought into the requirements analysis and knowledge elicitation work that the resulting design will be appropriate. Early user involvement in the evaluation of the first prototype and subsequent versions is essential. One element, which can be carried out by an agent outside the development team, is to introduce a quality assurance initiative as a means of early constructive support rather than only providing detailed criticism at the end. This kind of intervention can also be used throughout the design and development process to ensure that requirements are implemented and that vital matters such as the setting of acceptability criteria are attended to.

The scope of the evaluation is, ideally, extended to the whole environment into which the system is being introduced and the complete task attributes of the users, rather than being confined to the user-system interaction (Bjorn-Anderson, 1984). In establishing the general aims of the evaluation exercise, it is necessary to define them in terms of suitability for the task at hand from the end-user perspective. The first goal of user evaluation is to provide feedback on the design and operation of the system and convey the results into the next stage of the design and implementation work. The scope of what is to be evaluated will depend upon the context but will usually include general design features of the user interface, the accuracy and appropriateness of the expert system advice, and the reliability, performance, acceptability and ease of use of whole system. In establishing evaluation criteria with users and user management, it is important that appropriate assistance is provided by an evaluation co-ordinator whose role is to support and record, rather than to impose prescriptions or ready made, inflexible guidelines. In addition, the development team will, of necessity, need to establish its own evaluation criteria and to relate these to the users' criteria.

Collecting clear accurate data which can be readily transferred to the next stage of the design is very important. Structured interview formats, devised from taped unstructured interviews, can provide more accessible results than *ad hoc* conversations. However, feedback during initial training or informal discussion about the early system use and related activities are useful to monitor. The users in the present project were encouraged to record their observations about the prototype user interface on a 'scratch pad', or write notes during use. In addition, automatic time-stamped recording took place. Using the data gathered from these different sources provided a more complete picture of events. Because of the possibility of variation in views between management and end-users, the evaluation co-ordinator(s) must be alert to conflicts of opinion.

The evaluation of the stand alone user interface must, primarily, involve end-users. Their reaction, faced with the first direct experience of the projected system, can confirm any doubts about the matching of the design to their needs and be a means of articulating requirements. The possibility that the users might not use the system, if it is the case, is then apparent to the whole team. A complete reassessment of the design concept is only likely to be made when it is apparent that the users are likely to reject the system.

The installation of a stand alone user interface in this case study made it possible to evaluate that component separately from the knowledge base. One advantage was the early identification of issues requiring change in the user interface. It was thus possible to carry out a limited number of changes prior to the installation of the whole system. With the linking of the user interface and knowledge base, the identification of those design functions and features attributable to the expert system, and the architecture as distinct from the user interface, was possible. In a later stage, when the expert system output was evaluated independently of system use, despite the high degree of accuracy, users were not readily convinced that they could use it. Thus, it appears that an evaluation of functional performance, in the form of accuracy of advice given without direct operational experience with the whole system, has limited value from an end-user perspective. Separate user interface evaluation also provided an opportunity for the users to become familiar with the software and for the development team to gain immediate feedback about its use and appropriateness. However, it was made clear that there would be differences when the full system was installed. As a result of the user interface evaluation exercise a number of changes were made prior to complete installation. These changes had limited impact on the design of the user interface. They ranged from alterations to wording and type of input required, to modifications in the specification of machines from individual machines to machine groups.

Some issues were found to be of paramount importance to users. In particular, the reliability and performance of the prototype system which was perceived by some as 'Mark 1' of an evolving system in spite of protestations to the contrary. It is essential that, even with a prototype, it must be reliable because of the likely impact on user co-operation and confidence. A lack of robustness and reliability in the system can influence the results of the evaluation in two ways: firstly, by preventing the users from carrying out a sufficiently thorough evaluation; and, secondly, by affecting the users' attitudes to the system as a whole and their confidence in the development. The performance of the expert system in the sense of its level of expertise, the accuracy and completeness of its advice, was critically important to user management. The prospective end-users were more concerned about response times and the length of time taken to complete the whole task using the system. More important than this was the information such an evaluation yielded in relation to the design concept itself. This led to a reconsideration of aspects of the whole system and of the design and development process being employed.

Issues which emerged more explicitly included the difference in perspective between the end-users and management. The latter had a more positive view of the system design and thought that more training would overcome initial resistance. On the other hand, the prospective end-users did not see how they could usefully incorporate it into the estimating task because it focused on the final and, from their perspective, least significant part of the process. The general view was that the method used was likely to slow them down. It was clear that the performance of the system was critical in a number of respects, not least of which was the accuracy and completeness of the advice from the expert system.

It was the evaluation of the user interface that was instrumental in making certain issues, concerning the design of the whole system, explicit. It became clear that the procedure used up to this point had allowed some significant matters to remain implicit for too long. The immediate outcome was a change in project organization and procedures. The new design process adopted places more emphasis on end-users and the user interface early in the process. The application development teams were made inter-establishment, divided into design and technical rather than user interface and knowledge base, and the co-ordinating roles included a user company representative.

THE DESIGN AND DEVELOPMENT MODEL

From the experiences in expert system development that have given rise to the views expressed above, it can be seen that there are a number of overlapping elements which must be reconciled. In order to address the problems associated with requirements analysis and knowledge acquisition in the context of user-centred design and organizational realities, it is

113

necessary to adopt a development model which recognizes the complexity of that process. The phased incremental approach is limited because it supposes that the initial design concept is basically correct and that subsequent iterations will involve amendments to the first implementation. The model adopted as a result of the project described supports two main discrete stages: firstly, an exploratory design prototype which is thrown away and secondly an evolutionary prototype arising from the ashes of the initial design which is incrementally improved. It is, in essence, consistent with that of Eason *et al*, (1988). See Figure 1.

In the feasibility study, the application is identified (Stow, op. cit.), the design team established, the corporate context determined, and the feasibility of a project assessed. Assessment of feasibility involves establishing the business case, ensuring that the system can deliver significant, perceived benefit to the company, planning the project and organizing the design team. Having determined the business case, the design team then carries out the exploratory user task analysis and the first definition of requirements. Once the initial round of knowledge engineering and architectures work is complete, the first prototype is constructed quickly using the most appropriate tools for the purpose. These do not have to conform to the final delivery hardware or software base. Once the prototype has been evaluated it is discarded. When the team is confident of the design,

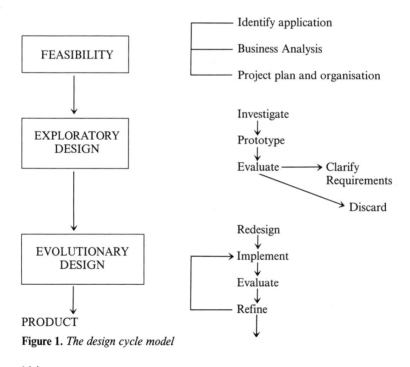

Figure 1. *The design cycle model*

the approach becomes an evolutionary one whereby each successive design is evaluated and refined until it is deemed to be satisfactory.

A critical difference in this model from the initial approach used in the case study, is that the exploratory user requirements specification predominantly precedes the knowledge acquisition activity. From the task analysis and requirements exploration a more detailed analysis of the task scope and user requirements emerges than has previously been obtained. Thereafter additional knowledge acquisition is warranted, there being a much clearer picture of what is required in terms of procedural, operational and factual knowledge. For example, in the present project it was discovered that more knowledge about the role of drawing information in specifying the set of machining actions on a part, (an operation layout) had to be elicited. In this way the user requirements analysis and specification impinges directly on knowledge acquisition work. The requirements specification defines the information, transformations and communications involved in the task, requiring knowledge-based support and conventional information access, and hence delineates for the knowledge engineer the scope of the knowledge required. In this case, the software architecture and specific knowledge representation employed in the first prototype were discarded, whilst the domain knowledge itself was carried forward to be refined and extended in the evolutionary prototype phase.

The establishment of ground rules that can be agreed no matter which culture the participants come from is vital in the early days of the project. For example:

- involve the end-users as early, as often and as much as possible;
- iterate round an 'elicit/design/prototype/evaluate' cycle in design and development;
- educate, inform, and manage the expectations of management at all levels;
- agree a coherent design, development methodology and organization and apply it.

The design team must include end-user representatives responsible for ensuring that a useful, usable system is produced, an expert 'owner' of the knowledge and experienced systems professionals. The corporate context in which the system will be deployed is important and should be included in the task analysis and evaluation. The project's objectives must be integrated with corporate strategies and goals, and the criteria by which its success will be judged must be defined. Both corporate and line management should be involved in this process, and should be asked to make clear the scope that the project team has for engineering changes in reporting structures, working practices and organization.

Plans must be kept realistic and achievable. Some useful guidelines are:

- the horizon for detailed planning should not be more than about three months;
- overall project objectives should be stated in fairly general terms (rather than specifying detailed requirements at the outset);
- keep the use of milestones and specific deliverables limited to the detailed planning horizon;
- overall project objectives should be formally reviewed in line with the planning cycle.

In applying the model, it is necessary that the requirements and contributions of corporate management, line management, domain experts and computer department management be recognized and reconciled with those of the end-users. But with such a broad spectrum of contributors to the design, it is inevitable that requirements will change during the life of the project. Changes can be caused by staff turnover, real-world changes and the development of ideas brought about by interaction with prototypes and the introduction of early versions of the system. The oldest chestnut of software engineering – that 'designing to meet a requirement is like walking on water – it helps if it is frozen' was always an impractical ideal. When developing systems with knowledge-based components it is essential to adopt a design and development model which recognizes and accommodates requirement and design changes as an inherent part of the development process. It is also important to recognize that the design and development model itself is only a framework which will be adapted to the particular circumstances of a project. Different companies have different procedures for defining and funding projects: departmental managers have different degrees of freedom as to how far they can take projects without corporate backing. Company management styles vary from the democratic and problem-oriented to the bureaucratic and dogmatic. Thus, for example, giving its end-users an absolute right of veto (or even a say) over a system design may seem obvious and natural in one company, and be regarded as runaway anarchy in another.

CONCLUSION

In a case study concerned with the introduction of an expert system into a manufacturing environment certain important factors for success have been identified or emphasized. It is particularly important that the design and development process focus on certain problems:

- the requirements of different categories of users;
- the relationship of knowledge acquisition to requirements analysis;
- mechanisms for enabling users to articulate requirements;
- the organizational context.

A design model has been presented in which the design team, which must include user representatives, follows an iterative process. In this model, the identification and refinement of requirements is seen to continue well into the system development process. A particular feature that can be employed is the use of a prototype stand alone user interface to assist with the early requirements analysis.

Underlying the work reported here has been a concern to learn from systems theory; it is suggested that Checkland's notion of 'soft systems methodology' needs urgent attention in the context of the debate about design and development methods for expert systems in particular and computer systems in general.

ACKNOWLEDGEMENTS

The authors are members of a much larger team concerned with all aspects of the project. They are grateful to all members of the team, especially the users. Particular mention must be made of Mark Buckley who made valuable contributions to the case study of the project and commented on earlier drafts of this chapter. The work was funded as part of the an Alvey Programme as project Alvey IKBS 058.

REFERENCES

AHIC report (1987). *Human Interface Issues in the IT 86 Programme*. AHIC discussion document prepared for Alvey Directorate.

Avison, D.E., Fitzgerald, G. and Wood-Harper, A.T.(1988). Information systems development: a tool kit is not enough. *The Computer Journal*, Vol 31, No 4, pp. 379–80.

Benyon, D. and Skidmore, S. (1987). Towards a toolkit for the system's analyst. *Ibid.*, Vol 30, No 1.

Berry, D.C and Broadbent, D. (1984). On the Relationship between Task Performance and Associated Verbalizable Knowledge. *Quarterly Journal of Experimental Psychology*, **36A**, 209–31.

Bjorn-Anderson, N. (1984). Challenge to Certainty. In *Beyond Productivity: Information Systems Development for Organizational Effectiveness*, Th.M.A. Bemelmans (ed.). Elsevier Science Publishers (North-Holland), IFIP.

Buckley, M., Candy, L. and Edmonds, E.A. (1988). Determining Requirements and Prototyping the User Interface. Paper presented at *Human and Organizational Issues of Expert Systems*, joint ICL/ Ergonomics Society Conference, Stratford, May.

Candy, L. and Edmonds, E.A. (1988). Expert System Development for an Office Environment: Users, Evaluation and the Design Process. *Proceedings IFAC Conference on Man-Machine Systems*, Oulu, Finland, June.

Candy, L. and Lunn, S. (1988). Design Strategies for Expert Systems : a case study. Paper presented at *Human and Organizational Issues of Expert Systems*, joint ICL and Ergonomics Society Conference, Stratford, May.

Checkland, P.B. (1984). Systems Theory and Information Systems. In *Beyond Productivity: Information Systems Development for Organizational Effectiveness*, Th.M.A. Bemelmans (ed.). Elsevier Science Publishers (North-Holland), IFIP.

Damodaran, L. and Eason, K.D.(1981). Design Procedures for User Involvement and User Support. In *Computing Skills and the User Interface*, M.J. Coombs and J.L. Alty (eds), 373–88.

Downs, E., Clare, P. and Coe, I. (1988). *SSADM: Application and Context*. Prentice Hall, London.

Eason, K.D., Harker, S.D.P., Raven, P.F., Brailsford, J.R. and Cross, A.D. (1987). A User-Centred Approach to the Design of a Knowledge-Based System. *Proceedings of Interact 87*, H.J. Bullinger and B. Shackel (eds). North Holland, IFIP.

Edmonds, E.A. (1982). The man-computer interface: a note on concepts and design. *International Journal of Man-Machine Studies*, **16, 5**, 231–36.

Edmonds, E.A. (1987). Good Software Design : What does it mean?. *Proceedings of Interact 87*, Bullinger, H.J and Shackel, B. (eds). Proc Interact 87. North-Holland, IFIP, 333–5.

Green, M. (1985). Report on dialogue specification tools. In Pfaff, G.E. (ed.), *User Interface Management Systems*. Springer-Verlag, North Holland, Amsterdam.

Hayward, S. (1987). The KADS Methodology : Analysis and Design for Knowledge-Based Systems. *ESPRIT report Y1: P1098*, STC Technology Ltd.

Hayward, S., Wielinga, B.J., and Breuker, J.A. (1987). Structured Analysis of Knowledge. *International Journal Man-Machine Studies*, **26**, 487–98.

Hekmatpour, S. and Ince, D.C. (1987). Evolutionary Prototyping and the Human-Computer Interface. *Proceedings of Interact 87*, H.J. Bullinger and B.Shackel(eds). North-Holland, IFIP.

HM Treasury (CCTA) (1985). Information Technology in the Civil Service: Expert Systems–Some Guidelines.

Ince, D.C. and Hekmatpour, S.(1987). Software Prototyping in the Eighties.

Information technology briefings, Dept of Computing, The Open University, UK.

Long, J. (1986). People and Computers: Designing for Usability. *Proceedings of 2nd Conference BCS HCI Specialist Group, People and Computers: Designing for Usability*, M.D. Harrison and A.F. Monk (eds), CUP.

Mulhall, T. (1989). Touche Ross Management Consultants, (personal communication).

Mumford, E. (1983). *Designing Participatively*. Manchester Business School, Manchester University, UK.

Nosek, J.T. and Sherr, D.M. (1984). Getting the requirements right vs. Getting the system working – Evolutionary development. In *Beyond Productivity: Information Systems Development for Organizational Effectiveness*, Th.M.A. Bemelmans (eds). Elsevier Science Publshers (North-Holland), IFIP.

Pollack, M.E., Hirschberg, J. and Webber, B. (1982). User participation in the reasoning processes of expert systems. *Proceedings of AAAI-82*, 358–61.

Schon, D. (1971). *Beyond the Stable State*. Temple Smith, London.

Schon, D. (1983). *The Reflective Practitioner*. Temple Smith, London.

Senn, J.A. (1985). *Analysis and Design of Information Systems*. McGraw-Hill, London.

Shackel, B. (1986). Ergonomics in Design for Usability. *People and Computers: Designing for Usability, Proceedings of 2nd Conference BCS HCI Specialist Group*, M.D. Harrison and A.F. Monk (eds).

Slatter, P., Nomura, T. and Lunn, S. (1988). A Representation for Manufacturing Sequencing Knowledge to Support Co-operative Problem Solving. Paper presented at joint ICL/ Ergonomics Society Conference: *Human and Organizational Issues of Expert Systems*, Stratford.

Stow, R., Lunn, S. and Slatter, P. (1986). How to identify business applications of expert systems. *Proceedings of 2nd International Expert Systems Conference*, Learned Information, Oxford.

Vitalari, N.P. (1984). A critical assessment of structured analysis methods: a psychological perspective. In *Beyond Productivity: Information Systems Development for Organizational Effectiveness*, Th.M.A. Bemelmans (ed.). Elsevier Science Publishers (North-Holland), IFIP.

Wasserman, A.I, Pircher, P.A, Shewmake, D.T and Kersten, M.L.(1986). Developing Interactive Information Systems with the User Software Engineering Methodology. *IEEE Transactions on Software Engineering*, **12, 2**, 326–45.

Wilkinson, G.G. and Winterflood, A.R. (eds) (1987). *Fundamentals of Information Technology*. John Wiley and Sons, London.

Wood-Harper, A.T., Antill , L. and Avison, D.E.(1985). *Information*

Systems Definition : The Multi-View Approach. Blackwell Scientific Publications, Oxford.

Ernest Edmonds and Linda Candy
LUTCHI Research Centre, Department of Computer Studies
Loughborough University of Technology
Loughborough
Leics LE11 3TU, UK

Philip Slatter and Steven Lunn
Telecomputing PLC
244 Barns Road
Oxford OX4 3RW, UK

Chapter 7

Methods for the Development and Application of Knowledge-Based Systems: Some Features, Constraints and Issues

Martin Colbert, John Long and David Green

INTRODUCTION

In order to exploit the potential of new computer technology, organizations require methods for the development and application of knowledge-based systems (KBSs). This chapter concerns the initial specification of one such method for Research Associations. This specification, it is considered, will help those attempting to specify other such methods. First, the requirements of the method and an approach to the specification of methods are outlined. Then, the process and product of specifying the method for RAS are presented. Finally, some human and organizational issues arising from the specification are considered.

REQUIREMENTS OF THE METHOD

Organizations need to use knowledge effectively. KBSs have the potential to satisfy this need. However, to realize this potential, organizations require methods for the development and application of such systems.

The research associations (RAs) are organizations which operate within specialist engineering domains, such as hydromechanics and welding, to provide engineering consultancy. The RAs have the ability to distribute specialist engineering knowledge to UK industry. They provide information, advice, research and development services, and related technical support including software. Consequently, they attract financial support from public bodies, such as the Department of Trade and Industry, and from many UK industrial and manufacturing companies.

To supplement and extend their activities, the RAs require a method for the development and application of KBSs. This method must satisfy a number of requirements. It must enable the development of KBSs which perform a variety of tasks within a variety of engineering domains. It must be appropriate for use by present RA personnel; that is, by hydromechanical or welding engineers and traditional software engineers with limited experience of developing KBSs. The method must also make current KBS development activities less informal and less *ad hoc* whilst maintaining flexibility.

Some of these requirements are likely to be shared by other organizations. For example, an objective of the RAs is to use artificial intelligence techniques to sensitize existing databases to particular tasks. A valve manufacturer's catalogue might be sensitized to component selection. Other requirements of the method, however, may be unique to the RAs. For example, the method must be appropriate for developing a wide variety of KBSs. The KBSs will be used within a number of task contexts, including selection, diagnosis and design, and within a number of organizational contexts, including the RAs and their member companies. The KBSs will also vary in size and in their degree of integration with other systems. Other organizations may have less varied requirements.

AN APPROACH TO THE SPECIFICATION OF METHODS

The need expressed by the RAs formed the basis of collaborative research. An approach to the development and application of KBSs was outlined (Green, Colbert and Long, 1987). They proposed that a method that satisfied the particular requirements of the RAs was unlikely to be specified by drawing analogies with currently available methods, since all potential analogies were significantly different from this case. Consequently, the method for RAs was specified by constructing a range of possible methods and then selecting an appropriate option from within this range. More specifically, the method was specified by identifying some critical features of the method for RAs, some possible values of these features and some constraints imposed by particular values of these features. A feature, here, is the most basic unit of description of the method. A constraint is a limitation imposed by a particular value of one feature of the method on the possible values of other features of the method. The features and values identified were then used in a process of explicitly accepting or rejecting constraints. For example, 'representation' is a feature with possible values 'booklet' and 'manual'. The particular value 'booklet' constrains the possible values of another feature, namely 'level of description' to high. A booklet provides insufficient space for a detailed, that is, low level of description. The acceptance of the constraint imposed by 'booklet' means that only a high level of description is possible. For example, rather than describing in detail the steps by which one conducts a particular technique, the method would simply state that the technique was to be used.

This process of accepting or rejecting constraints resulted in the specification of a suggested method. This specification is presented below in terms of some of its critical features, their possible values and constraints. Since critical features are likely to be common across methods, these examples should assist others attempting to specify other methods for the development and application of KBSs.

THE SPECIFICATION OF THE METHOD

The method specified is a mixed, or hybrid method. It is to provide both declarative and procedural knowledge, knowledge of various levels of certainty, and knowledge expressed at different levels of description. It is to cover all stages of the development and application of KBSs and be represented in the form of a booklet and an on-line knowledge base. The subsequent sections specify the method in more detail, consider some human and organizational issues arising from this specification, and finally, suggest possible future development of the method in the light of its potential strengths and weaknesses.

SOME FEATURES OF THE METHOD AND THEIR POSSIBLE VALUES

A method is defined as a representation which provides a user, who has a goal, with the control knowledge for performing a task, meeting certain criteria using certain instruments in a given organizational context. This definition identifies a number of specific features of the method, namely, 'representation', 'user', 'control knowledge', 'organizational context', 'goal', 'task', 'criteria' and 'instruments'. These features and their possible values are described below and constitute potential sources of constraint on the method.

The feature 'representation'

This may take a number of values, including 'manual', 'computer program' or 'journal article'. In the case of the RAs this is a booklet together with an on-line knowledge base. 'Booklet' and 'on-line knowledge base', then, constitute particular values of the feature 'representation' of the method for use by RAs.

The feature 'user'

This can be described in terms of level of skill in the application of appropriate techniques. ('User', here, refers to users of the method rather than end-users of the KBS.) A number of factors contribute to level of skill, including experience of KBS development, educational background, attitudes and preferences. Users in the RAs have some skill. They are, typically, domain experts and traditional software engineers who have limited experience of using intuitive techniques to develop demonstration and/or prototype KBSs. Such users contrast with, for example, domain experts unfamiliar with KBSs or expert knowledge engineers.

The feature 'control knowledge'

Control knowledge determines what the user should do next. It may be of different types, be described at different levels of description and possess different levels of certainty. For example, a method can provide procedural control knowledge which might read: 'Do a card sort, then do a cluster analysis', or it may provide declarative control knowledge, which might read '*If* the knowledge provider knows the requirement for knowledge, *then* the length of his or her turn in an interview can be long'.

Control knowledge can also be described at different levels. Levels of description can be distinguished in terms of the degrees of freedom a user of control knowledge is allowed – higher levels of description allow greater freedom. For example, a task in which an unstructured set of concepts, represented as outline drawings, is transformed into a structured set of objects represented in terms of spatial location on a computer screen, may be described, at a high level, as 'concept assignment'. At a low level of description it may be described as 'on-line icon sorting' or 'card sorting'. In this example, the high level of description allows the freedom to perform the task on- or off-line; the low level of description does not allow such freedom.

Control knowledge can also possess different levels of certainty. Uncertain control knowledge might be based on an hypothesis derived from one particular experience. Certain control knowledge, in contrast, might be supported by a generally accepted theory.

The method devised for the RAs is to provide both declarative, high-level, uncertain control knowledge (referred to here as heuristics), and procedural, low-level certain control knowledge (referred to here as algorithms). This contrasts with, for example, a method which provides either heuristic or algorithmic control knowledge, but not both, or one which provides some other type of control knowledge, such as uncertain, high-level, procedural knowledge.

The feature 'task'

This is a feature of the method which varies in terms of the stages of system development. It may take the possible values of 'requirements analysis', 'specification', 'implementation', or 'evaluation'. The task also varies in terms of the extent to which it can be specified. For example, it may be possible to specify the task of developing a prototype KBS for demonstration purposes well. However, the task of developing a large, integrated KBS capable of meeting the needs of real users may, in the absence of models of tasks and domains (see Kidd and Sharpe, 1988), be difficult or impossible to specify. The method devised for the RAs is to cover all stages of KBS development and application. These stages can, at present, only be ill-specified. Where resources allow however, it may be possible to specify well certain sub-tasks of knowledge elicitation. The method for use by RAs contrasts with one which guides a single stage of system development, such as implementation, or one which attempts to specify all stages of system development well.

The feature 'goal'

This may also take a number of values. The goal of the RAs is to develop, now, systems which make a significant contribution to knowledge use within themselves and within their membership. This contrasts with, for example, a KBS developer whose goal is to explore the potential of KBSs or to discover the demands that the development of such systems will place on the organization(s) concerned.

The features 'criteria', 'instruments' and 'organizational context'

The criteria applied to the method include acceptability (how willing users of the method, that is knowledge engineers and knowledge providers, are to perform KBS development tasks using the method); usability (how able the users are to perform the task using the method); functionality (the extent to which the task is performed as required using the method); and utility (the extent to which use of the method is cost effective). A method requires the use of different instruments. For example, a computer-based method for KBS development may be compatible with specific hardware. An off-line method may require the use of intermediate representations, recording equipment and means of data analysis. The method devised for RAs is compatible with the computer systems which they currently use. The organizational context for a method is contributed to by such factors as prior experience in KBS development, the attitude to training, the importance of confidentiality, the consequences, in terms of employment (for example, for those assisting in KBS development) and the availability of knowledge providers and their obligation to participate. For the RAs, the state of the client relationship is of considerable importance.

Figure 1 summarizes the values of the features of the method devised for the RAs.

---

* representation := on-line knowledge base and booklet
* user := domain expert and traditional software engineer with some skill in KBS development
* control knowledge := heuristic, and algorithmic in parts
* task := all stages of system development ill-specified
  some sub-tasks of knowledge elicitation well-specified
* goal := real systems and now
* criteria := acceptable, usable, functional and utilizable
* instruments := wide compatibility
* organizational context := confidentiality ensured

Figure 1. *High level specification of the method for developing and applying KBSs for Research Associations*

In the Figure, the fact that a feature of the method takes particular value is written as 'feature := value'.

In order to explain how and why these features were selected, and why other options were rejected, it is necessary to consider some constraints on the method.

SOME CONSTRAINTS ON THE METHOD

A constraint is a limitation imposed by a particular value of one feature of the method on the possible values of other features of that method. For example, since appropriate models of tasks and domains do not currently exist, the task of KBS development can, for present purposes, be only ill-specified. Thus, the particular value 'now' of the feature 'goal' constrains the value of 'task' to 'ill-specified'. Future research into tasks and domains may be more or less successful. Thus, the constraint imposed by the value 'future' of the feature 'goal' is treated as unknown.

Further, the ability to specify the task constrains the type of control knowledge provided by an appropriate method. A generally accepted principle of computer science is that ill-specified tasks are controlled most effectively by heuristics. Well-specified tasks are controlled most effectively by algorithms (Davis and Lenat, 1982). Thus, the particular value 'ill-specified' of the feature 'task' constrains possible values of the feature 'control knowledge' to 'high-level, declarative and uncertain'. The value 'well-specified' constrains other values to 'low-level, procedural and certain'.

Different types of control knowledge place different demands on the user. Algorithmic control knowledge can be applied easily and directly by users familiar with the operations required. However, in order to apply heuristic control knowledge, the user must re-describe that knowledge and reason with it. A user must also be able to diagnose and recover from the errors in task performance which, as a result of the uncertainty of the knowledge, inevitably occur. Thus, the particular value 'heuristic' of the feature 'control knowledge' constrains the possible values of the feature 'user' to 'skilled'. The value 'algorithmic' constrains values to 'less-skilled'.

To summarize, then, the KBS development task is currently ill-specified. Consequently, the RAs can provide heuristic control knowledge for immediate use. Heuristic control knowledge needs skilled users (see Figure 2).

These constraints helped to define the problem of specifying a method. Current RA personnel have limited skills in KBS development. The RAs would therefore like to have algorithmic control knowledge. However, they cannot have this type of knowledge now. The solution to this problem consists of two elements. First, the value of the feature 'user' is to be changed from 'less-skilled' to 'skilled'; that is to say, personnel are to be trained. Second, where possible, the value of the feature task is to be changed from ill-specified to well-specified, thus enabling some algorithms to be developed for aspects of knowledge transfer. Alternative solutions might have been: – to change the goal of KBS development from 'now' to 'sometime in the future', by which time it may be possible to specify well all stages of KBS development; – to increase usability and acceptability at the expense of functionality, ie to change the criteria and to apply an algorithmic method to an ill-specified task.

Knowledge of the features of the method, together with their consequences as constraints, although uncertain and possibly incomplete, was nevertheless sufficient to enable explicit and informed decision making during the specification of the method for the development and application of KBSs for use by RAs. Since other methods for developing and applying KBSs are likely to be similar to the method specified here, the features,

goal := ⟶ task := ill-specified

task := ill-specified ⟶ control knowledge := heuristic

control knowledge := heuristic ⟶ user := skilled

Figure 2. *Some constraints on the method*

In the Figure, the fact that a feature of the method takes a particular value is written as 'feature := value'. Constraint is imposed left to right and is represented by arrows pointing from the source of constraint towards the object of constraint.

values, and constraints identified should assist others specifying methods. However, additional values, features and constraints are likely to be relevant to other applications. For example, if the application involves issues of safety, the additional value 'formal' of the feature 'control knowledge' may be important – formal control knowledge provides greater guarantees. If the method is to be up-dated, the additional value 'modular' of the additional feature 'representation' may be important – it is easier to modify control knowledge represented as separable units. Thus, method developers need to consider, not only what has been presented here, but also what is relevant to their own applications. Additional features and values of possible relevance may be found in Long *et al* (1982), which lists 35 variables that influence the attitudes of users and non-users to the introduction of an interactive computer system.

ISSUES RAISED BY THE SPECIFICATION

The process and product of specifying the method for use by RAs raised a number of issues which required consideration for the proposed development and application of KBSs to be effective.

First, specifications may be highly constrained by a particular value of just one feature. The influence of this feature is propagated throughout the method as the acceptance of one constraint necessitates the acceptance of other constraints. For example, in this case the critical value 'now' of 'goal' constrained the value of 'task' to 'ill-specified', which in turn constrained 'control knowledge' to 'heuristic', which in turn constrained 'user' to 'skilled'. Changing this key feature influences other, apparently loosely-related features of the method. For example, a method for use in the future may be applied by different kinds of user. Second, in order to develop and apply KBSs an organization may need to change. In this case, change in the organization was manifest as training.

Third, both the requirements (of the method) and the solution (in the form of a method) may impose and experience constraint. For example, the requirement that the method for use by RAs must control the development and application of KBSs by users with some skill, and control it now, constrains the solution. However, since only a partial solution to these requirements could be found, that is, a method to be applied by current personnel some time in the future (and not now), the solution begins to constrain the requirements. Either a different method for use now must be sought or the requirements relaxed and the available method used only in the future. Such problems in specifying a method may precipitate a process of negotiation between the procurers of the method and its developers.

Fourth, the heuristic '*If* the knowledge provider has an engineering background *then* try representing knowledge in look-up tables', guides the design of knowledge transfer tasks so that KBS development is sensitive to particular conditions. (Engineers, in this case, are familiar with look-up tables.) Such sensitivity will require flexible mechanisms for knowledge transfer. If currently available tools cannot provide such flexibility, new kinds of tool, for example ones with configurable interfaces, may need to be developed (see Cockton, 1988).

Fifth, an organization needs to consider the extent to which it really does want to provide its personnel with algorithmic control knowledge. There is no guarantee that algorithmic control knowledge will ever be appropriate for all tasks. Some tasks, for example those which involve dealing with people who know something you do not, may not be completely specifiable. Even if KBS development can eventually be specified, heuristic knowledge may be perfectly adequate to control tasks performed to the criteria generally held by KBS developers. Thus, it may be impossible to specify KBS development well; or, if possible, there may be no need.

Sixth, and finally, it is apparent from the options presented earlier that methods for the development and application of KBSs need not all be of the same type. For example, a hybrid method was contrasted with heuristic and algorithmic methods. Additional options, not considered here, also exist such as methods which provide high-level, relatively certain procedural knowledge. If an organization is to develop and apply KBSs effectively, it must consider which, of all the options, is the type of method they need.

POTENTIAL STRENGTHS AND WEAKNESSES OF THE METHOD AND ITS FUTURE DEVELOPMENT

A potential strength of the method is that it provides a structure into which knowledge from a number of sources, including the literature and the experience of method users, can be organized and integrated. For example, a list of rules can be categorized with respect to the feature of the method to which they refer or to the conditions under which their application is appropriate. In addition, the method can easily be up-dated. This facilitates both the incorporation into the method of future knowledge as it emerges – an additional rule may simply be added to the list – and the incremental development of the method. Rules which specify intended KBS development tasks, for example, could be added to the method before other types, such as rules which guide the diagnosis of errors or difficulties in the implementation of the task. A potential weakness of the method is its complexity and lack of usability.

For the method to transfer engineering research knowledge to the RAs effectively, the strengths of the method must be fully exploited and its potential weaknesses overcome. To this end, it is envisaged that selection criteria will be developed to filter out inadequate knowledge as it is recruited into the method and that procedures for using the method will be specified.

ACKNOWLEDGEMENTS

This research was undertaken under an SERC grant awarded to Dr D.W. Green and Professor J.B. Long and as part of an Alvey project (098).

REFERENCES

Cockton, G. (1988). User interface managers, interface components and reuse. Paper presented at *IEEE Computing and Control Division, Colloquium on Formal Methods and HCI: II*, 22nd February 1988, Digest No 1888/82.

Davis, R., and Lenat, D. (1982). *Knowledge-Based Systems in Artificial Intelligence*. McGraw Hill, New York.

Green, D.W., Colbert, M. and Long, J. (1987). Towards a transaction approach to knowledge-based system development. In *Proceedings of the Third International Conference on Expert Systems*, London, 4th–6th June, 1987. Learned Information, Oxford.

Kidd, A.L. and Sharpe, W. P. (1988). Goals for expert systems research: an analysis of tasks and domains. In D.S. Moralee (ed.) *Research and Development in Expert Systems IV*. Cambridge University Press.

Long, J., Hammond, N., Barnard, P., Morton, J. and Clark, I. (1982). *Introducing the interactive computer at work: the users' views*. Report No HF060, IBM UK Laboratories Ltd, Hursley Park, Winchester, Hampshire, United Kingdom.

Research Associations: British Hydromechanics Research Association Cranfield, Bedfordshire MK43 0AJ, UK.

Martin Colbert, John Long and David Green
Psychology Department and Ergonomics Unit
University College London
26 Bedford Way
London WC1 0AP, UK

Section III
Towards Effective Interfaces

It has been conventional to describe an expert system as consisting of a knowledge base, an inference engine and an input-output interface. In some sense the ordering of these elements reflects the amount of importance that has been attached to them. Most of the early research effort went into developing different knowledge representations and inferencing procedures. Considerably less attention was paid to the user interface. In recent years the crucial importance of the interface has become more and more apparent. One of the clearest lessons learned from the early pioneering expert systems is that excellent decision-making performance in itself is not sufficient to guarantee user acceptability. Users must be able to communicate effectively with the complex systems which they are supposed to use. It is interesting to note a similarity here with conventional system design. In the early days of information systems the emphasis tended to be on the construction of a good database. After some years of experience developers then started to emphasize the need for effective and helpful interfaces to enable users to access the databases.

There are, therefore, established principles for interface design in relation to information systems. Expert system designers should not ignore these otherwise, at best, they will 'reinvent the wheel' and, at worst, their systems will be inadequate. However, it is not simply a matter of applying previous work on human-computer interaction to the area of knowledge engineering. Expert systems are intended for use in situations involving professional judgement and uncertainty. As mentioned in the previous section the background, skills and needs of expert system users will often be different from those of information system users. Moreover, consultations with expert systems are typically different from those with information systems. In many situations expert systems must be able to support brief interactions and must be able to respond flexibly to the specific and changing needs of the user.

The convention of viewing the input-output interface as one of three components has also led to the misconception that it can be developed almost independently of the other two. It is simply not the case that attention can be turned to the interface in the later stages of a project after the knowledge base and reasoning methods have been developed. The system must be designed from the outset with the needs of the intended users in mind. In the previous section Edmonds, Candy, Slatter and Lunn (Chapter 6) asserted that the interface is so important that a prototype interface should be used as a means of system specification and knowledge elicitation. Similarly Kidd (1987) suggests that, 'a key part of the knowledge acquisition process must be to analyse certain key aspects of prospective users. Too often, consideration of users is a last minute icing on the cake.' Kidd argues that the users' needs should actually constitute the minimal 'dietary requirements'. She proposes that knowledge acquisition must include an

identification of the different classes of users, an analysis of their requirements and an analysis of the types of knowledge which they bring to bear on
the problem-solving process. It is clear that without a thorough understanding of user needs and requirements system developers may fail to provide
crucial capabilities and the resulting systems may have limited utility.

The interface between the system and user is particularly important
because, after all, it is the sole means by which users supply information and
understand the resulting inferences. Many early systems were rejected
because they only allowed for rigid system-oriented dialogues, with little or
no user-interrupt facilities. Explanation facilities were very primitive and the
dialogues were generally text-based, whether or not this was appropriate for
the particular application. In recent years research has been aimed at
improving these various deficiencies. The three chapters in this section
exemplify some of the progress in this area.

Dodson (Chapter 8) starts from the position that the burden of
understanding in human-computer interaction must lie with the user, rather
than with the computer. Only the users can be fully aware of the context,
subtleties and special features of a particular case. As Dodson stresses,
people need to understand computers because the likelihood of computers
understanding users is almost non-existent. He suggests that simple text
output is a very poor medium for many types of application and that
graphical output can offer a much richer environment. 'A picture speaks a
thousand words' can be very applicable in this context, provided that the
pictures are used in a way which is helpful to the users. Dodson describes
different types of connection diagrams and explores the potential of such
representations for current and future systems. There is therefore a need for
a greater understanding of how such representations are viewed by users and
how they can best be employed. It is all too easy to be beguiled by the
technology and to use it because it is there, rather than because it is a good
solution to a real problem.

The other two chapters describe experience in the use of various
interfaces. Hanne and Hoepelman (Chapter 9) discuss the relative merits of
natural language, direct graphical interaction and formal languages. They
warn against the dangers of users over-estimating the capabilities of systems
on the basis of the interface, particularly in the case of natural language
processing. They describe the various forms of deixis used in communication and the importance of deixis in human-computer interaction. Their
implementation incorporates deixis with multi-windows and language
processing, and is an interesting multi-modal communication.

Kuczora and Eklund (Chapter 10) describe two tools which make use of
conceptual graphs. Their experience in knowledge engineering suggests that
people find it much easier to refine a knowledge system which is presented
to them in the form of conceptual graphs than by more conventional

methods. In particular, they describe the power of such tools in knowledge elicitation from experts. Note the similarity between this view and that expressed by Edmonds, Candy, Slatter and Lunn in Chapter 6. In each case the system developers believe that the most effective way of specifying or assessing the performance of a system is to see it in operation.

It should be noted that the chapters in this section are concerned with the interface between a system and an individual user. The emphasis has been on how information should be presented, rather than what should be presented and when. These other aspects are obviously important. Furthermore, when designing and evaluating systems it is necessary to consider not only the direct effects on immediate users, but also indirect effects on other personnel within an organization. This will be covered in the final section of the book.

REFERENCES

Kidd, A.L. (ed.) (1987). *Knowledge Acquisition for Expert Systems. A Practical Handbook*. Plenum Press, New York.

Chapter 8

Interaction with Knowledge-Based Systems through Connection Diagrams: Where Next?

David C Dodson

INTRODUCTION

Since we cannot rely on computer systems to understand us reliably and efficiently, computer users need reliable and efficient understanding of the computerized cognitive systems with which they wish to communicate. This need is of vital importance for many expert system users, not least as a basis for the trust without which communication cannot be reliable and efficient. It is therefore a fundamental consideration in the construction and maintenance of KBSs in general.

Interactive connection diagrams (ICDs), a type of interactive graphics, have begun to play an important role in serving this need. ICDs can help users understand KBSs much better, but that is by no means all. They can also serve as a medium through which KBSs can be built, modified and used. ICDs have begun to boost the effectiveness of human communication with KBSs and could make many KBS applications much more usable.

Connection diagrams show interconnections as graphic links (or 'arcs') connecting objects shown as graphic nodes. Figure 1 is a simple example concerning surfboard faults. This diagram employs a very simple connection-diagram language comprising a few syntactic and semantic conventions. Connection diagram languages include many other convenient schemes for abstract graphical explanation.

Animated connection diagrams of KBSs can show progressive change in the knowledge state of a system, thus showing knowledge processing at work. ICDs go a step further, using graphical input to allow direct manipulation (Shneiderman, 1987; Hutchins *et al*, 1986) both of diagrams and, via diagrams, of knowledge. The mnemonic ICDOK (ICD of Knowledge) is used throughout this chapter as shorthand for an ICD used as a medium of interaction with a knowledge base or KBS. ICDOKs are directly-manipulable graphical explanations through which knowledge and knowledge processes can be accessed and modified.

ICDs have become popular in user interfaces to KBSs and other systems.

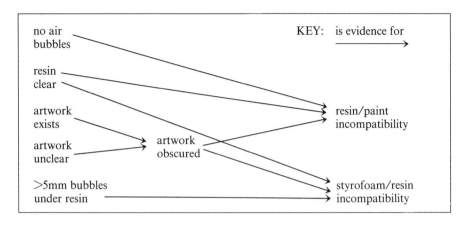

Figure 1 *A simple connection diagram*

In particular, an increasing number of KBS programming environments embody ICDOK facilities, commonly termed 'browsers' or 'graph browsers'. There is little doubt that generally available ICDOK implementations, which have tended to provide similar functionality, can be effective aids to knowledge engineering. However, many knowledge engineers feel that they are less useful than attractive, for their functionality is impaired by significant shortcomings in usability. Specifically, they are limited in representational power and lack appropriate means of displaying incremental progression in dialogue context and content. Rarely are they appropriate for use in end-user interfaces. Yet many interface designers believe that improved ICDOK facilities will enable major advances in interface effectiveness, even for end-users. Clearly, much remains to be done to unlock the potential of ICDs.

We need to develop and apply broader and more systematic conceptions of ICDs than are evoked by current, early exemplars. We need to understand the universe of diagrammatic languages which computer graphics can support, not just the flat-earth world of static, 2-D diagrams. We must also identify and exploit the enormous scope for better ways of selecting and modifying what an ICD shows and how it shows it. Such advances are badly needed if the matching of ICD facilities to KBS applications is not to remain a hit-and-miss affair.

This chapter surveys human and computational aspects of ICDs which are important in their development and use as a medium of interaction with KBSs. These issues fall within a broader area of questions about the means, extent and effectiveness of access to knowledge, explanation and justification by KBS users. The following sections offer a pragmatic perspective on

137

the value of ICDs as a medium for cognitive communication with KBSs, characterize available implementations, outline the scope for advance in representational power, discuss problems with ICDOK usability which invite computational approaches to their solution, address some further human aspects, present a working hypothesis on the applicability of ICDOKs and, finally, summarise key points.

COMMUNICATING WITH KNOWLEDGE SYSTEMS

We need to build joint cognitive systems (Woods, 1986) which integrate human and computer cognition. This demands cognitive communication between a person and a KBS: that is, communication at the conceptual level rather than just data communication. Yet for some decades to come, whilst computer cognition will evolve in complexity and power, it will remain impoverished, inflexible, and qualitatively different compared with human cognition. Were it not for this complexity-but-dissimilarity, there would be no knowledge acquisition bottleneck and no fundamental obstacles to the creation of effective end-user interfaces to KBSs. As it is, we are still discovering what is natural or effective in human-computer communication, scarcely keeping pace with the increasing sophistication of computer systems.

It is becoming clear that cognitive communication requires that at least one party 'understands' the other, in the sense of having a good model of the communicative ability and state or situation of the other. For communication to be reliable and efficient, this understanding must likewise be reliable and efficient. Yet for some decades to come, we will not be able to rely on computer systems to understand us reliably and efficiently. Users must therefore reliably and efficiently understand the computerized cognitive systems with which they wish to communicate.

It is easy to imagine people and computers interacting in entirely natural language. It is tempting to believe we can soon make computers use and understand language just like humans. But this is not feasible in this century. To begin with, efficient linguistic communication with humans depends on leaving unsaid a great deal that the recipient can understand in context (Grice, 1975; McCawley, 1981). This in turn depends on reliable use and update of a vast amount of knowledge of what can be understood. This latter includes not only knowledge of disambiguating facts, which may be sought from the user by a computer which did not have access to them, but also knowledge of ambiguating facts, such as homonymies and multiple occurrences of entities matching a description. Knowledge is also needed of pragmatic practices and users' goals which, as Suchman (1985) points out, are in general rather inaccessible to computers, given their impoverished sensory and cultural environment. In short, computers are in general far from being ready to bear the burden of understanding us reliably.

The more conventional approaches to human-computer interaction also have serious shortcomings. Formal command languages need extensive practice to be learnt and are readily forgotten without frequent use. Restricted natural languages have these limitations too, though to a lesser extent. However they can also seductively evoke a dangerous anthropomorphism, giving users an impression of more human-like ability than is available. Users get 'lost' in hierarchical menu systems of any size. All of these approaches raise very considerable problems of skill transfer between systems, and all of them place the burden of understanding on the user without providing strong support for the user's understanding of system state. Finally, program-driven dialogues assume that the user needs no insight into system state beyond what is evident from memory of recent interactions and any concurrently displayed information. There is another approach however.

Direct manipulation (Shneiderman, 1987; Hutchins *et al*, 1986) has emerged as a key design concept for reliable, efficient and understandable computer systems. It demands the adoption of a visual 'language' for representing the world of interest according to some representational metaphor, and the adoption of a corresponding language for user action on that world, or just on its representation, through graphical or spatial input. The use of good direct manipulation interfaces is readily learnt and retained. Moreover the way in which user input can refer to what is already shown (Draper 1986) can enable high efficiency and reliability of use, and thence highly effective interaction as a whole.

In a KBS, the world of interest is one of concepts, propositions, inferences, inference processes and their interconnections. Connection diagrams are ideally suited to visual representation of such a world, both for explication and direct manipulation. They offer an otherwise impossible degree of freedom of arrangement, without which the irregularity of knowledge structures could not be accommodated. They greatly aid users in cross-referencing between related knowledge units without losing track of where they were. This is very beneficial, provided that the interconnections shown serve users' interests. Immediacy of cross-reference in turn helps users to abstract, comprehend and compare subsets of the structural arrangement of knowledge, a facility especially relevant in knowledge engineering and instructional applications.

Thus ICDOKs, as a direct manipulation medium, place squarely on the user the burden of understanding a system, but can give strong support to this understanding through clear representation of system state. As yet though, the real limits to the effectiveness of ICDs cannot be identified. Current implementations hint at the potential of the medium but also misrepresent it. They are bound by limitations of current supporting technology and by limitations of conceptualization of the diagram which are only slowly being weaned away from those of hand-crafted diagrams. A radically new kind of language medium has been born. Its evolution – subject to the logic and human factors of spatio-temporal arrangement and to quasi-natural processes of variation, accretion and selection – has just begun.

CURRENTLY AVAILABLE ICDOK FACILITIES

A variety of ICD facilities are available in computational environments used in knowledge engineering. Each presents a window onto an ICDOK which in many cases outlines a network of frames. The connections shown are usually tuples of a partial ordering relation (such as 'is-a' or a-cyclic 'is-

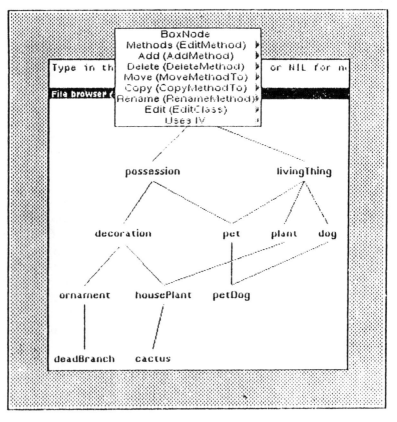

Figure 2. *The loops browser*

evidence-for') which in frame-based ICDOKs may be defined by slot values.

In typical ICDOKs the nodes take the form of a rectangular array of character cells or just a row of characters, often with no enclosing border-line. Connections or links are binary (linking two nodes) and appear as single-pixel wide straight lines, occasionally with optional arrowheads and/or link type coding by line types or labels. There is an overall 'directionality' to which one or more link type is committed, eg downwards in Figures 2 and 3. Automatic diagram layout is often provided but the result usually warrants manual editing to make it more usable.

Figure 2 is a screen dump from the browser in the seminal LOOPS system from Xerox. This browser works with inheritance hierarchies only, but can draw them in a variety of styles. The layout of this figure, including the menu placement, is automatic and unedited. The menu, which can be moved, appeared upon clicking on the hidden, uppermost node. Menu items turn to inverse video when under the cursor. Each triangular icon to the left of a menu item points to where a sub-menu will attach if the item is selected. Upon selecting an item in the 'Edit' sub-menu, the upper text panel of the browser invites the user to key in a change to the super- or sub-classes (depending on the sub-menu selection) of the selected class. Upon entering such a change, the diagram is computed afresh, possibly changing its size.

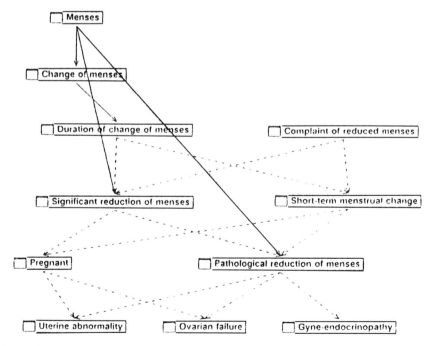

Figure 3. *A diagram in note cards*

Figure 3 shows a diagram constructed in the browser of another Xerox system, NOTECARDS. Panels (not shown here) attached to the diagram window include a key to the link types. Here solid links show attribute dependency; dotted links show evidence flow. Two novice minutes were spent adjusting the initial automatic layout to make this diagram more compact, and there is still considerable room for improvement. A 3-D version of this diagram could further clarify its structure, for example by placing the evidence-flow network in a geometric plane but articulating the attribute dependency hierarchy outside of that plane.

ICDOK user input facilities usually encompass the following:

- view control (see below);
- layout editing (usually by moving one node and its links);
- content editing (eg adding and deleting nodes and links, editing displayed 'active value' data);
- access to non-displayed data (usually via menus).

Conventional view control facilities allow the user to control general diagram attributes (eg orientation and the appearance of nodes and links) and to trigger automatic layout. Scroll bars may also be used to select the portion of a large diagram to be displayed in the available window. In some systems such as KEE from Intellicorp, this latter facility is complemented by a small auxiliary panel in which the position of the main window is marked on a miniature sketch of the overall diagram. Moreover, scrolling may be controlled not only by the user, but also by the system to keep its locus of control in view. This can cause abrupt changes of view which tend to be very disorientating.

One or more styles of menu interaction (pop-up, pull down, etc) give access to a repertoire of user input functions. Data associated with objects in the diagram can thus be accessed and edited, and associated actions can be triggered. As hinted at in Figure 2, pop-up menus may hide precisely that part of the diagram which the user would like to refer to in making a selection.

There are many further variants on such schemes. For example, simulation-oriented knowledge engineering environments often support schematic diagrams of physical structures like those commonly used in industrial control, but with interaction facilities more like those described above.

ICDOK systems such as these are powerful tools for knowledge engineers, yet often fall short of the functionality that is warranted. Their limitations reflect the 'prototypical tradeoff' (Norman, 1986) between features which increase informativeness and the space and time they consume. Yet hardware keeps improving in raw power and graphics system architectures better suited to ICDs are becoming available. We can expect consequential advances in expressive power and in the use of computation to package functionality into effective, usable forms.

Semnet, a research tool developed at the Microelectronics and Computer Corporation, provides a glimpse of things to come. This system provides 3-D ICDs which can be navigated using a 'helicopter' metaphor. It also supports hierarchical decomposition of nodes into sub-networks, allowing this to take place without losing view of the surrounding nodes and links. In addition, all the nodes linked to a selected node may be made to spring close to that node even if they were out of view. A limited automatic layout facility is illustrated in the video publication on SemNet (Fairchild and Poltrock, 1986), but this makes extensive manual post-editing indispensable for human convenience.

LANGUAGES OF DIAGRAMMATIC REPRESENTATION

We can view an interactive diagram paradigm as comprising a 'language' of diagrammatic output and a dependent language of diagrammatic input. Both can be analysed as comprising separate syntactic and semantic components. In practice, it is convenient to specify diagrammatic input languages using state transition formalisms which also define the interrelation between input and output events. These formalisms may themselves be connection-diagrammatic. Such formalisms facilitate defining the meaning of input language utterances as a function of what is on display in the representational language. Cockton (1988) provides an up-to-date perspective on state transition formalisms suited to defining direct manipulation input languages in general. In contrast, our main concern here is with the representational capabilities of diagrammatic output, which limit diagrammatic input in a similar way.

In a connection-diagrammatic output language, the syntactic component delineates grammatical assemblies of diagram elements including nodes, links and labels. The semantic component is compositional, defining the meaning of well-formed assemblies of syntactic elements as a combination of the meaning of their elements, typically in a straightforward way. It also provides semantic conventions for individual diagram elements. For example, a given type of node with a simple text label may represent the proposition (or entity or event) named by its label.

The existence of semantic conventions for nodes and for their interconnections need not exclude other conventions. Meaning can for example attach to some coordinate(s) of a node's position, or to a node containing or touching another. The size, shape, colour and texture of diagram elements can all be meaningful as can depiction of physical objects (as in exploded

143

parts diagrams). Three-D diagrams enrich the representation of connectivity, allowing distinct connection types the visual prominence of a distinct directionality. Hiding can have meaning independent of relative depth since ordinary hiding by near objects of those behind them is optional. Change over time is also semantically versatile. In animation, program time represents real time, but time can also represent another dimension, or be represented by another, and can convey depth in simulated viewer motion.

Representational conventions can themselves be combined compositionally (MacKinlay, 1987), provided that the problem of diagram layout remains soluble and no ambiguity is introduced. MacKinlay demonstrated the composition of conventions in APT, a tool which generates, selects and then uses 2-D diagrammatic languages to display relational data. The result is often a connection diagram. More generally, connection-diagrammatic paradigms can be constructed to accommodate almost any visual appearance whilst also delineating cognitive structure in what is shown. The combination of physical imagery and diagrams proposed for Knoesphere (Lenat *et al*, 1983) would be well served by such a paradigm.

Semantic compositionality, both within languages and in merging languages, is hardly unique to the medium of diagrams. However, the way in which this dual compositionality manifests itself in diagrammatic languages has some special characteristics which deserve attention. In particular, diagram semantics is in some sense highly tractable and transparent, whereas semantic composition in natural languages is not easy to account for. We may note, for example, that 'digested biscuits' are not in fact biscuits at all; also there is a difference of meaning between 'A politician kissed every baby' and 'Every baby was kissed by a politician'. Theorists have dealt with this kind of surface discrepancy by appealing to a level of abstract or deep structure at which semantics is neatly compositional. This transfers the burden of supporting an economical account of semantics to complex systems for mapping semantics onto syntax. In contrast, diagrams can put deep structure plainly in sight. This seems fundamental to the advantage ICDs can have over natural language for effective interaction with computers. More insight into such differences is needed.

In contrast to the situation regarding semantics, usable formalizations of ICD syntax are potentially much more complex than the syntax of linear language. This reflects the greater spatial dimensionality of the diagrammatic medium. As in a syntactic account of a linear language, ICD syntax must have a component specifying acceptable ways of putting syntactic units together. At an abstract level, this will specify a set of acceptable diagram structures. One such structure might for instance be specified as comprising two nodes A and B of specific types, each with some annotation, and some particular type of left-going link from A to B. Of course, this example is trivial. The diagrammatic analog of 'phrase structures' may in general need to be more structurally sophisticated than conventional phrase structure trees. Beyond this, there also needs to be a lower level of analysis, somewhat analogous to morphology. This must specify the permitted geometry of the various types of links and nodes and their junctures. For diagrams undergoing gradual change it should also specify how their geometry may vary in time.

Our conceptualizations of the scope of ICDs have been impoverished primarily because of our limited understanding of the kinds of syntactic features that can be employed. Dodson (1988a) offers a preliminary ontology of ICD features, primarily concerned with diagram syntax. Adequate ontology is critical as a basis for rigorous description and comparison of ICD paradigms. Without it, it is very hard for human factors evaluations of ICD implementations to articulate what they actually pertain to.

An indefinite number of different schemes of diagram semantics can be employed to present the same information. Whilst this gives plenty of scope for choosing good schemes for given applications, it raises unbounded empirical problems in seeking to identify the best.

IMPROVING THE USABILITY OF ICDOKs

Increasing the representational power of ICDs will only be of value where it is usable. Adding features to an interface often diminishes its usability through increasing users' uncertainty, stress, error rates and so on. Yet incorporating more of the functionality needed to support users' tasks within an ICD has the opposite effect. This places emphasis on maximum uniformity of interaction and on getting features to support multiple functions. ICDs facilitate this in many ways. For example, in some ICDs of inference networks, nodes representing propositions can be annotated with ticks and crosses to indicate confirmation or disconfirmation. Figure 4 shows a diagram from KEE which illustrates this. This adds multiple functions, showing which inferences are being drawn, explaining how conclusions are supported, and explaining why information has been solicited. To obtain comparable explanatory function with text alone, users have to issue many requests and interpret lengthy responses, which imposes temporal and cognitive demands which tend to discourage explanation-seeking.

The usability of the current generation of ICDOKs is very limited however. This can be attributed to two sorts of problems. First, users may have difficulty in understanding the diagrammatic representations and the facilities for interaction with them. This depends on the type of user

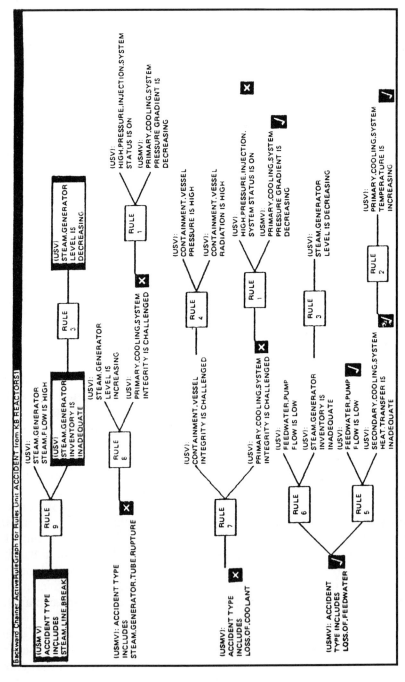

Figure 4. *A KEE 'active rule graph' (from Kunz, 1987)*

involved. Relevant factors here include cognitive style, (this is touched on in the next section), extent of involvement and experience in knowledge engineering, and frequency and extent of use. There is of course considerable scope for improvement in the extent and quality of help facilities, including ready access both to a full graphic key to the conventions used in a diagram and to instructive and summary information about user input facilities.

The second and more fundamental shortcoming is the lack of convenient facilities for controlling the content of diagrams in ways that support users' tasks. This raises further research topics of key importance:

- the variety and structure of tasks in interaction with KBSs;
- criteria for what to show in a diagram;
- criteria for satisfactory layout of dynamic diagrams;
- algorithms for dynamic diagram layout;
- mixed initiative navigation of diagrams.

Task Structures

Knowledge of the range of task structures relevant to ICDOKs is largely subjective. Methodical analyses are needed. Adopting Moran's (1983) ETIT terminology, we need to study both the 'external' tasks of knowledge engineering *per se*, and the 'internal' tasks these map onto in the context of ICD interfaces. However, improved tools can enable better but different strategies of working. Studying the tasks performed with card punches and readers would have been of little help to the design of screen editors and filestore access facilities. It may thus be dangerous to rely too much on analysis of existing task structures in designing the forthcoming generation of ICD tools.

What to Show

Showing knowledge structures is explaining: 'laying-out', etymologically. Ideally, we might like KBSs to explain themselves like a human expert/tutor. Studies of natural, co-operative dialogues show that explanations are often volunteered as well as being provided in response to requests. As with advice, the content of explanations is often a matter to be negotiated to ensure their usefulness (Draper, 1988; O'Malley, 1988). Results such as these highlight the need for co-operative, mixed initiative dialogue, which holds irrespective of dialogue medium.

Diagram Presentation

Two objectives of considerable importance in the interests of usability are frequently in conflict. On one hand it is desirable to support progression in the content and context of dialogue through structurally dynamic ICDs. On the other hand, it is important to maintain continuity or persistence in diagram arrangement. Unless there is enough space available to display the entire knowledge base, a compromise is needed. If dialogue can be predictably decomposed into discrete contexts, diagram decomposition into a hierarchy of pages may be workable. Otherwise, intuitively, such a compromise demands progressive but gradual changes both in the set of diagram components on display and in their arrangement.

Probably the best way to support this kind of gradual change involves maintaining 'displayworthiness' metrics for each knowledge unit the presence of which in a diagram is to be variable (Dodson, 1986; 1988b). Informing in this way the selection of what is to appear may also serve as a basis for controlling diagrammatic fish-eye views (Furnas, 1986). There then remains a need to develop criteria and methods for usable layout and re-layout of diagrams, the components of which are changing.

Dynamic Layout

Criteria and algorithms for diagram layout are of central importance. Extensive work has been done on these topics in the case of static 2-D connection diagrams. Tamassia *et al* (1987) review the literature and propose an integrating approach. Dealing with progressive change of diagram content has received less attention. Batini *et al* (1984) note the need for incremental layout methods to achieve this, but significant details of appropriate criteria and techniques are in short supply. Intuitively, the arrangement of diagram elements should be conserved as much as possible, even upon re-appearance after a period of absence. In addition, any multiple instantiation of non-ground structure should tend to follow a recognizable pattern. In many KBS contexts, the expedient of using a manually-edited overall arrangement as a guide for an incremental layout function, approximating to viscous elastic distortion, could be a major step forward. Even then, the speed of layout computation is likely to be critical for responsiveness and may often warrant parallelism. Alternatively, incremental presentation may be made relatively tractable by adopting specialized diagram paradigms (eg Rector, 1986) which simplify the layout problem.

Mixed Initiative Control

An approach has been proposed for obtaining system-generated measures of displayworthiness for inference network elements reflecting their importance in an inference task (Dodson 1986, 1988b). Heuristic mixing of such measures with user-determined parameters provides a basis for a variety of techniques of mixed initiative control. User control may thus be effected through a combination of browsing interaction and simple adjustment of

ICD control parameters. It is apparent that such an approach can integrate concurrent explanation-seeking and explanation-volunteering and can be extended to handle the inspection and comparison of hypothetical (What-if?) contexts. Powerful and graceful forms of co-operative, mixed initiative diagrammatic dialogue are thus possible.

SOME OTHER HUMAN FACTORS ISSUES

Diagram Size

Appropriate diagram size in terms of number of elements displayed is likely to be a controversial issue for some time. Current experience with ICDs and conventional guidelines favour small numbers of nodes (say, less than 20). This would seem likely to facilitate rapid incremental layout since layout time complexity is usually high. It would also seem to be necessary in order to avoid a confusion of detail. Against this, it is not clear that diagrams with many nodes would typically require a much higher rate of re-layout, in terms of nodes per second say, than small ones. Also it is not clear that the conventional wisdom about display complexity need apply, given good layout persistence, the fundamental cross-referencing property of connection diagrams, and distinctive and balanced visual coding to help users recognize nodes and follow pertinent links. It may be that factors such as these will enable a significant increase in the amount of information that it is useful to display at any time. If this is so, it will become more important as the size of displays increases.

Individual Differences

It is often said that diagrammatic interfaces suit a minority of people highly-oriented to visual representations, but are unsuitable otherwise. Individual differences along this dimension clearly exist but it is not clear that they would apply so fiercely to use of the type of ICDs envisaged here. Such ICDs remove the burden of diagram design from the user. Also, their primary diagrammatic effect is the provision of links which function to signpost and lead the eye. One researcher who has designed a specialized ICD paradigm admitted to having a marked lack of ability at using diagrams before becoming keen on ICDs. Increasing cultural penetration of effective ICDOKs is sure to motivate increasing interest in comprehending the use of the medium.

Standards

One area of limitation to usability is likely to be the emergence of a highly redundant variety of ICD languages. Variety in ICD design will of course be a mainspring to the evolution of ICD languages, but as in other interface areas it will have bad effects:

– wasteful duplication of Research and Development and poor integration of facilities;
– increased risk attaching to application implementation decisions;
– poor portability of applications and diagram data;
– reluctance of potential users to adopt ICDs.

Ample scope exists for seeking a standard but extendible, logical framework for interfacing ICD presentation layers to their neighbours. Many will no doubt argue that it is too early to begin seeking standards. Yet as no software standards of any complexity have appeared without serious weaknesses, the sooner we begin learning the lessons of attempting to create them the better.

THE APPLICABILITY OF ICDOKs

In which situations and to what extent can user interfaces incorporating ICDOKs be more effective than those without? The straightforwardness of such a question belies the difficulty it poses. To begin with, it is not clear what is to be compared with what. Such a question leaves unspecified the non-ICD interface modalities with which an ICD modality might be merged or compared. Moreover it is not clear how we could identify, in any given situation, an ICD facility representative of the level of effectiveness ICDs could offer. If we consider only extant ICD implementations, we cannot be sure of the extent to which they might be improved as a result of more advanced ICD technology, or just better design choices.

There are so many avenues for improvement. The scope for, and rate of, improvement in the effective application of ICDs and contrasting media is thus necessarily very uncertain. The available wealth of pertinent evidence is growing fast but there will always be much subjectivity in assessing its broad implications. Highlighting the need to live with this uncertainty, Brooks (1988) identifies three kinds of results as being of scientific interest: findings, observations and rules-of-thumb. These might be characterized, respectively, as firm scientific results, modest generalizations from experience, and rather broader generalizations which investigators are willing to support. As yet, little more than the latter kind of answer can be given to our question about the applicability of ICDs.

It is important that we develop an idea of the situations in which interfaces incorporating ICDOKs will be more effective than those without. The following characterization is essentially my own best assessment. It is expressed with somewhat spurious precision, in preference to vagueness, to enhance its value as a hypothesis to test and refine. Issues raised by the non-ICD modalities which might be combined or merged with ICDs have been assumed to be second-order issues and have been disregarded here.

WORKING HYPOTHESIS

Incorporating ICDs in a KBS user interface will yield significant gains in effectiveness if *and only if* each of the following apply:

1. The users have a significant interest in understanding the knowledge systems which they are using, ideally in order to serve a significant decision-making need. The user's role may for example be that of a knowledge engineer, an author, an evaluator, an end-user needing joint cognition (Woods, 1986) to facilitate problem solving, or a trainee.
2. The ICD language has adequate representational power and an adequate semantic mapping to the knowledge that needs to be represented. (This is easy to satisfy for KBSs presently inhabiting simple shells.)
3. If an ICD knowledge representation is seen through a limited window:
   Either: The user is a knowledge engineer or patient knowledge author;
   Or: Gross alterations may occur in what is seen through the window (eg by scrolling) but for most of the time the window contains appropriate dialogue context without alteration. Specifically, no such change should be required for about 80 per cent of non-view-altering interactions (if manually altered), or about 90 per cent of such interactions (if automatically altered);
   Or: Diagrammatic dialogue is conveniently decomposable into discrete subjects for which there is a corresponding hierarchy of diagram pages – pages appear in full and most non-paging interactions (at least about 80 per cent) require no page changes;
   Or: The ICDOK supports good incremental layout of relevant content, following problem-solving activity with an acceptably low average rate of change of diagram content and layout. The acceptable rate of content change is plausibly of the order of one incoming and one outgoing node per non-layout interaction on average.
4. Any change in the position or presence of diagram elements within the window is gradual and the user has at least a suspend/resume control on automatic change.
5. There is compliance with appropriate general guidelines. In particular the user has had time to learn the representational conventions of the

ICDOK, and to overcome any problems of skill transfer from a system with syntactically similar but semantically different conventions.

This preliminary assessment leaves many issues open, such as the dependency of ICDOK effectiveness on other interface modalities, on domains of application and on KBS architectures. Before we can make much headway on such matters, much more attention will need to be devoted to the creation and experimental application of much more advanced ICD tools.

This chapter has focused almost exclusively on human rather than organizational issues. It should however be noted that knowledge suppliers are frequently unwilling to allow users to inspect the knowledge that they otherwise make available in a KBS. This secrecy may sometimes be motivated as much by the need to hide rough-handed or unmanageable knowledge formalizations as by the need to keep valuable knowledge secure. Even with text-based facilities for inspecting knowledge bases, poor quality knowledge may be much more difficult to detect than with the aid of graphical exposition. The provision of ICDs may thus turn out to be a valuable indicator of knowledge base quality.

SUMMARY

This chapter surveys key issues for the technology and use of interaction with knowledge-based systems (KBSs) through interactive structure diagrams (ISDs). To begin with, it has argued that for KBSs to be widely, efficiently and reliably usable, they must provide more open and genuine, cognitive communication with users. This echoes Michie's (1988) conclusion that 'The only computer-based decision structures which can be regarded as safe are those amenable to conceptual debugging by non-programming personnel.' Attempts to meet these needs with intelligent natural language interfaces commit a fundamental anthropomorphic fallacy, placing on computers a burden of understanding which they are not in general ready to sustain with high reliability. Direct manipulation interfaces which use ICDs as the medium for interactive access to knowledge structures, are needed to cut through this impasse. It is thus important to grasp how little the scope for diagrammatic interaction has been exploited. We need to separate the issues of the usability and applicability of ICDs in general from the issues of the limited usability and applicability of current exemplars.

The stage is set for dramatic increase in the representational power of ICDs. This will make appropriate forms of graphical explanation available for increasingly complex paradigms of KBSs structure. Three-D and dynamic displays will play a major role in extending this power well beyond the scope of the familiar domain of 2-D diagrams. Moreover the technology needed for making graphic displays dynamic and 3-D can reside entirely on very large scale integration (VLSI), with obvious implications for decreasing cost.

There will also be major advances in making ICDs more usable. This will begin to transform what is still a very passive and inflexible medium into one which co-operatively and fluently supports a new immediacy of mixed initiative dialogue. For many kinds of application, the most usable KBSs will co-operatively explain their reasoning and dialogue context in gracefully dynamic interactive diagrams. Moreover, such diagrams will be readily adjustable by the user as a means of exploring and interacting with KBSs.

Much forward-looking and systematic research needs to be done to achieve and integrate the various kinds of advance in ICDs sketched here. Particular attention has been drawn to the need to study diagrammatic paradigms and the layout and mixed initiative control of dynamic diagrams. Meanwhile, caution is needed in assessing the value of available ICD facilities for KBSs. In particular, we should not assume that available ICD facilities provide much indication of the riches the medium holds in store.

ACKNOWLEDGEMENTS

Particular thanks are due to Tom Green and Cathy Carter at Rank Xerox EuroPARC for their help with LOOPS and NOTECARDS; to Intellicorp and Artificial Intelligence Limited for demonstrating KEE; to British Telecom and the Open University for demonstrating KEATS; and to many others who shared their experiences with these and other systems.

REFERENCES

Batini, C., Nardelli, E., Talamo, M. and Tamassia, R. (1984). A Graph Theoretic Approach to Aesthetic Layout for Information System Diagrams. In *Proceedings of the 10th International Workshop on Graph-Theoretic Concepts in Computer Science*, Berlin, 1984.

Brooks, F.P. (1988). Grasping Reality Through Illusion-Interactive Graphics Serving Science. *Proceedings of CHI'88*, Washington, 15-19 May. *SIGCHI Bulletin* (special issue). ACM/Addison Wesley, May 1988.

Cockton, G. (1988). Generative Transition Networks: A New Communication Control Abstraction. In D. Jones and R. Winder (eds), *People and Computers IV*. Cambridge University Press.

Dodson, D.C. (1986). Explanation Explanation ... A Brief Sketch. In *Proceedings of the First Alvey Explanation Workshop*, University of Surrey, March 1986. IEE.

Dodson, D.C. (1988a). Interactive Structure Diagram Graphics: A Preliminary Ontology. In *Proceedings of Third Alvey Explanation Workshop*, University of Surrey, September 1987. IEE.

Dodson, D.C. (1988b). Structure-Diagrammatic Interaction for a Medical Advice System: Ideas in Visual Coding. *Ibid.*

Draper, S.W. (1986). Display Managers as the Basis for User-Machine Communication. In D. Norman and S. Draper (eds), *User-Centered System Design*. Lawrence Erlbaum Associates.

Draper, S.W. (1988). Spontaneous Explanation. In *Proceedings of Third Alvey Explanation Workshop*, University of Surrey, September 1987. IEE 1988.

Dudman, J. (1988). AI Expert calls for the human touch. *Computing* **21 4** 1988.

Fairchild, K. and Poltrock, S. (1986). SEMNET (video). *Technical report HI-104–86*, Microelectronics and Computer Technology Corporation, Austin, Texas.

Furnas, G.W. (1986). Generalized Fisheye Views. In *Proceedings of CHI'86*, Boston, April 1986. SIGCHI Bulletin (special issue). ACM.

Grice, H.P. (1975). Logic and Conversation. In P. Cole and J. Morgan (eds) *Syntax and Semantics 3: Speech Acts*. Academic Press.

Hutchins, E.L., Hollan, J.D. and Norman, D.A. (1986). Direct Manipulation Interfaces. In D. Norman and S. Draper (eds), op. cit.

Lenat, D.B., Borning, A., McDonald, D., Taylor, C. and Weyer, S. (1983). Knoesphere: Building Expert Systems with Encyclopedic Knowledge. *Proceedings of Eighth International Joint Conference on Artificial Intelligence*, Karlsruhe, August 1983.

MacKinlay, J. (1987). Automating the Design of Graphical Presentations of Relational Information. *ACM Transcript on Graphics*, Vol 5 No 2, April 1987.

McCawley, J.D. (1981). *Everything that Linguists have Always Wanted to Know about Logic*. Blackwell Scientific, Oxford

Michie, D. (1988). As reported in Dudman (1988). op.cit

Moran, T.P. (1983). Getting Into a System: External-Internal Task Mapping Analysis. *Proceedings of CHI'83*, Boston, 12-15 December. SIGCHI Bulletin (special issue) ACM.

Norman, D.A. (1986). Cognitive Engineering. In D. Norman and S. Draper (eds), op. cit.

O'Malley, C. (1988). Understanding Explanation. In *Proceedings of the Third Alvey Explanation Workshop*, University of Surrey, September 1987. IEE.

Rector, A. (1986). Graphical Presentation of Explanation in a Decision Support System based on Browsing and 'Co-operative Search'. In

Proceedings of the Second Alvey Explanation Workshop, University of Surrey, January 1987. IEE.

Shneiderman, B. (1987). *Designing the User Interface: Strategies for Effective Human-Computer Interaction.* Addison-Wesley.

Suchman, L. (1985). *Plans and Situated Actions: The Problem of Human-Machine Communication.* Report ISL-6, Xerox PARC, Palo Alto, California.

Tamassia, R., Batini, C. and Di Battista, G. (1987). Automatic Graph Drawing and Readability of Diagrams.*IEEE Transactions on Systems, Man and Cybernetics.*

Woods, D.D. (1986). Cognitive Technologies. *AI Magazine*, Vol 6, No 4.

David Dodson
Department of Computer Science
The City University
Northampton Square
London EC1V 0HB, UK

Chapter 9

Natural Language and Direct Manipulation Interfaces to Expert Systems (Multimodal Communication)

Karl-Heinz Hanne and Jaap Hoepelman

HUMAN-COMPUTER INTERFACES IN EXPERT SYSTEMS

Expert systems usually require user interaction. From a user's point of view the capabilities of the system, the shell and the application are determined by the user interface. In recent years, the interfaces used in traditional data processing applications have become more and more interesting. As a result, effective interface techniques have been developed for end-user systems. This progress is closely connected to developments in the field of artifical intelligence research and technology (eg development environments and tools for expert systems).

Human-computer interfaces (HCIs) to expert systems, with distinct modes such as 'pure' direct manipulation or natural language, have advantages and disadvantages but they can be improved by a combination of modes. This idea of multimodal interaction leads to problems of the presentation of the user's 'world', and of deictic expressions and screen-oriented pointing to 'objects of interest' anchored in the user's world. Such considerations led to the design and implementation of a direct graphical manipulation interface system. System architecture and structure are based on layered models. The systems are developed and implemented on SUN workstations in 'C' and are PROLOG based on UNIX. They provide a set of modules and a communication layer for combined (multimodal) interfaces, thus allowing the inclusion of deictic/natural language references to objects represented on the screen. Several applications have been developed, including a pure direct manipulative interface to an expert system in the domain of aircraft design, and other systems allowing a combination of natural language and direct manipulation queries.

156

GENERIC INTERACTION MODES

Based on the interface model presented in, for example, Faehnrich and Ziegler (1984), three generic communication modes can be identified.

Natural Language

The most common medium in human communication is natural language (NL). NL processing is one of the major topics of HCI research largely because of its 'naturalness'. Most people can use it and would not have to learn a new, possibly difficult, formalism before interacting with a natural language interface. As possible application fields for NL systems the following are worth mentioning:

- dialogue systems;
- question and answer systems;
- communication with knowledge-based systems;
- creation, manipulation and query of databases in NL;
- programming in natural language;
- automatic translation;
- linguistic word processing: automatic spelling correction, testing of text consistency, automatic summary, automatic retrieval of strings, text generation;
- automatic theorem proving;
- combined language and graphic systems.

Some well known American systems are LIFER (Hendrix *et al*, 1978), PLANES (Waltz *et al*, 1976), LUNAR (Woods, 1972), and SHRDLU (Winograd, 1972). German systems include PLIDIS (Berry-Rogghe *et al*, 1980), USL (Zoeppritz, 1984), and HAM-ANS (Nebel and Marburger, 1982). A commercially available American system for data bank query is INTELLECT.

NL is an adequate tool for the creation of references to objects, actions and abstract facts in bitmap-based environments. Methods have been developed for managing effective dialogues and creating complex consistent texts. In addition, NL allows for quantification, time reference, negation and deixis (that is, pointing operations, like 'this', 'that', 'here', 'there'). As NL is always used in a particular situation, at a particular time and in a particular place by people (or systems) who share a great deal of both general knowledge and situational perception, the comprehension of NL depends on these factors and can be expressed by means of deictic expressions. Traditional categories of deixis are person, place and time (Hoepelman *et al*, 1986; Schmauks, 1986); categories of discourse deixis and social deixis can be added. However, place deixis is of particular importance

157

in screen-oriented HCI. The use of NL in the user interface not only considerably increases the number of potential users but is also of great value for the 'professional' user, as the expression of the user's intentions is no longer inhibited by an artificial language.

On the other hand problems arising from the application of NL in the user interface must not be ignored. The most natural means of communication between people is not necessarily the most 'natural' one between human and computer. Many aspects of NL can neither be understood theoretically nor described algorithmically. Most systems contain, at best, a limited fragment of NL which in addition is usually restricted to a specific field of application. As a result of the illusion that the system understands NL, there is a constant danger that users will over-estimate capabilities of the system. This may lead to disappointments and misinterpretations, whereby semantic over-generalizations ('semantic overshoot') may result in inefficiency. It is very important in the implementation of NL interfaces that the user is always aware of the system's capabilities.

Direct (Graphical) Manipulation

The basic idea of direct manipulation (DM) is the visual presentation of the working environment, as well as the objects of immediate interest in a symbolical or mnemotechnical form, on a suitable screen, and a possibility to interact directly with the respective screen objects (Shneiderman, 1982; Faehnrich and Ziegler, 1984). These are usually implemented in the new generation of systems, equipped with a high resolution bitmap display, and a pointing (or selecting) device such as a mouse, joystick, or touch-screen.

Communication with Formal Languages

In this context formal language essentially denotes formal language in the mathematical sense, especially programming and command languages, and other classical 'user-initiated' interaction modes with restricted conceptual and semantic models. An overview is given in Faehnrich and Ziegler (1984). There have also been several approaches to improve formal or command languages using AI-methods (eg Zoeppritz, 1984).

COMBINED (MULTIMODAL) COMMUNICATION

In conventional systems only one of these modes is used at a time. In many real-world situations, however, a combination of these communication modes would be considerably more effective. Combined multimodal human-computer interfaces aim to exploit the advantages of the different generic communication modes and to avoid their disadvantages. In particular, combination of direct (graphical) manipulation and NL interaction presents advantages (eg Bijl and Szalapaj, 1984; Hayes, 1986; Hanne *et al*, 1986; Kobsa *et al*, 1986). In the many computer applications which already use graphic objects, there is the simple possibility of combining natural language and graphic objects by pointing or selecting objects and operations. The expressive power of such combined NL/direct manipulation interfaces in HCI lies in the possibility of allowing deictic interactions on screen-oriented objects.

An obvious and powerful application of deictic/DM interaction allows users to 'talk' about objects for which they have no name, or to use simple pointing actions such as pointing on a map instead of giving complicated spatial descriptions. The use of maps can facilitate talking about temporal aspects using spatial relations, if there is an implicit or explicit time axis. Objects which are already synthetic, in that they are created by the system, are well suited for combined deictic interaction; an example is business graphics.

Unfortunately, this combination of NL and DM cannot be achieved at the display level, but needs some form of common representation. The system has to create a 'link' between the selection and the user-intended object on the screen in order to understand, for example, a question. If all generic communication modes exist in the system, their combination can introduce multi-dimensional redundancy into the interface. For example, graphical output of a table or a chart can be presented with an accompanying text such as a summary. Communication defects that occur in one communication mode can be clarified by changing into another one.

COMBINED ENVIRONMENTS

There have been attempts to combine knowledge-based and graphic NL systems. The SWYSS system (Hussman and Schefe, 1984) from the University of Hamburg combines a knowledge-based scene analysing system with a dialogue system that is based on a phrase structure grammar. ISOBAR (Masdo *et al*, 1984) is a system developed in Japan that accepts language as well as 'pictorial' input. It contains a common representation for parts of the symbols that are used in meteorological charts and a fragment of NL referring to meteorological data. MOLE (Bijl and Sazalapaj, 1984) from the Edinburgh EdCAAD group, allows the design of architectural objects through quasi-natural specifications. Other systems that have been developed in Edinburgh are based on Stiny's shape grammars (Krishnamurti and Giraud, 1984; Stiny, 1975). They allow the construction of graphics on the basis of knowledge concerning their forms and relations. An American system for the construction and manipulation of graphic objects is described in Brown and Chandrasekaran (1983).

Other systems based on the philosophy of combined environments include the Japanese intelligent interface system FGS (Moto-Oka, 1983), the systems developed at BBN, (Brachman *et al*, 1979), the VIEW System (Wilson and Herot, 1980), the 'Put-That-There' System, MIT (Bolt, 1980) and the Krine System, (Ogawa *et al*, 1984).

The remainder of this chapter discusses aspects of system design and implementation, and describes implemented versions of DM/NL query environments in business and technical applications. Deixis will be defined as a reference to an object mentioned in an utterance by means of a pointing gesture – for example, John points at a desktop icon and says: 'This' ↑ 'is my paper' with the arrow marking approximately the chronological order of the pointing gesture in the course of the utterance. Usually, conversational dialogues contain a rich variety of deixis (eg Hoepelman *et al*, 1986; Schmauks, 1986) as humans try to make reference wherever possible, thus avoiding complicated, inexact, sometimes even not verbalizable, object descriptions. The latter are particularly important when asking about unknown objects.

A form appears to be very suitable for the investigation of deictic phenomena in graphical interfaces. When asking questions, the user refers to objects on the form. Most of these are unfamiliar and at best, the user can describe their visual structure. The FhG/IAO prototype DIS–QUE (deictic interaction system – query environment, described by Wetzel *et al*, 1987) investigates such phenomena in the light of the following main questions:

– How can deixis be included in a reasonable way in NL dialogues between user and machine?
– Which strategy would be adequate to solve multiple references to concepts and overlying objects?
– What might a question/answer system satisfying the mentioned dialogue requirements look like and how should it be structured?

OBJECTIVE AND THEORY

Related approaches and theoretical work are documented by Faehnrich *et al* (1984), Hoepelman *et al* (1986) and Hanne, (1986). An overview of the field of deixis and its classification can be found in Hoepelman *et al* (1986). A detailed investigation into pointing gestures is reported by Schmauks (1986).

Place deixis denotes pointing actions at, for example, objects, individuals and directions. It can be divided into two phases. These are reference specification (pointing) and reference identification (recognition of the object pointed at, whereby this object is the demonstratum). Deixis would be quite easy to handle if there were always just one possible demonstratum, as in cases where the speaker points at one unambiguous object and the listener recognizes exactly this object as demonstratum.

Graphical Semantics of Forms

In form deixis, consisting of pointing actions at objects on a form, the problem is simplified as there is no space left between the pointer and the demonstratum. The pointing action is made in the context of a human computer dialogue with the help of a pointing device in the two-dimensional space of the screen. This means that all those cases where several possible objects lie spatially behind or near each other are excluded from reference identification. However, this does not mean that deixis is no longer ambiguous. In the case of forms, there is the additional problem of interlocking similar objects because the apparent flat and unambiguous form can actually have a complex topology. If the user is not familiar with the terminology, even an additional description of the object is difficult, if not impossible. In short, in form deixis, reference is made to three different groups of objects:

- to directly visible objects on the form, such as input sections, texts, pages, etc;
- to data in the input sections;
- to concepts associated with the objects on the form or with the data in the input sections.

DIS–QUE (deictic interaction system – query environment)

In DIS–QUE, deictic user requirements are reduced to a minimum. Firstly, the pointing action is included in the sentence; that is, between two input words and indicated by an arrow symbol ↑.

Secondly, the user has to activate the actual pointing action by pressing a button on the mouse. The local information thus acquired is then used in combination with heuristics in order to determine which object or concept was intended. Obviously, no set of heuristics is good enough to invariably find this object. This is also a problem that appears in human conversation. If the inquirer receives a wrong answer, he or she will ask again or rephrase the question more precisely.

The heuristics of DIS–QUE are based on three principles:

- start globally and go into detail;
- try to find alternatives;
- choose the hierarchically nearest object with respect to objects mentioned in the last question.

Implementation

The implementation was carried out in two phases, the first of which used CPROLOG (Clocksin and Mellish, 1986) on a VT240 graphics terminal under UNIX on a Vax 750 (Hanne, 1985). This was then transferred to a SUN workstation with a bitmap-oriented screen under BIM PROLOG (BIM, 1986), C and UNIX, and a number of additional tools developed at the FhG/IAO (Hanne and Graeble, 1987) for the connection of window systems, graphics, and input.

The PROLOG/C communication system PROCI (Graeble and Hanne, 1987) facilitates the connection of different programming languages and processes via process-process communication channels, and the passing of program parts written in C to the PROLOG program (see Figure 1). The same technique allows for the transfer of time consuming PROLOG elements to 'C' without changing the structure of the entire system. In further developments the transfer of graphic calculations and of the parser to'C'will be taken into consideration. Additional tools allow graphic-oriented input and output. Other components presented in the diagram are based on PROLOG.

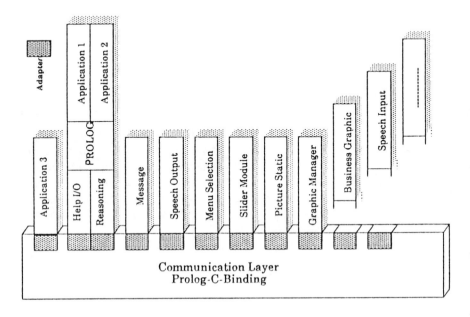

Figure 1. *Implementation structure*

ARCHITECTURE

The structure of DIS–QUE is divided into seven different basic components as demonstrated in Figure 2. The parser works top-down and breadth first. The grammar is a syntax and semantic controlled phrase structure grammar. The NL part of the system represents a fragment of the English language restricted to simple query sentences, simple statements, and more complex nominal phrases in connection with pointing actions. The graphic manager handles the solution of positional attributes in natural language. Form data are stored in a file as a hierarchy of form objects together with the graphical and descriptional information. The data are structured in two hierarchies, a form object hierarchy, and a concept hierarchy representing the underlying concepts and their relations. The connection between the two hierarchies is established by values in the form's data section and by associative relations between objects of both hierarchies. The knowledge base manager pre-processes form data for problem solving. The problem solver (with the answer generating component) receives the semantic representation from the parser, analyses it, and decides what was asked with the help of the graphic manager and the knowledge base manager. The glossary is a term definition lexicon which is used by the system and contains about 200 words of the form's domain.

USER INTERFACE

The user interface has been designed to make use of the special features of the SUN workstation (see Figure 3). The dialogue between user and

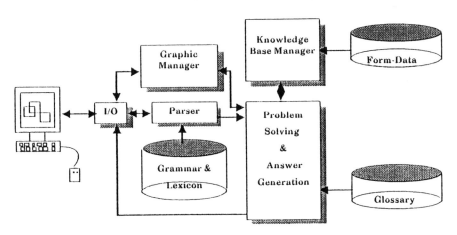

Figure 2. *System overview (DIS-QUE)*

163

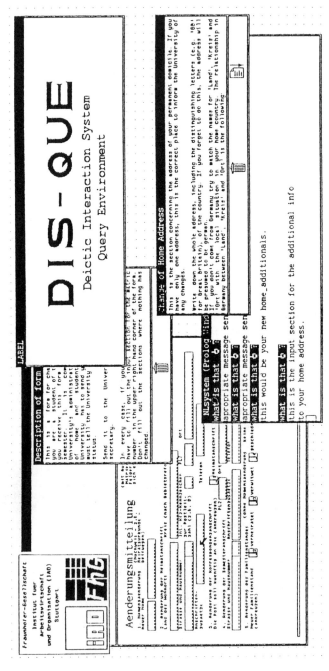

Figure 3. *Example of the system's user interface – business application (English)*

program is presented in several different windows. Textual entries made by the user are simple English sentences which may contain pointing actions: eg

What is that ↑? What does this ↑ text mean?

What text is this ↑?

What does the text above that section ↑ mean?

This ↑ is Stuttgart. What section is that ↑?

For simplification reasons, most questions use the verb to be or to do because most statements can be expressed in this way. The system permits a large degree of complexity concerning positional information about the inquired object, eg:

What does the text above ↑ that under that text ↑ beside that section ↑ mean?

For system control there is also the possibility of command input. It is possible to add a text-to-speech board for an acoustic output of text.

DISCUSSION AND FUTURE WORK

Despite its restrictions DIS–QUE can demonstrate the importance of pointing actions in human-computer dialogues. This is of particular interest in communication especially with unskilled users and in explanatory systems. Here, a common problem is that users have to talk about things which they cannot, or can only partially, put into terms. This problem can be elegantly solved by deictic references. As one of the most complex but natural forms of human dialogue, deixis will gain more and more importance, for example in the field of optical recognition of movement and of recognition and production of speech.

The implemented tool-set facilitates the prototypical development of user interfaces in accordance with established principles of HCI and provides a basis for future applications dealing mainly with NL/DM dialogues on business graphics.

In the near future the NL input may be acoustic using a speaker-dependent speech recognition system. This feature will enhance the acceptance of combined interaction by the intended users. Text understanding systems on different levels are available on the market. For the application with screen-oriented interaction it is possible to use a restricted the application. A training session, in order to adjust a speaker-dependent system to the specific user, is possible too. The use of such systems would, from our point of view, enhance the acceptance of the described communication modes.

ACKNOWLEDGEMENTS

The approach and the systems introduced in this paper are investigated and developed in the context of the ESPRIT project 107: 'A Logic-Oriented Approach to Knowledge and Databases Supporting Natural User Interaction' (LOKI), and are partly supported by the Commission of the European Communities. The development of the DIS–QUE system was done by R P Wetzel, and the development of the communication and graphics modules has been done by A Graeble. We would like to thank the partners and participants in the LOKI project (BIM, Belgium; SCICON, UK; SCS, Germany; Cretan Computer Institute, Greece; Technical University of Munich, Federal Republic of Germany; University of Hamburg and INCA, Federal Republic of Germany; Cranfield Institute of Technology, UK) for their co-operation.

REFERENCES

INTELLECT (1980). *Query System User's Guide*. Artificial Intelligence Corporation, Waltham, Massachusetts.

Berry-Rogghe, G.L., Kolvenbach, M., Lutz, H.D. (1980). Interacting with PLIDIS, a Deductive Question Answering System for German. In Bolc, L. (ed.), *Natural Language Question Answering Systems*, Hanser.

BIM (1986). BIM PROLOG manual, Everberg, Belgium, September 1986.

Bijl, A., Szalapaj, P. (1984). Saying What You Want with Pictures and Words.In Shackel, B. (ed.), *Proceedings of the 1st Conference on Human-Computer Interaction INTERACT 84*, London.

Bolt, R.A. (1980). 'Put-that-there': Voice and Gesture at the Graphics Interface. *Computer Graphics*, Vol 14, No 3, pp. 262–70.

Brachman, R.J. *et al* (1979). *Research in Natural Language Understanding*. BBN report No 4274, annual report from BBN.

Brown, D., Chandrasekaran, B. (1983). *Design Considerations for Picture Production in Natural Language Graphics Systems*. Department of Computer & Information Science, Ohio State University.

Clocksin, W.F., Mellish, C.S. (1986). *Programming in PROLOG*. Springer, Berlin.

Faehnrich, K.P., Ziegler, J. (1984). Workstations Using Direct Manipulation as Interaction Mode – Aspects of the Design, Application and

Evaluation. In Shackel, B. (ed.), *Proceedings of the 1st Conference on Human-Computer-Interaction INTERACT 84*, London.

Faehnrich, K.P., Hanne, K.H., Hoepelman, J., Ziegler, J. (1984). *The Role of Graphics*, report E3, (LOKI Pilot phase FhG/IAO).

Graeble, A., Hanne, K.H. (1987). Integrated PROLOG Graphics Direct Manipulation Interface System. Programmer manual and internal manual (ESPRIT-LOKI reports KRGR 6.2.2 and 6.2.3, FhG/IAO).

Hanne, K.H. (1985). *A System for Graphic Assisted Knowledge-Based Querying Combining Direct (Graphical) Manipulation and Natural Language Interaction in PROLOG, Combining PROLOG and Graphic Standard Systems – Connecting PROLOG to a Graphic Terminal.* ESPRIT-LOKI report Kr-Gr 2 and 4, Part 1 and 2, FhG/IAO.

Hanne, K.H. (1986). *Investigation into the Literature of Combined Graphics Textual Systems.* ESPRIT-ACORD report, FhG/IAO.

Hanne, K.H., Graeble, A. (1987). Design and Implementation of Direct Manipulative and Deictic User Interfaces to Knowledge-Based Systems. In Bullinger, H.J. and Shackel, B.(eds), *Human Computer Interaction INTERACT '87*, pp. 1067–73.

Hanne, K.H., Hoepelman, J. Ph., Faehnrich, K.P. (1986). Combined Graphics/Natural Language Interfaces to Knowledge-Based Systems. In *Proceedings Conference on Artificial Intelligence and Advanced Computer Technology*. TCM, Liphook.

Hayes, Ph. (1986). Steps Towards Integrating Natural Language and Graphical Interaction for Knowledge-Based Systems. *Proceedings European Conference on Artifical Intelligence ECAI '86*, Vol 1, pp. 456–65.

Hendrix, G.C., Sacerdoti, E.D., Sagalowicz, D., Slocum, J. (1978). *Developing a Natural Language Interface to Complex Data. ACM TODS*, **3, 2**, pp. 105–47.

Hoepelman, J. Ph., Hanne, K.H., Oellinger, W (1986). *Classification of Deictic Phenomenona in Natural Language*. ESPRIT LOKI report KRGR 5.1A, FhG/IAO.

Hussman, M., Schefe, P. (1984). The Design of SWYSS, a Dialogue System for Scene Analysis. In Bolc, L. (ed.), *Natural Language Communication with Pictorial Information Systems*. Springer.

Kobsa, A. *et al* (1986). *Combining Deictic Gestures and Natural Language for Referent Identification*. XTRA-Project, report 7, University of Saarbrucken.

Krishnamurti, R., Giraud, C. (1984). *Towards a SHAPE Editor*. Department of Architecture, University of Edinburgh, UK.

Masdo, Y. *et al* (1984). Language-Picture Question-Answering through Common Semantic Representation and its Application to the World of Weather Reports. In Bolc, L. (ed.), *Natural Language Communication with Pictorial Information Systems*. Springer.

Moto-Oka, T. (1983). The Intelligent Interface System. In Scarrott, G.G. (ed.), *The Fifth Generation Computer Project, State of the Art Report*, pp. 101–14. Pergamon Infotech, University of Tokyo, Tokyo, Japan.

Nebel, B., Marburger, H. (1982). Das naturlich-sprachliche System HAM-ANS: Intelligenter Zugriff auf heterogene Wissens- und Datensbasen. In Nehmer, J. (ed.), *Proceedings 12, GI-Jahresagung*. Springer.

Ogawa, Y., Shima, K., Sugawara, T., Takagi, S. (1984). Knowledge Representation and Inference Environment: KRINE, an Approach to Integration of Frame, PROLOG and Graphics. *Proceedings Conference on Fifth Generation Computer Systems*, pp. 643–49.

Schmauks, D. (1986). *Form und Funktion von Zeigegesten. Ein interdisziplinärer Überblick, Bericht Nr 10, XTRA-Project, Universitat Saarbrucken.*

Shneiderman, B. (1982). *The Future of Interactive Systems and the Emergence of Direct Manipulation. Behaviour and Information Technology*, Vol 1, No 3, p. 237.

Stiny, C. (1975). *Pictorial and Formal Aspects of SHAPE Grammars*. Basel.

Waltz, D., Finin, T., Green, F., Conrad, F., Goodman, B., Hadden, G. (1976). *The PLANES System: A Natural Language Access to a Large Database*. Report T-34, University of Illinois, Urbana.

Wetzel, R.P., Hanne, K.H., Hoepelman, J. Ph. (1987). *DIS-QUE, Deictic Interaction System – Query Environment*. ESPRIT-LOKI report, KRGR 5.3 FhG/IAO.

Wilson, G.A., Herot, C.F. (1980). Semantics vs. Graphics – to show or not to show. *Proceedings Annual Conference on VLD*, Montreal, pp. 183-96.

Winograd, T. (1972). *Understanding Natural Language*. Academic Press.

Woods, W.A. (1972). Semantics and Quantification in Natural Language Question Answering. *Advances in Computers*, Vol 17. Academic Press, New York.

Zoeppritz, M. (1984). *Syntax for German in the User Speciality Language System*, Tubingen.

K.H. Hanne and J. Ph. Hoepelman
Fraunhofer Institut fur Arbeitswirtschaft und Organisation
Holzgartenstrasse 17
D-7000 Stuttgart 1
West Germany

Chapter 10

A Conceptual Graph Implementation for Knowledge Engineering

Paul Kuczora and Peter Eklund

INTRODUCTION

The exercise of knowledge acquisition, where a domain expert's expertise is extracted and encoded into an expert system, is rapidly developing the reputation of being a problem area within the field of knowledge engineering. Based on the premise that an expert system development environment is only as good as its weakest ergonomic element, a major strand of our work over the past few years has been dedicated to the development of a range of graphically-oriented interfaces for knowledge engineering, which employ modelling techniques such as semantic or associative networks.

This chapter describes the design philosophy which underlies a working implementation of conceptual structures (Sowa, 1984; Sowa and Foo, 1987); a graphical form of knowledge representation based on linguistics, psychology and philosophy which allows for a richer description of the world than that provided by the semantic network representations currently employed by network-based expert system development environments. This implementation allows the knowledge engineer/domain expert to describe conceptual graphs in a WIMP (windows, icons, mouse, pointer) style of interface, and then maps these onto an intermediate object-oriented representation for subsequent translation into a number of knowledge representations, including frames, production rules, PROLOG and a limited form of natural language. In addition, we discuss the pitfalls which can occur when using such network-based knowledge representation techniques. In particular, the problem of ambiguity detection and resolution are discussed in relation to taxonomic inheritance hierarchies (specifically multiple inheritance hierarchies where a sub-class may inherit properties from more than one super-class), and rule-based inferencing systems.

The prototype conceptual graph tool (CGT) works in conjunction with a semantic network editor VEGAN (Kellett, Winstanley and Boardman, 1987) which maps out the associational properties of concept-to-concept relations in a rule-based frame system (RBFS), (Barber, Marshall and

Boardman, 1987; Eklund, Barber and Teskey, 1987). The intention is that the conceptual graphs will replace production rules, resulting in a greater productive power at the knowledge engineering interface. Conceptual graphs are a form of knowledge representation which use a graph structure to model the underlying semantics of a knowledge base. Conceptual graphs are used as a vehicle to provide a common language or framework for the development of KBSs. In the system described in this chapter, conceptual graphs provide a mechanism for describing the logical dependencies inherent in a particular domain. Another graphical knowledge representation, semantic networks, is used in conjunction with conceptual graphs to build and describe object-relation taxonomic hierarchies. The two representations work in tandem; semantic networks provide a description of the knowledge base and the conceptual graphs are used to represent procedural and heuristic information based on the existence of generic or individual objects in the problem domain.

USING GRAPHICAL INTERFACES FOR KNOWLEDGE ENGINEERING

The RBFS is an expert system development architecture which integrates the knowledge representation techniques of semantic networks, information frames and production rules with a backward-chaining inference engine. It runs on SUN workstations using the POPLOG programming environment, and has been ported on to the Apple Macintosh using the ALPHA-POP language. VEGAN, the Visual Editor for the Generation of Associative Networks, provides an interactive graphical editor which allows the knowledge engineer to generate and manipulate associative networks on a computer workstation screen in a natural and accessible way, while simultaneously maintaining the underlying frame base on which the RBFS inference engine operates.

The RBFS/VEGAN development environment has proved useful in the development of a number of non-trivial expert system solutions in the domains of functional test generation for electronic circuits (Knowledge Representation Automaton for Functional Test Strategies – KRAFTS – developed in conjunction with Schlumberger Technologies ATE division), (Lea, Brown, Katz and Collins, 1988); plan generation (Professional Intelligent Project Planning Assistant – PIPPA – developed in conjunction with Rediffusion Simulation Ltd); (Marshall, Boardman and Murray, 1987); and project expedition (eXpert Project Expedition Reasoning Toolkit – XPERT – developed in conjunction with Babcock International), (Barber, 1987). With production rule bases containing hundreds of rules, and semantic networks containing a similar number of nodes, these systems have demonstrated the need for the knowledge engineer and domain expert to be able to 'navigate' around a complex knowledge base as development of the system proceeds. The success of the use of graphical network tools for knowledge engineering was amply demonstrated during the development of XPERT system, where the VEGAN semantic network produced by the knowledge engineer was used as a basis for discussion with the domain expert, a project manager with no experience of AI-based tools. As development of the system progressed, the domain expert began to use the VEGAN editor to modify the system's knowledge base as a natural part of the knowledge engineering process, something which would have been impossible with a system based on, say, a raw PROLOG implementation.

As well as offering the usual graphical manipulation facilities (such as adding and moving a node or link, block moves and deletes, pan and zoom) VEGAN is also provided with more powerful features which have been found to be necessary during expert systems development. Thus, all nodes and links on the VEGAN view-surface are 'active', and can be accessed via an 'inquire' operation which allows the user to view their detailed structure and properties. (It should be noted that VEGAN only displays the nodes and links of the semantic network. Each node has a detailed frame structure which underlies it, but to display all this information on the screen at once would result in a display so cluttered that it would be impossible to read.) In addition, VEGAN employs a system of user-definable filters which can be used to 'mask' the network so that only a tractable sub-set of the network is displayed on the view-surface at any one time. This feature allows an uncluttered display of sections of large-scale networks, which may potentially consist of hundreds of nodes and links. An animation facility also allows the user to view the generation of a network as reasoning proceeds, thus providing a useful debugging aid to the knowledge engineer.

Over the course of its use it has been observed that, due to aesthetics and ergonomic appeal of the VEGAN network editor, inexperienced knowledge engineers have tended to place an unnecessary emphasis on building, modifying and updating the semantic network. Often this has occurred at the expense of the production rule knowledge base definition, even when easier solutions were at hand through encoding or re-coding the production rules. Thus, in some ways, the VEGAN editor has become a victim of its own success. While the metrics for success for a human-computer interface (HCI) are difficult to quantify, there is no doubt that all users of computer systems have an intuitive grasp of the concept of 'usability'. In the meantime, the WIMP style of interface has become a *de facto* standard for many applications, which is an indication of its ergonomic soundness. These issues are discussed in greater detail by Kellett and Esfahani (1988). The explanation for this phenomenon is considered to be that the rule encoding mechanism lacked intuitive appeal in comparison with the graphical semantic network editor. A recent development called KET (Esfahani and Teskey, 1987) is a software tool which goes some way to redress the balance by providing a graphics map of the production rule knowledge base and a HCI for describing production rules to the system.

This system has met with some success, although the underlying knowledge representation remains undisturbed. In our view, the production rule representation is insufficient to describe all domains, and ideally the system as a whole would be better served by replacement of goal-directed production rules by a conceptual graph, to propositional logic translator. The result has been a concerted effort towards a unified knowledge engineering paradigm centred on graphical knowledge representation techniques. This has resulted in the adoption of the dual conceptual graphs/ semantic networks approach.

CONCEPTUAL GRAPH NOTATION

For those unfamiliar with conceptual graph notation, the following section gives a partial summary of conceptual graph theory and syntax. Conceptual graphs are a form of knowledge representation based on linguistics, psychology and philosophy, and which can be represented in either a textual or graphical form. In many ways conceptual graphs can be seen as an extension of the semantic or associative networks currently used by many expert system development environments, but which provide a richer descriptive environment than those simpler representations. In a semantic/ associative network, concepts are represented as nodes and the relationships between concepts are represented as named links. Thus, the statement 'the cat sits on the mat' can be represented in a semantic network as shown in Figure 1.

This representation is fine as far as it goes, but it cannot support more complex descriptions of the world, which may be required for the development of more advanced expert systems. In particular, a semantic network representation is limited in relation to the statements which can be made regarding properties and relations which have been modelled as links in the network. Thus, if we wish to model the statement that 'the cat sits quietly on the mat', this can only be done by replacing the 'sits-on' link with a link named 'sits-quietly-on', as shown in Figure 2.

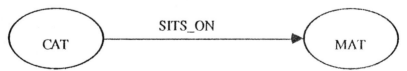

Figure 1. *A semantic network model of a cat sitting on a mat*

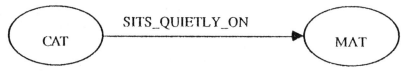

Figure 2. *Such a model does not capture the act of sitting quietly*

While this may model the situation in a crude way, the system is completely unaware that there is any connection between the concepts 'sits-on' and 'sits-quietly-on', and so is unable to perform any reasoning based on connections between these concepts.

In a conceptual graph representation two types of node exist, namely concept nodes which represent entities, attributes, states and events (as in semantic networks), and relation nodes which show how concepts are interconnected. Each type of node is connected to the other by directional arcs to establish relationships but, unlike semantic networks, the arcs are not labelled in any way. Using this form of representation it is possible to model the case cited above in a much more meaningful way, as shown in Figure 3.

In order to rule out conceptual graphs which fail to make sense, it is possible to develop a theory of semantics that imposes selectional constraints on permissible combinations of words. A meaningful graph is thus defined to be 'canonical' if it subscribes to selectional constraints taken from a grammar in the form of a conceptual lexicon. The idea is to include all 'relevant' vocabulary and shorthand in the dictionary and in doing so provide a more limited discourse domain and semantic relevance. The canonical dictionary can be generated either directly from the semantic network model or by the knowledge engineer encoding conceptual graphs libraries.

Formulation rules can be used to combine existing canonical graphs to form new canonical graphs. Sowa talks of three ways of forming canonical graphs (perception, formulation rules and insight) and then develops a generative grammar for conceptual graphs: the COPY, RESTRICT, JOIN and SIMPLIFY operations for mapping canonical graphs. As an example, consider two conceptual graphs based on the situation of a cat sitting quietly on a mat, as described in Figure 3. The COPY rule simply states that an exact

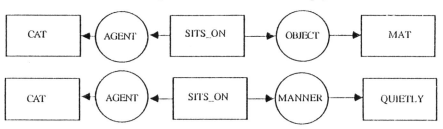

Figure 3. *Conceptual graphs for a cat sitting quietly on a mat*

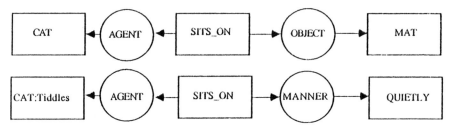

Figure 4. *The result of applying the RESTRICT rule*

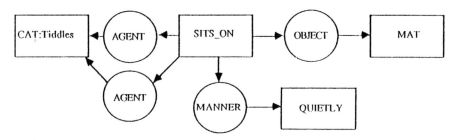

Figure 5. *The result of the JOIN rule*

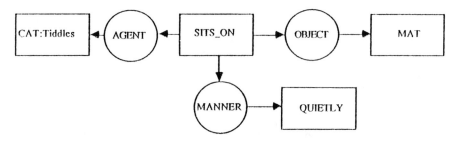

Figure 6. *The result of the SIMPLIFY rule*

copy of a canonical graph is also canonical, which requires no further explanation. The RESTRICT rule can be used to replace a type label of a concept with the label of a sub-type, so that in the example above [CAT] may have been derived from [ANIMAL], or to convert a generic concept such as [CAT] to an individual concept such as [CAT: TIDDLES]. Thus applying this restriction to the graphs in Figure 3 produces the new graphs shown in Figure 4.

The JOIN rule can now be used to merge identical concepts, resulting in a single graph as shown in Figure 5.

As a result of the JOIN operation, some relations in the resulting graph may become redundant, as in the case of the (AGENT) relation above. One of these duplicates can be erased by applying the SIMPLIFY rule, resulting in the final graph, shown in Figure 6, which states that a cat called Tiddles is sitting quietly on a mat, although which mat is not specified. From this simple example it can be seen that conceptual graphs hold the promise of providing the knowledge engineer with a much richer descriptive framework than that offered by the combination of semantic networks and production rules.

APPLYING CONCEPTUAL GRAPHS TO EXPERT SYSTEMS

A major challenge facing both expert systems in particular, and KBSs in general, is that of coping with those aspects of reasoning which are non-monotonic. In the context of expert systems, a common form of non-monotonic reasoning is default reasoning where the system is required to reason about entities which generally inherit properties from the class to which they belong, but occasionally exhibit properties which are exceptions to a generalization. A famous example is Tweety, who is assumed to be able to fly due to being a bird, until discovered to be a penguin.

Two distinct forms of knowledge representation have been employed in attempts to implement such forms of reasoning. These are higher order logics such as Reiter's default logic (Reiter, 1980), McCarthy's circumscription (McCarthy, 1980) and Doyle's truth maintenance system (Doyle, 1979); and inheritance reasoners based around the associative networks described by Findler (Findler, 1979) and others. While first order logic's properties of expressive power, soundness, completeness and well-defined semantics offer great advantages as a knowledge representation for monotonic applications, it has become increasingly apparent that the use of higher order logics for default reasoning may lead to less than satisfactory results. In particular, such reservations have been expressed by McDermott (1986) who has been one of the leading proponents of logic as a knowledge representation technique. A salient analysis of the problem has been carried out by Reichgelt (1988), whose argument can be summarized as follows:

> Default logics work on the basis of rules of the form 'If x implies y, and it is consistent to assume y, then conclude y on the basis of x'.
>
> However, in order to show that y is consistent, it is necessary to determine that $\neg y$ is inconsistent (that is, cannot be proved on the basis of the information available to the system). Such an operation is beyond first order predicate calculus, which is only semi-decidable and would require that any type of reasoning system perform a complete expansion of search space,

resulting in a loss of computational tractability. The problem of such undecidability can be overcome for a first order logic by using heuristics to limit the search, leading only to a loss of completeness. For a default logic this would result in some pieces of information being assessed as consistent when evidence to the contrary is ignored due to the limiting of the search. Thus loss of completeness in a default logic must necessarily lead to loss of soundness as well. With completeness and soundness lost, and ongoing problems with defining a semantics for such logics, Reichgelt concludes that the very concept of a default logic must be viewed as suspect.

Reasoning with defaults in a system employing some form of inheritance network is based on a philosophy which is quite different to that of default logic. Default logic is based on the premise that it is not possible to list explicitly all the exceptions which a system will encounter. It is therefore considered necessary that the system is able to reason non-monotonically in order to be able to retract reasoning when it is discovered that an assumed default is actually incorrect, although whether such new information is inferred or supplied externally, and when, seems obscure. Thus Tweety is considered first as a bird, and hence able to fly, until the system 'later' discovers (somehow) that Tweety is actually a penguin and therefore flightless. (Unless, of course, he is being shipped to a zoo on a Boeing jet, the argument can seemingly be prolonged *ad absurdam*.)

In an inheritance network, defaults can be handled almost trivially, although multiple inheritance systems (where a sub-class may inherit from one or more super-class) require some care, as discussed at greater length in the following section. Exceptions to defaults are handled without problem as long as sub-class/super-class relationships are strictly monotonic and a 'closed world assumption' is used at system run-time. The closed world assumption is perhaps best illustrated by a comment from a colleague to the effect that : 'If I was implementing a system, and a piece of information was relevant to the operation of that system, then I would include it in the system'. With such an approach, non-monotonicity is transferred to the knowledge engineering process, and manifests itself during the rapid-prototyping development cycle. Thus early prototype systems will believe that all birds can fly until development shows that information 'outside' the scope of the closed world assumption is required (because the system is producing spurious output) and the knowledge engineer refines the inheritance hierarchy downwards a level from 'bird' to 'penguin', 'eagle', 'sparrow' and so forth. When Tweety is instantiated as a penguin, the inheritance reasoner simply ensures that sub-class information always overrides super-class information, and inheritance remains monotonic and hence tractable.

While inheritance reasoners may be capable of dealing with default reasoning, it is undeniable that the expressive power of the production rules which they employ for inference is strictly limited in comparison to that of a first order logic. Given the problems involved with implementing default reasoning using logic, and the lack of expressive power of production rules for inference, we believe that the notion of using non-monotonic logic for inference within the context of an inheritance reasoner offers the potential for a powerful reasoning system. Our intention is to produce a default reasoning system which goes some way towards exploiting the best features of each form of knowledge representation. Work currently in hand is aimed at mapping the representation of conceptual graphs produced by an interactive conceptual graph editor onto an intermediate representation (such as POP11 or PROLOG) which can be procedurally attached to individual nodes of an RBFS inheritance network, thus providing a distributed inferencing system based on conceptual graph notation. Given that we are committed to using inheritance networks on pragmatic and HCI grounds, the ability to exploit conceptual graph holds the promise of increasing the expressive power of such a system, while maximizing user accessibility via ergonomically sound graphical interfaces. These interfaces will be based on a common object-oriented template described by Eklund (1988), with the reasoning system itself eventually being implemented using object-oriented programming techniques.

AMBIGUITY DETECTION AND RESOLUTION

As described in the previous section, it is important to note that conceptual graphs will be used within the context of semantic networks which are used to represent a taxonomic inheritance hierarchy. In a multiple inheritance hierarchy, where sub-classes may inherit properties from one or more super-class, non-monotonicity can enter the system in the form of either redundancy leading to ambiguity (as in Figure 7 where Clyde's colour is ambiguous); or direct ambiguity (as in Figure 8 where Nixon's pacifism is ambiguous). These are issues which must be addressed by any inheritance reasoner.

The 'inferential distance ordering' proposed by Touretzky (1986) offers a theoretically sound and intuitively appealing mechanism by which redundancy and ambiguity may be detected and handled correctly. Inferential distance ordering states that an individual or class A is 'nearer' to class B than to class C if, and only if, A has an inheritance path through B to C.

Inferential distance ordering implements a system called 'on-path pre-emption' to assign priorities in the inheritance network, so that in the case of Figure 7, the Royal Elephant node will be considered as containing more

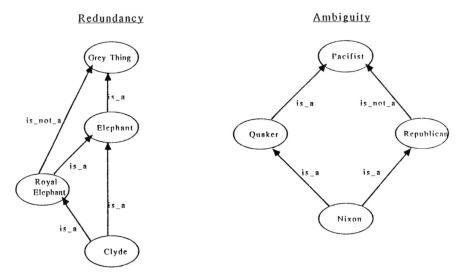

Figure 7. *Redundancy leading to ambiguity*   **Figure 8.** *Direct ambiguity*

specific information about Clyde than the Elephant node. This is due to the fact that there is a path through Royal Elephant to Elephant, so that inherited information from Royal Elephant pre-empts that from Elephant. Sandewall (1986) has proposed a more liberal system of 'off-path pre-emption' which can be used to resolve situations which on-path pre-emption will assess as amibiguous. In Figure 9 the introduction of the African Elephant node results in a network where on-path preemption will report Clyde's colour as ambiguous, although it seems intuitively acceptable for Clyde to be reported as being not-grey.

The situation is not completely clear cut, since Touretzky (Touretzky, Horty and Thomason, 1987) has demonstrated that off-path preemption may prove to be too liberal. The network shown in Figure 10 has a topology which is identical to that of Figure 9, but it is no longer immediately clear whether it is correct to insist that George is not a beer drinker, as will be the case with off-path preemption. Given that identical topologies must necessarily be treated identically, it must be the case that our intuition regarding Clyde's colour in Figure 9 was flawed in some way. This questions the validity of off-path preemption itself. Touretzky comments that the most relevant missing piece of information in Figure 10 is the relative rates of beer drinking among marines and chaplains; if most marines drink beer and only some chaplains abstain, then the most likely conclusion may be that George drinks beer. There are a number of partial inheritance techniques which can be employed in order to assign some measure of confidence to the

On-path vs Off-path Preemption

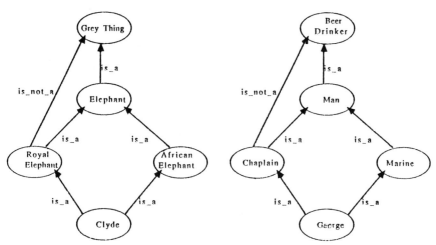

Figure 9. *Off-path pre-emption insists that Clyde is not grey, which seems reasonable*

Figure 10. *An identical topology to figure 9, but is it reasonable to insist that George does not drink?*

inheritance links themselves, giving the possibility of some form of secondary reasoning strategy which the system could employ when inheritance reasoning provides ambiguous results.

In the case of probability-based methods such as Dempster's Rule (Ginsberg, 1984), Sandewall (1985) notes that there may be a problem when propagating probabilities through the network. For example, a chain of ten 'is_a' links, each with a confidence factor of 90 per cent , might in the worst case result in an overall confidence factor as low as 35 per cent for the entire chain. The use of fuzzy chains for partial inheritance reasoning has been proposed by Graham and Jones (1987), but they admit that parametric sensitivity is a major problem encountered when using this technique.

Many of the problems faced by Touretzky in handling non-monotonic multiple inheritance are due to the NETL style representation which he is committed to using. The system of defeasible links used for inheritance in NETL does not correctly implement sub-class/super-class relationships, and so ambiguity results from the topology of the NETL representation in an arrangement such as the Nixon diamond (see Figure 8); where Nixon's pacifism is ambiguous due to his being both a Quaker and a Republican. The fact the NETL architectures have their own particular problems does not mean that other systems are free from the need to address the issues of redundancy and ambiguity. In a frame-based system such as RBFS, a redundant 'level-skipping' 'is_a' link is a potential source of incorrect reasoning unless it is identified via inferential distance ordering. Ambiguous topologies such as the Nixon diamond do not exist in RBFS because the system does not operate with is_not_a links, but it is quite possible for ambiguous properties to be inherited directly from multiple super-classes, or for the firing of erroneous production rules to produce ambiguous inferences. Modifications to the current RBFS shortest-path reasoner are being made with a view to resolving these issues.

The revised system employs inferential distance ordering to pre-process the inheritance network, allowing redundant links to be identified and 'tagged' so that they will not interfere with inheritance reasoning. To detect and report ambiguity during reasoning, it will be necessary for the system to perform a more exhaustive search of the inheritance network than is currently the case. It will then employ user-definable heuristics to decide whether ambiguity has resulted from the values obtained, providing the system with a limited meta-reasoning capability. The resolution of ambiguity is beyond the scope of a pre-processor, as it is possible for values derived via procedural calls or production rule inference during reasoning, to lead to ambiguity later in the reasoning process. Should this technique report a value as being ambiguous when it is inferred via the inheritance structure, the system can resort to a secondary form of reasoning in an attempt to resolve the ambiguity. A software switch will allow 'ambiguity detection' to be 'toggled off' in situations where maximum speed of execution is required.

While it can be argued that a model containing redundancy or ambiguity is a bad model, and should therefore be revised, this must have the effect of placing further constraints on the knowledge engineer. In addition, recent liaison with industry has shown that there is a requirement for expert systems to be developed whose knowledge bases can be modified by domain experts rather than by knowledge engineers. If expert systems are to be modified by their users in this way, there is a strong requirement that they are able to reason correctly in the presence of both redundancy and ambiguity, or at the very least they should be able to detect and report such features when encountered. A shortest-path reasoner is incapable of performing these functions and so it is necessary to modify the operation of such inheritance reasoners in order to allow them to cope with non-monotonic multiple inheritance.

THE CONCEPTUAL GRAPH TOOL (CGT)

Sowa points out that a conceptual graph has no value or meaning in isolation. It is only through unifying basic concept/relation types to a broader semantic network that we can derive a context for the conceptual graph. An important point to note is that a semantic network and a conceptual graph are distinct. The conceptual graph asserts a single proposition, while a semantic network includes a node for each type of concept known, a taxonomy or class hierarchy (to distinguish subordinate classes), and procedural information in the form of links to more complete knowledge bases.

Our objective is to produce an AI environment which demonstrates the principle of distinguishing the two knowledge representations from a knowledge engineering perspective, but at the same time, unifying the two representations into a single knowledge base. In much the same fashion as the semantic network editor can be used to build up taxonomic object-relation hierarchies, the conceptual graph editor is used to construct conceptual graphs which qualify the relationship between objects in the expert domain. The two knowledge representation tools co-operate in ensuring that unknown concepts or relations defined within the conceptual graph can be located in the semantic network description of the knowledge base. In addition to this simple constraint check, a mechanism is in place to allow the knowledge engineer to construct a lexicon of re-usable, canonical, conceptual graphs which can later be recalled in the form of a conceptual library. This goes some way to assuring that only semantically correct conceptual graphs are used. This notion lends support to the idea of clustering libraries of semantic networks and conceptual graphs for well-known domains. This has been applied by Kellett in the area of project planning and expedition and is reported in Kellett and Esfahani (1988). The objective is to provide both expert guidance in the construction of a model and to critique models by comparing the current model with a control model.

CONCLUSIONS

We maintain that the results of this study are important from two standpoints. Firstly, the system incorporates a number of current AI techniques into KBS development which help to alleviate problematic human-computer dialogue issues. Secondly, while direct applicability of inferential distance ordering to frame-based systems may be limited, the importance of redundancy and ambiguity detection in model building should not be overlooked.

While there is no doubt that the specific mechanisms which have been introduced through this paper (conceptual graphs, non-monotonic taxonomic inheritance, inferential distance ordering) have individual merit, the principle of producing an environment which is ergonomically balanced, from a HCI perspective, must be paramount.

APPENDIX – CONCEPTUAL GRAPH THEORY

For those unfamiliar with conceptual graph notation, this appendix gives a partial summary of conceptual graph theory and syntax. Readers who do not wish to delve into these more abstract considerations can ignore this section.

In conceptual graph theory we define a 'formula operator' (ø) which maps *n*-adic abstractions into *n*-adic lambda expressions.

If a conceptual graph μ contains k generic concepts assign a distinct variable symbol $x_1, x_2, \ldots x_k$ to each one.

For each of the c_i generic concepts in μ let y_i be a variable assigned. The referent of c is the assigned value if c is an individual.

Then ø(μ) has a quantifier prefix $\exists y_1, \exists y_2, \ldots, \exists y_k$ and a body consisting of the conjunction of all predicates for the concepts and conceptual relations of μ.

Example

$$[CAT{:}FELIX] \rightarrow (STATUS) \rightarrow [SIT] \rightarrow (LOCATION) \rightarrow [MAT]$$

Recognize the two generic concepts $[SIT]$ and $[MAT]$

> assign y_1 to $[SIT]$
> assign y_2 to $[MAT]$

The two conceptual relations map to

> $stat(FELIX, y_1)$
> $loc(y_1 y_2)$

ø(μ)=>

$\exists y_1 \exists y_2 (CAT(FELIX) \; \hat{} \; STATUS(FELIX, y_1) \; \hat{} \; SIT(y_1)$
$\hat{} \; LOCATION(y_1, y_2) \; \hat{} \; MAT(y_2))$

To rule out conceptual graphs which fail to make sense it is possible to develop a theory of semantics that imposes selectional constraints on permissible combinations of words.

A meaningful graph is thus defined to be canonical if it subscribes to selectional constraints taken from a grammar in the form of a conceptual lexicon. The idea is to include all 'relevant' vocabulary and shorthand in the dictionary and in doing so provide a more limited discourse domain and semantic relevance.

Formulation rules can be used to combine existing canonical graphs to form new canonical graphs. Sowa (1984) talks of three ways of forming canonical graphs (perception, formulation rules and insight) and then develops a generative grammar for conceptual graphs, the COPY, RES-TRICT, JOIN and SIMPLIFY operations for mapping canonical graphs.

$[GRAY]<-(COLOUR)<-[ELEPHANT:Clyde]<-(AGENT)<-[PERFORM]$
$\rightarrow(LOCATION)\rightarrow[CIRCUS]$

v is the differentia for defining *CIRCUS–ELEPHANT*

$[ELEPHANT:*x]<-(AGENT)<-[PERFORM]\rightarrow(LOCATION)\rightarrow[CIRCUS]$

The following graph is thus the projection $\pi v \mu$ to z.

$[GREY]<-(COLOUR)<-[CIRCUS-ELEPHANT:Clyde]$

In the next stage type contraction replaces the type label to form the graph.

$[GRAY]<-(COLOUR)<-[CIRCUS-ELEPHANT:Clyde]<-(AGENT)$
$<-[PERFORM]\rightarrow(LOCATION)\rightarrow[CIRCUS]$

The canonical dictionary can be generated either directly from the semantic network model or by the knowledge engineer encoding conceptual graphs libraries.

REFERENCES

Barber, T.J. (1987). Pragmatic project control using a heuristic algorithm and an intelligent knowledge-based system. Submitted to *Proceedings of IEE*.

Barber, T.J., Marshall, G., and Boardman, J.T. (1987). A philosophy and architecture for a rule-based frame system (RBFS). *International Journal of AI in Engineering*, July 1987.

Doyle, J. (1979). A truth maintenance system. *Artificial Intelligence*, **12** 231–72.

Eklund, P. (1988). *A template for HCI construction using POPLOG flavours*. ITRI/R/44, Brighton Polytechnic.

Eklund, P., Barber, P.J. and Teskey, F.N. (1987). An AI environment for knowledge-based systems development. In *Proceedings of the KBS '87 Conference*. On-Line Publications, London.

Esfahani, L. and Teskey, F.N. (1987). KET: A Knowledge Engineering Tool. In *Proceedings of the First European Workshop on Artificial Intelligence*, University of Reading.

Findler, N.V. (1979). *Associative Networks – Representation and Use of Knowledge by Computers*. Academic Press, New York.

Ginsberg, M. (1984). Non-monotonic reasoning using Dempster's rule. In *Proceedings of the 4th National Conference on AI*, Austin, Texas.

Graham, I. and Jones, P. (1987). A theory of fuzzy frames. In *Proceedings of Expert Systems '87*, Brighton, UK.

Kellett, J. and Esfahani, L. (1988). VEGAN and KET: An integrated graphical approach to knowledge representation and acquisition. In *Proceedings of the Joint ICL and Ergonomics Society Conference on Human and Organizational Issues in Expert Systems*, Stratford, UK.

Kellett, J., Winstanley, G. and Boardman, J. (1987). A methodology for knowledge engineering using an interactive graphical tool for knowledge modelling. Submitted to *International Journal of AI in Engineering*.

Lea, S., Brown, N., Katz, T. and Collins, P. (1988). Expert system for the functional test program generation of digital electronic circuit boards. *Proceedings of IEEE International Test Conference*, Washington, DC.

McCarthy, J. (1980). Circumscription – A form of non-monotonic reasoning. *Artificial Intelligence*, **13**, 27–39.

McDermott, D. (1986). A critique of pure reasoning. Technical report, Department of Computer Science, University of Yale.

Marshall, G., Boardman, J. and Murray, P. (1987). Project formulation and bidding in the flight simulation industry using knowledge-based techniques. In *Proceedings of the Royal Aeronautical Society International Conference On the Acquisition and Use of Flight Simulation Technology in Aviation Training*, London, UK.

Reichgelt, H. (1988). The place of defaults in a reasoning system. *Workshop on Reason Maintenance Systems and their Applications*, University of Leeds.

Reiter, R. (1980). A logic for default reasoning. *Artificial Intelligence*, **13**, 81–132.

Sandewall, E. (1985). A functional approach to non-monotonic logic. In *Proceedings of 9th International Joint Conference on Artificial Intelligence*, Los Angeles.

Sandewall, E. (1986). Non-monotonic inference rules for multiple inheritance with exceptions. In *Proceedings of the IEEE*, **74**, (**10**) 1345–53.

Sowa, J.F. (1984). *Conceptual Structures – Information Processing in Mind and Machine*. Addison Wesley, Reading, Massachusetts.

Sowa, J.F. and Foo, N.Y. (1987). *Conceptual graphs for knowledge systems*. (In preparation, Stockholm.)

Touretzky, D. (1986). The mathematics of inheritance systems. In *Research Notes on Artificial Intelligence*. Pitman, London.

Touretzky, D., Horty, J. and Thomason, R. (1987). A clash of intuitions: the current state of non-monotonic multiple inheritance systems. In *Proceedings of 10th International Joint Conference on Artificial Intelligence*, Milan.

Paul Kuczora
Information Technology Research Institute
Brighton Polytechnic
Sussex, UK

Peter Eklund
Department of Computer Science
Linkoping University
Sweden

Section IV
Consequences For Individuals and Organizations

Most expert systems are used by people and people generally work within organizations. One might imagine that if systems are designed to meet the needs of 'users' then they will automatically meet the needs of the organization. This is not necessarily the case however. To start with, the notion of a 'user' is not well defined. Some people will be regular users of a system, others will be infrequent users, and many more people will receive information which has been influenced by the use of the system. It is in fact conceivable that everyone in an organization could be an indirect system user. In general, organizations are very complex entities which change their nature with time and as a result of forces from both the inside and outside. They have a dynamic nature owing to the interactions between the very many people and groups of people of which they are constituted. Some people may have more power and effect than others, but all affect and are affected by each other. While the people may have individual perspectives, interests and motives, these all contribute to the systemic behaviour.

Since organizations are very complex, the task of modelling them is very difficult. It is desirable to model them in such a way as to be able to predict the effects of change which is deliberately introduced, bearing in mind that there are likely to be other similar changes which have not been planned. It must be remembered that in a complex system a small change can have far reaching effects on the system as a whole. This is a well known principle in mathematical modelling. Predicting these 'ripple effects' can be as difficult as giving long-term weather forecasts.

Assessing the effects of change is further complicated by the fact that it is necessary to distinguish between the actual process of change, the period of disequilibrium, and the period after the change is complete; that is, the new state of equilibrium. It is essential to separate transitional effects, that only occur during the change process, from longer term effects which result from use of the new system. Another complication is that the introduction of new technology may actually be part of wider organizational changes. When assessing the effects of the introduction of a certain type of system it is necessary to separate these from the effects of other deliberate organizational changes, such as modernization or restructuring. Even when one limits oneself to considering direct changes caused by the introduction of a particular system, it is possible to distinguish between changes that result from the actual use of the system and those that result from the fact that people now think about the domain in a different way. Clearly, not all effects are detrimental, nor are they inevitable. What actually happens in practice will depend on such things as the type of organization, the nature of the application, the type and amount of information available, the way the project is managed and the attitudes of the people involved.

Despite these complications, if expert systems are to be introduced to effect then there must be some attempt at modelling the organizations for which they are intended. There is no consensus in the field about how this should be done. Taylor, Hardy and Weaver (Chapter 11) describe a large scale project within the UK Government's Department of Health and Social Services, which is reputed to be the largest administrative body in Europe. They recount how their initial conception of the proposed system changed as they became immersed in an analysis of the organization, and gradually appreciated the subtleties and varieties of decision making and knowledge. Their work was continually constrained by the politics of the situation as well as the practical considerations of how the knowledge could be validated, how it should be presented to users, and how it could subsequently be maintained. They comment that some people have thought their domain to be inherently unsuitable for expert systems, but they believe that this domain merely focuses issues which are likely to be present, albeit to a lesser extent, in other organizations.

Hollnagel (Chapter 13) argues the case for intelligent decision support systems for the very reason that decision making is a complicated procedure. He points out the relative strengths and weaknesses of human and machine expertise. Two common fears about expert systems are that they cannot be thoroughly proven, and that they do not behave in the same way as people. Hollnagel believes that these are not necessarily serious enough to outweigh the potential benefits of expert systems. He compares expert systems with other forms of automation and makes conclusions about responsibility issues, the types of explanation which a system should provide and possible ways of designing with safety in mind. However, he warns that the introduction of technology cannot be neutral and that it is difficult to predict the effects of the changes.

Diaper (Chapter 12) is also aware of the issues of responsibility, quality control, and the effects of the system on users and the organization. He stresses the importance of planning, testing, training and maintenance. While these should be established practice in software engineering, they are often ignored in knowledge engineering. The neglect of such good practice in expert system development can have very far reaching effects. Diaper disagrees with some authors in this volume, notably Edmonds, Candy, Slatter and Lunn (Chapter 6). He believes that it is possible, at least in some cases, to specify requirements away from the delivery vehicle and he proposes a methodology which incorporates this. He identifies two groups of people involved in any project, namely the designers (whether these be external or in-house) and the clients. He asserts that the modelling process must take account of these two groups. Diaper advocates that there should be a two-part contract between the designers and clients. The purpose of the first stage is to produce a complete specification of the system and to cost the full project. The second stage, if the clients agree to it, is the delivery of the final system. Diaper identifies the need for an applied psychology of people and organizations that goes beyond consideration of the end-users.

All three chapters describe implications of expert systems for users and organizations. A wider concern is the potential effect on the status of knowledge, both within the organization and outside it. Deciding to codify an element of knowledge in the system and not to codify another is likely to affect the status of those elements. It is possible that ultimately knowledge will be defined as that which is in the system or capable of being introduced into the system. In order to avoid this misconception it is necessary to educate people about the power and limitations of expert systems, as well as to train them in their use. While it is impossible to predict the social effects of expert systems, it is certainly interesting to look at the history of other systems of coding, for example writing and musical notation. These had the effects of standardizing and distributing, making some notations more respectable than others, and of facilitating some messages and making others very difficult to represent. Knowledge is associated with power, and it is important that people retain control. This means that they must see technology in perspective, and use it effectively. Asimov's Laws, as cited by Hollnagel, sound a warning note for expert system designers.

Chapter 11

The DHSS Local Office Demonstrator: A Systemic Approach to Organizational and Human Issues in Knowledge-Based System Design

Andrew Taylor, Virginia Hardy and Julie Weaver

INTRODUCTION

The majority of writings on expert systems report either on the development of small-scale, limited scope systems or on theoretical issues of knowledge-based systems development. Unfortunately, neither of these approaches is likely to raise, or adequately address, major organizational issues. In contrast, the work described in this chapter involved a major system design and development carried out as part of the Alvey 'DHSS Large Demonstrator' project. This was a £7,000,000, five year project which aimed to develop demonstration systems which would show the potential for advanced technology in producing decision-support systems for large, legislation-based organizations. The work was carried out within the UK Government's Department of Health and Social Security (DHSS) which is reputed to be the largest administrative body in Europe. Our concern was with the Social Security aspects of the DHSS' work which includes the administration of social welfare payments, according to legally defined procedures. The UK Social Security system is administered by a network of more than 500 local offices which provide the point of contact between the DHSS and the public. A central focus of the work has been on supporting legal decision making, which takes place in these DHSS local offices, relating to the assessment of entitlement to Benefits. This decision-making task is carried out by legally empowered 'adjudication officers' who are required to apply the law in an explicitly unbiased and correct manner. Decisions made by adjudication officers may be appealed against in which circumstance they are passed to Appeals Tribunals – the highest levels of which are chaired by commissioners who are able to make important Case Law rulings on the cases.

One of the distinctive aspects of the work has been its scope – in terms of the scale and complexity of the legislative conditions, the central importance of the task for the organization, and the extent and complexity of interrelations between the various organizational groups responsible for carrying out the task. Our belief is that by addressing such extensive organizational requirements we have identified many essential requirements for knowledge-based system developments which smaller scale, or more localized developments have managed to avoid. This chapter firstly explains how our understanding of the requirements of the local office demonstrator has changed during the project – from a large, but otherwise straightforward, expert system to a more elaborate set of capabilities to support various aspects and stages of decision making. Secondly, it describes the overall design of the system and the specific features that have been developed. Finally it extracts some of the general and specific lessons which have (in some cases painfully) been acquired through the work.

UNDERSTANDING THE LOCAL OFFICE REQUIREMENTS

There are a number of easily identifiable issues facing the legal decision-making tasks of the DHSS which encourage a belief that a large 'traditional' expert system which incorporated the complex legal conditions concerning benefit assessment would be of significant benefit to the DHSS. Unfortunately it became apparent that such a system would not address the problems which our analysis showed were real, critical and urgent for the organization and the various individuals and groups involved. In this part of the paper an attempt is made to explain why this is the case, and more particularly:

– why did we make the mistake of believing that a traditional expert system would be useful?;
– how have we tried to make sure that our demonstrator development does address these issues in our subsequent and remaining work?

Once we have explained what we now believe the requirements to be, we can move onto explaining, in the second part of the chapter, what we think we can do to support them.

Problems in the DHSS

In a significant number of cases the DHSS finds it difficult to maintain acceptable standards in the quality of its legal decision making. These difficulties are largely the result of the environment in which these decisions have to be made. Firstly, there is a high volume of decisions to be made; in 1984 approximately 24 million Supplementary Benefit decisions were made by over 10,250 adjudication officers. (Supplementary Benefit is one of the variety of Social Security benefits and is payable to people who are not in full-time work and whose income is less than their needs. This benefit has recently been replaced by the new Income Support scheme.) Additionally, the scale and complexity of the legislation is vast and that relating to Supplementary Benefit alone was contained in two large loose-leaf volumes of approximately 500 pages, each called the S-Manual. These legislative conditions are constantly being amended, repealed or added to as a result of commissioners' decisions and policy changes. Consequently, the adjudication officers in local Offices have to be kept up-to-date with these changes and reference supporting legislation and Case Law for each decision.

Not only are there problems associated with the volume of decisions to be made and the degree of updating, there are additional problems to do with the legal language in which the legislation is written, making it difficult to understand for people without a significant legal training. To address this, the DHSS produces volumes of guidance and procedures on the interpretation and application of the law. The responsibility for producing this guidance, and indeed for monitoring the standard of legal decision making, lies with the Office of the Chief Adjudication Officer (OCAO) currently located in Southampton. The guidance and procedure for Supplementary Benefit was contained in the S-Manual and was supposed to be one of the main reference sources for local office staff administering the Supplementary Benefit scheme. With the introduction of the new scheme following the Reviews of Social Security in 1986, a complete set of guidance for all benefits is to be available in the 11 volumes (*circa* 1,000 pages per volume) of the Adjudication Officers Guides. Even with this guidance, there remain a number of specific areas of decision making that prove particularly difficult and cause recurring problems. In a monitoring exercise carried out by OCAO, criticisms were made in more than 30 per cent of those cases in the sample (Annual Report of the Chief Adjudication Officer, 1987). In addition there are many appeals; and in the same monitoring exercise one third of the appeals considered resulted in a review and revision of the original decision.

There are many factors which can be seen to contribute to this state of affairs, including the high turnover of staff, the pressure on staff resulting from the large volume of cases and other administrative responsibilities, and the variety of complex cases which can, potentially, arise. The main point that emerges is that legal decision makers in local offices must necessarily have high demands placed on them concerning the quality of their decisions, and although there are plans for computer developments to support large parts of the local office administrative tasks, the area of adjudication stands out as a prime candidate for more sophisticated support. It was for these reasons that we saw this area as presenting a major possibility for expert system developments.

Initial conception of appropriate support

In the initial stages of the project we thought it reasonable to consider the task of the local office Supplementary Benefit decision maker, at a general level, as involving the collection of appropriate claimant data and the identification of the corresponding rule in the S-Manual. It is not then difficult to conceive of a KBS which represented all the rules in the S-Manual, collected claimant data and was then able to assess the claimant's entitlement to Supplementary Benefit by the application of its rules to that data. The main problems we would have to address, on this model of our project's objectives, would be how to scale up the size of our knowledge base to be able to incorporate all the conditions and their interrelationships. It was generally acknowledged that there would also be a requirement for detailed modelling of the optimum means for collecting the necessary claimant data, and probably an interaction model which ensured that the users maintained their feeling of autonomy and control in the decision making process, but in some senses it was felt that these issues were 'secondary'.

At this stage of the project we also thought it was reasonable to develop three separate demonstrations covering the handling of relatively straight-forward decisions; the support of discrete 'highly interpretative' or 'discretionary' decision making; and a 'training' mode of use of the system. This approach proved, according to our detailed analysis of tasks, to be over-simplistic and essentially misdirected – a fact which may not be surprising. Indeed it is misleading to imply that we ourselves felt that there were no limitations with our planned approach (after all, given the scope of the problem, we had to limit the objectives of our project in some ways). Our reason for presenting this initial conception in such an extreme way is really to suggest that simplistic conceptions of the task they are intended to support can often permeate the design of expert systems to a greater extent than most of us would like to think appropriate.

The recurring result of our analysis was that the real requirement was subtle and complex, and that any failure to appreciate these subtleties would have severe implications for the success of our work and the relevance of the system. For example, it was by no means clear that knowledge of the legal rules was in fact a major problem – there was far greater concern with identifying which of the known rules would be applicable for a particular case, how those rules should be interpreted, what additional information was necessary before a decision could safely be arrived at. Equally, it was clear that it was dangerous to try to separate the treatment of 'hard' and 'easy' cases – not least because until a case is finished it is difficult to be sure what kind of case it is. Nor could the training task really be separated from the decision making process – it proved to be essential to support the

195

development of staff during their decision-making activities. It seemed that we had fallen into the trap of tending to 'spend more and more time and use even more refined technological tools for solving the wrong problem more precisely' (Bjorn Anderson, 1984). The failure to appreciate the issues of organization and human decision making is, we would suggest, typical of much of the work in expert systems. Indeed, our own experiences have helped us to understand why many expert systems suffer from a number of significant limitations. Firstly, most developments have had a limited impact on the organizations in which they are placed – applicable to specific, narrowly defined and explicitly controlled decision making in small, discrete areas of organization activity, and seldom in areas of strategic business importance. Secondly, because the capabilities of such systems are usually inferior to those of the human expert, and more importantly fail to communicate significant aspects of the knowledge to their users, they tend to have a de-skilling effect. A third limitation is that systems are often designed so as to address clearly defined and almost routine problems when the organization is more often faced with having to respond and adapt to unexpected and difficult-to-describe changes in its environment and task.

These limitations on the surface may appear to be limitations in the specific technical design of existing developments. Our experience has led us to believe that they are actually symptomatic of failings in approach, analogous to many of the mistakes in traditional system design and that expert systems developments are young enough to be still reproducing these mistakes. These approaches are dominated by the taking of a single perspective – usually that of a single domain 'expert' and defining the problem according to that perspective. By ignoring the organizational context they fail to address other perceptions and issues relating to the organization's overall objectives. This 'narrow' problem definition leads to a narrow analysis of the task. Most noticeably they neglect the issues of how organizations monitor and control the quality of decision making, along with the associated issues of the role and significance of 'experts', the varied status and usage of 'knowledge', and the verification or evaluation of specific individual decisions. As a result the systems fail to link into the existing organizational procedures and objectives and so under-achieve their real potential.

Our analysis work has therefore attempted to take a more 'systemic' approach which acknowledges the different interest groups, perspectives and decision-making priorities, and which tries to link the system design to specific and important user requirements. To illustrate what we mean by this we need to reconsider the 'problems' and requirements of the DHSS legal decision maker in more detail. We suggest that these can be looked at as four major conceptual tasks requiring support.

196

Problem Structuring and Information Collection

The most frequent criticisms made by commissioners of assessment decisions are that they are based on inadequate information and that they are insufficiently argued. In one sense this can be seen as just reflecting the time and other pressures placed on the decision maker. On closer analysis, however, we have found that it often indicates an underlying difficulty with the initial development of an overall approach to a case, ie knowing what kind of case it is, what problems there are with it, how it should be treated. This is understandable, given the number of cases that a decision maker may have to deal with, many of which are genuinely routine and straightforward. In such circumstances it is easy for the decision maker to adopt a standard approach to certain types of case and so ignore or neglect aspects of the less straightforward cases which require more careful treatment. Similar problems can be found with 'novice' decision makers in other organizations – for example Articled Clerks in a legal practice will typically only be given specific 'sub-problems' to deal with, while the experienced lawyer is responsible for the overall approach to, and handling of, the case. The problems which arise if an inadequately experienced person is structuring the case can be as a result of the wrong strategy being adopted (ie the ordering of the handling of 'sub-problems' is inappropriate), or by failure to recognize the importance of certain features of the case. It can lead to situations where the wrong questions are asked, either of the claimant or of the legislation, with the result that there is insufficient or inadequate information upon which to decide the case.

It is this aspect of decision making which we have found to be most dependent upon the experience and expertise of the decision maker. The only mechanisms currently available in the DHSS for supporting this aspect of decision making are the provision of published guidance and the support of less experienced staff by more experienced ones. Clearly, it is not just a question of providing decision makers with guidelines and procedures to follow, but rather of providing ways of perceiving and addressing problems. Indeed this is apparent from the training courses provided for the adjudication officers which continually emphasize the underlying principles and role of adjudication rather than the specifics of certain problem types. The overall aim in supporting this initial aspect of the decision-making process is to reinforce the role of the local office staff as autonomous legal decision makers while ensuring they are aware of and consider all the relevant factors and information in a case.

Domain Complexity

The DHSS Social Security legislation has been characterized as particularly 'messy' and 'complex' (Ogus and Barendt, 1982). Indeed, the quality of the

197

drafted legislation is generally considered to be poor in many cases. All the indications are that this complexity leads to many types of mistakes. The volume of rules and variety of possible circumstances often leads to situations where a rule is forgotten, where a rule is misapplied, or the wrong rule is applied. The relationship between sets of rules can be misunderstood, leading to 'routing' mistakes or mistakes concerning the precedence of one rule over another. Even in those cases where the rules themselves are clear, the number of steps in the process can be sufficient to lead to mistakes concerning where the decision maker has got to go in the process. Difficult procedures in the DHSS include those involving excessive memory loads, a large number of sub-procedures and those where the procedure is poorly specified or ambiguous. These complexities of domain and procedure are further exacerbated by the skill and experience levels of DHSS staff and by the frequency of changes to the system. In this sense the issues of the identification and application of relevant rules are of much greater relevance to the DHSS local office than they may be in other large legislation-based organizations, employing legally trained and experienced staff.

We have to be careful to understand correctly the nature of this difficulty, however. In particular, it is not a problem which could simply be solved by a Supplementary Benefit expert system, or by the presentation of the complete legal conditions to the decision maker. This is because it is not simply a problem of taking fixed input data and applying a large number of rules across this data. Rather it has to be seen as a problem of how to describe the 'real world' facts that the claimant is declaring in such a way that it is possible to select the appropriate legal rules. Problems arise because decision makers cannot identify the relationship between the 'real-world attributes' and the 'legal attributes' – just knowing what the legal attributes are, and how they are interrelated, is not sufficient. The requirement for this aspect of the decision making is some mechanism for guiding the decision maker through the alternative ways of describing the facts presented to them by the claimant and highlighting the legal conditions which may be relevant, along with a statement of what additional information is required in order to determine which conditions are of primary relevance.

Interpretation and Use of Case Law

Questions of interpretation arise with considerable frequency throughout all aspects of DHSS Social Security decision making. Interpretation arises whenever a vague or so called 'open-textured' term is used (eg When is a house 'hard to heat'?, When should two people be considered to be 'living together as husband and wife'?). More obviously there are many cases when the legal conditions explicitly refer to the concept of 'reasonableness' or 'in the opinion of the adjudication officer'. These questions frequently require reference to appropriate Case Law rulings by Commissioners. The volume of potentially relevant Case Law is considerable. Furthermore, searching the Case Law to find appropriate references to factors relevant to the case is time consuming and difficult without considerable experience of what the Case Law contains. There are particular difficulties for people without a legal background using Case Law to support a decision. For example it is important to establish the status of the commissioner's decision with regard to the issue being addressed, and to ensure that no subsequent ruling or legislative change has overturned this status. Consequently it is not sufficient, and can even be dangerous, simply to present all the Case Law referring to aspects in common with the case the decision maker is dealing with.

These issues are particularly significant in considering what information could best support the local office decision maker. It is easy to imagine situations where the local office decision maker could be confused rather than helped by references to Case Law. There may be too many apparently relevant cases; the relevance of the case may be obscure, there may be conflicting or competing relevant cases which it is difficult to resolve; the status of the Case Law with regard to the question facing the decision maker may be uncertain.

Ideally, therefore, support is needed:

– in the identification and retrieval of relevant Case Law;
– to explain to the decision maker the key aspects of the commissioner's decision and its scope and status;
– in helping the decision maker to resolve conflict between the alternative interpretations.

We should also expect that the variety and extent of information presented should take into account the skill and experience level of the decision maker, as well as the significance of the issue being considered.

Maintenance and Validation of the Knowledge Base

The scale of the relevant knowledge, and the frequency of its change, are two of the major issues facing the organization in its attempt to maintain the consistency and quality of decision making. It has been established that many local offices do not have access to all the relevant guidance or legislation, and the versions which are available are typically out of date and inadequately maintained. A computer-based system promises a way around this problem, but in the process generates problems of its own. The validity of the knowledge base has to be assured to those who develop the guidance, and there have to be clear mechanisms for identifying any problems and feeding these back for revision. Consequently some of the most crucial issues facing our development concern the support given for the people who will have to construct, validate and maintain the knowledge.

The issue of the 'correctness' of the knowledge base is particularly problematic in a legislative context. It has become apparent, for example, that we cannot expect any DHSS authorities to take our 'final' system and test its correctness. They must be able to examine and review the contents of the knowledge base in a manner that will assure them of its general validity. We now believe that even this 'after the event' review would not be sufficient. While it is conceivable that the published guidance can itself be reviewed on its completion, the main guarantee of its correctness is provided by the control mechanisms applied during its development. A similar requirement then seems necessary for a 'knowledge-based system' version. In addition to these considerations, given the scale and the rate of change of the knowledge, it would not be appropriate for the knowledge base construction to be carried out by a 'knowledge engineer' as a once-off activity. Rather, it is necessary for us to incorporate the process of creation and maintenance of the knowledge base into the existing organizational procedures and expertise. The knowledge base will have to be maintained in a manner analogous to the way that the current knowledge and guidance is maintained – and probably by the same people as are currently responsible. Finally, it must also be the case that changes to the knowledge base must be possible within the same time constraints and with at least the same reliability as are the changes with the current scheme.

General Requirements

The previous sections have described some of the main functional requirements based on the different key decision-making tasks facing an adjudication officer. In addition, however, there are numerous additional requirements resulting from the context in which these tasks take place. Firstly, there are certain support tasks including the accessing of cases for assessment, the production of a detailed justification of a decision, and the possible re-examination/re-working of the case in circumstances when appeals arise. More importantly, there are many 'environmental' factors, not all of which can be described in detail here, but their extent can be indicated by a number of examples.

We have already mentioned the work pressures in terms of volume of cases; this is compounded by a large number of interruptions during their decision making. In addition to their adjudication tasks they typically have other responsibilities like the supervision of staff, payment of benefit and other administrative duties. As part of the decision making on a case they will often require further information – either to clarify the claim, resolve an inconsistency or verify some declared item of information (eg value of savings, last wages). Contact may therefore be needed with the claimant, an employer, another DHSS section or Government department. One of the key 'tactical' decisions which the officer has to make is whether this additional information is essential to the decision on the case.

Adjudication officers undergo 19 weeks of training and receive 11 days training specifically directed at their adjudication role and the law. Some offices have a stable core of older and experienced staff at all levels, in many of the inner city offices, however, more than one third of the adjudication officers had less than six months experience. Any system must therefore be flexible to different skill levels of user. There is a particular concern that the skill of adjudication officers must be developed through the use of the system. There must be improved means for communicating the changes and developments in the legislation, guidance and case law. There is also a considerable need for some means of monitoring the areas of difficulty and focusing more support on these.

Underlying all of the requirements is a fundamental principle of independence of the adjudication officer. While they can be supported by guidance from OCAO, they are legally independent and are required to exercise an 'independent and impartial judgement'. Any system which threatened this independence – or even the explicit demonstrability of their independence – would be unacceptable.

Features of the Analysis

We have taken such lengths to describe the relative complexity of the user requirements for a local office demonstrator in order to indicate the importance of a 'deep' analysis of requirements before designing a knowledge-based decision support system. In fact the analysis results include far more subtle but equally essential requirements that we are not able to describe here (Taylor, Weaver and Loh 1987; Taylor *et al*, 1988). We have said little so far however about how these analysis results were derived, what their crucial features are, how we have selected areas of priority and appropriateness of support. Partly this is because we have no simple, or single answer to these questions. There are, however, three key points we can note.

Firstly, our understanding of requirements is based on a detailed analysis of the decision maker's tasks, in particular at a conceptual or cognitive level rather than a superficial 'observable' level. What emerges is that legal decision making, like any decision making is not 'one' thing at all but involves a variety of possible tasks each involving different types of knowledge and decision making. Solving a problem is relatively easy once it has been precisely and correctly defined. This is to say that the actual 'making' of a decision needs to be distinguished from the activities concerned with 'defining' the problem, deciding how to approach it, and establishing criteria for evaluation of the decision. Problems cannot be considered in isolation – any one problem is intertwined with other 'messy' problems. It is therefore necessary to consider the whole context in which the particular issues relevant for a decision become significant. Following on from this, collecting and categorizing information becomes a problem. The available 'facts' may be incomplete and of dubious reliability. With regard to those facts which are available there may be multiple and sometimes conflicting interpretations – they can be seen in different ways. It follows that there is uncertainty as to what would count as success in resolving the situation or what would count as a good decision. Only when some particular perspective has been taken can these issues be resolved and alternative actions evaluated. A 'good' decision can only be made once the criteria of success have been chosen and the problem defined.

Secondly, then, the analysis has had to build on an appreciation of the different organizational viewpoints and objectives associated with the whole process of adjudication decision making. What is immediately apparent in the DHSS is that this problem is not 'owned' by any single group at all, but impacts on the three major organizational groupings concerned with the social security system. OCAO, as we have mentioned already, are responsible for the guidance, and for monitoring the standard of legal decision making, attempting to ensure the legal correctness and impartiality of the system. The regional directorate is responsible for the administration of the regional and local organization, including training, operational aspects of adjudication and issues of administrative efficiency. Policy divisions are responsible for the overall effects of the Social Security system and in ensuring adequate responsiveness to political decisions. Taking virtually any of the factors determining the requirements of local office decision makers, it is possible to characterize at least three distinct but connected expectations of what the system should help to achieve. For example the rate of change of the legislative conditions can be seen as requiring consistent and correct application of the new conditions, ease of implementation and incorporation of the new conditions, and flexibility of response to policy decisions. It is not obvious that these would all be satisfied by any particular design choice, and the supporting organization procedures need to address any relevant claim to 'ownership of problems'.

Finally, there is a substantial variety of knowledge involved in any such 'rich' decision making situations – far more than it would be convenient to believe. There is an obvious requirement for knowledge of the legal conditions in the legislation and Case Law; which knowledge must extend well beyond a simple awareness of the existence of the various conditions to include an understanding of their significance. There must be an understanding of the structure and organization of the conditions, so that they can be identified when needed and so that the interrelations between the rules can be understood. Similarly there is a need to understand the range of possible appropriate interpretations and applications of the conditions. In addition to this knowledge of legal conditions, however, there is a much greater requirement for what can be called 'know-how' – the expertise, understanding and knowledge about the more pragmatic aspects of decision making which is typically developed through experience and from colleagues, training notes and letters to, or discussions with, experts. This know-how needs to include: awareness of the features of a case which makes it significant; experience of alternative approaches to certain types of case; the ability to recognize potential problematic issues; and the need for additional information, understanding of how to evaluate alternative courses of action, appreciation of the constraints arising from the local organization, the legal context and the claimants. This knowledge varies significantly in terms of its authority in law, its preciseness, its reliability, its usefulness to the local office decision maker, and its relevance for specific tasks. It cannot really be understood without a clear understanding of its sources, its differing relevance to different individuals and its importance as part of 'communication of expertise' throughout the organization.

The message which we are trying to convey is that anyone approaching any problem of this type thinking that it is susceptible to a relatively straightforward 'expert systems' solution must be either extremely insensitive to user requirements or extremely optimistic about the potential of such systems. It may be countered, however, that it is one thing to identify a requirement but what is the point if that requirement cannot be met by existing technology. Our suggestion is that developments are much more constrained by the analysts' and designers' lack of imagination than by the technology. Perhaps, however, some of these issues can be brought out more clearly by describing the main features of the system we have developed.

LOCAL OFFICE DEMONSTRATOR CAPABILITIES

In the previous section we outlined the results of our analysis of the decision making of the local office, legal adjudication officer. This has shown that the decision making task is not a single, discrete activity but a number of different processes. In determining the nature of the support appropriate for each activity we took into account the nature of the activity itself and its associated problems, the overall objectives of the organization and the objectives at the local office level. The approach we have taken leads us to identify the primary aim in developing a decision support system as the identification of the most appropriate kind of support for the particular organization's activities. Consequently, the central issue discussed in this section is the definition of the role or roles that the system should take in particular aspects of the decision making process. It was necessary to establish such a role definition before we could undertake any detailed analysis of the nature of the interaction between the user and the support system.

There are various degrees in which the computer system can contribute to the various decision making tasks. At a general level these can be seen as:

– situations where the machine can carry out the main elements of the task and, to a large extent, drive the interaction;
– those cases where the system stores and provides access to information and the interaction is directed by the user;
– those cases where a 'dialogue' or collaboration between machine and user takes place with each able to contribute in varying degrees to interaction.

It is soon apparent that within an organization like the DHSS the system taking the role of 'decision maker' would be inappropriate. The development of such a system would conflict with the organizational objectives of maintaining both the autonomy of the local office decision maker and their legal responsibility for authorizing the final decision regarding a claimant's entitlement to benefit. This requires that the user of the system has to understand the process by which the decision was arrived at. It is unreasonable to expect that the user of a decision making system would either trust the reliability of the system or more importantly be in a position to authorize a decision which effectively has been made without their direct involvement. In addition, having looked at the decision making process itself, it is apparent that there is a multiplicity of tasks to be supported. These tasks are interrelated and can occur concurrently within the process of assessing one claim for Income Support. Therefore no one kind of system role and associated support is sufficient to both support this decision-making process and meet organizational objectives. The general understanding of the decision-making tasks to be supported is that there are, effectively, different types of decisions requiring different types of support. Even within one 'problem type' it can be appropriate to support the decision maker in a variety of ways. Thus problems may involve:

– the (relatively) straightforward application of 'clear rules';
– the selection of appropriate rules by ascribing the case to a specific legal category;
– the interpretation of legal conditions;
– a sequence of procedures or decisions, depending on results of earlier decisions.

In addition there are issues concerning the adoption of an appropriate strategy for dealing with the case. Consequently the interaction is based on the principle of a 'managed negotiation' between the machine and user. In some contexts the system performs the majority of the task; in others it is mainly providing relevant guidance. In general, the interaction involves guidance from the machine, decision making by the user and the processing of the implications of the decision by the machine. However, the user is able to over-ride any decisions made by the system, except where they involve the manipulation of verified quantities.

From analysing the overall task of assessing a claimant's entitlement to Benefit, we identified a number of stages in this task.

1. Classification of the case and identification of possible approaches. In practice these are likely to involve the selection of a preferred approach, whilst maintaining awareness of alternatives which may later lead to a revision in overall approach.
2. Identification of aspects of the case requiring special attention. These may originate in the specific features of the case or result from a particular concern or unease of the individual decision maker.
3. Development of a detailed plan for dealing with the case. This is concerned with attempting to address comprehensively the potential relevant problems whilst minimizing the effort and time required from the decision maker.
4. Attending to the various aspects of the case and revising the detailed plan if necessary, eg stopping if a reason for ineligibility is found. The issues in the case may obviously be different in nature requiring different types of support.
5. Combining and summarizing the findings from each of the specific issues and completing the case assessment. This requires an evaluation of the correctness of the approach and a check of the overall coherence of the assessment – in particular whether anything has been missed.

It has been argued earlier that the identification of the relevant legal conditions is often problematic: their application relatively straightforward. Some legal conditions, however, are not easy to apply. These are the conditions that involve interpretation. The legislation, guidance on its interpretation and relevant Case Law are important elements in reaching decisions about the interpretive aspects of case assessments. An obvious answer would be to provide some capabilities for the retrieval of relevant text. Such systems may have a number of hidden dangers, however. In particular they may be dangerous if they give users access to knowledge which they don't know how to use properly. Equally, they may be effectively useless if the users don't know that they have a problem and that they are actually in need of guidance or if there are not easy ways of finding the relevant information from the mass which may be retrievable. Clearly, in terms of the scope of support such systems provide, one of their main limitations is that they do not provide support to the user in establishing whether a particular piece of information is appropriate to their task, neither are they capable of offering guidance on the application of this information. All the decision making is in effect carried out outside the support system. Our system provides access to the relevant legislation and guidance at all stages of the decision making task – from understanding what exactly the legislation means by 'board and lodging' accommodation when trying to determine a particular classification, to retrieving Case Law (with case features similar to those of the case being assessed) on a difficult area of adjudication such as 'living together as husband and wife' (Adam and Taylor, 1987).

Information directly related to the decision being made is available in this way. In addition, the legislation and guidance are presented as browsable text similar to the DHSS manuals used at present. In situations where a high degree of error occurs or where the legislation has recently been amended, this fact together with appropriate guidance is automatically brought to the attention of users. The system views the knowledge as a centrally-maintained resource, freely but appropriately accessible at local and individual level.

OCAO are responsible for producing guidance on Income Support legislation for local offices and therefore would be the natural owners of such a knowledge base. It is likely to contain upwards of 30,000 rules and if non-technical DHSS staff are required to maintain it they will need the appropriate tools to do so. Knowledge base development for the local office application is made up of a number of different activities, involving different types of individual and different support methods and tools. We are calling the two major stages 'knowledge analysis' and 'knowledge base building'. The first of these takes as its source the published legislation and guidance, developing structures for the knowledge with attached rules, and is carried out with a particular emphasis on the concerns, perspectives and require-ments of the DHSS 'experts' at OCAO. The second stage consists of turning these intermediate representations into the particular syntax required by the system and uses tools for the editing, browsing and checking of the knowledge base.

The previous sections have tried to explain the major functional areas of support described in the discussion of requirements. As we also noted in that discussion, however, there are some more general, pervasive, requirements which we are also looking to support. Firstly, there is the need to support tasks associated with, but essentially separate from, the assessment task. These include the retrieval of case decisions for the development of an appeal submission, the reviewing of particular decisions by people in a

206

supervisory role (be it in a local office or a training environment), and the more general monitoring of types of decision in order to identify and understand areas of recurring problems. To meet these requirements, the system must be able to present both the input data, the assessment, and (in some way) the method the user employed to arrive at the assessment. It should provide the capability to rework the decision with new information or to explore the relevance of alternative assumptions to establish the significance of parts of the decision making. There should also be a capability to allow selection of general types of case for review as well as the specific instances.

Secondly, there are interaction issues arising from the different levels of authority of the potential user, the status of the input data and the special handling of 'new' knowledge. There are a number of capabilities that are provided to support different users: 'fast paths' through the interaction for experienced users; 'unsolicited help' where guidance or warnings are felt to be so crucial that they are automatically displayed in the appropriate circumstances; 'different levels of explanation' covering both the 'Why do I need to answer this question?' and 'How did I get this result?' form of queries. In all cases we need to provide the facility for the user to 'override' the system, so that legal independence is maintained.

The status of information used is a fundamental and crucial element in the legal decision-making process. Two general issues arise, firstly the level of verification of the information and secondly the extent of interpretation which takes place in selecting, describing and declaring the information. Input data may have different levels of authorization or verification. In particular we believe we need to distinguish between:

- *told*: ie declared by the claimant on the claim form or in interview and contained in some form in the case details stored in the machine; any change to this information must be supported by a change in the contents of the stored case information.
- *assumed*: ie entered by the user as a 'worst case' guess or reasonable assumption in order to continue with the interaction and identify which information actually needs to be determined for the case assessment to be decided; this information can be changed freely by the user.
- *verified*: ie supported by appropriate authorization or evidence which confirms the statements of the claimant; typically this cannot be permanently removed during the interaction but it can be added to or reinterpreted in which case the existing circumstances hold, but earlier circumstances are catalogued for reference.

The significance of these categorizations is that they should be used by the system as one of the means to determine where there is 'inadequate information' for making the decision.

One of the major requirements of our support is that it should improve the handling of updates and amendments to knowledge used in decision making. It should therefore be made apparent to the user of the system when they are working on issues which have recently been the subject of changes in conditions or interpretation. The main support for this will be in providing 'unsolicited help' which in these circumstances may comprise a 'warning message' that changes have recently come into effect. One issue raised by this question is where a user wishes to use a fast path but the Knowledge base (KB) has been recently amended. The maintainers of the KB may well wish to draw these changes to the attention of the user, who will be working under the assumption that nothing has changed. A flagging of these changes may be sufficient or a forced 'slow path' through the amended area may be desirable.

The principal point about these capabilities that we have been establishing for our local office demonstrator is the need for an interconnected set of support capabilities corresponding to the inextricably connected organization activities surrounding what, on the surface, may have appeared to be a straightforward task. The initial reactions from the variety of users who would be involved in such a system have been very encouraging – they seem to recognize very quickly and with little or no prompting what the potential of the systems could be. The results of the work are currently being developed into a 'business case' for further developments which highlight the variety and extent of potential benefits including:

- improvement in the quality of legal decision making and of the explanations and justifications for their decisions;
- support in the training and skill development of adjudication officers as they carry out their work;
- improved flexibility in responding to changes in conditions resulting either from policy changes or case law rulings;
- facilities for monitoring areas of difficulty, highlighting them for potential changes in conditions or guidance;
- efficiency improvements in the handling of cases, particularly for reconsidering cases or preparing appeal submissions.

Such benefits would be of a major significance for the DHSS. What has become apparent is that such major changes depend upon sophisticated and varied support capabilities.

LESSONS TO BE LEARNED

What, then, are the more general lessons of this work – particularly with

0

208

regard to future developments of KBSs? Firstly, we believe that the major lesson concerns the importance of treating such developments as applications with many particular and often sophisticated requirements resulting from the organization's needs. This is to say that we do not feel it is possible to propose general solutions for organization problems of the type we have been addressing. The distinguishing features of these problems include, especially:

– that there are multiple, often inseparable, elements in the decision making: decision making is not one thing;
– that the decision-making process invokes issues concerning boundaries and cross-boundary communications: decision making cannot be localized to just one place, it involves different parts of the organization, each with different perspectives and priorities;
– that the decision-making process can involve many individuals with varying skills and sometimes a multiplicity of roles: there is no one type of decision maker;
– that there are many different types of knowledge used in the decision making, in terms of where it comes from, what it is about, what status, authority and validity it has and how useful, relevant and understandable it is for a specific purpose: knowledge is not one thing or one type of thing.

This variety of decision making, decision makers and knowledge types has evolved in order to address complex requirements which have arisen over many years. These requirements have arisen from such things as administrative law, the size and complexity of the organization and the variety of needs of claimants. Within the organization itself the decision-making process is seen to be inadequate in many ways. Change is achieved by the exercise of a complex balance of relationships. The designer of a support system for such an environment has to be particularly sensitive to these relationships and the effects which introduction of a system could have on them.

When we make these comments to people (particularly those in the 'expert systems community') a typical reaction is that we are working in an area of application which is inappropriate for the current 'state of technology'. Our feeling is that, even though the DHSS may be seen as an extreme example, all organizational decision making of any real significance to the typical organization involves these features to a greater or lesser degree. In contrast, many of the areas addressed by expert system developments are notable for their narrowly limited, almost closed, perspective. Surely the time has come when we have to face the major challenge and stop feeling that lessons of major impact can be found in the quiet corners of organizations.

The second general lesson concerns the requirements of any satisfactory analysis approach for these developments. In particular we believe that analysts have to be aware of three fundamental issues in the analysis task.

1. It must make explicit the multiple objectives and tasks of the various users and owners of the system, so that the implications of the designed task which the system will support are apparent and acceptable to those involved. In particular the system should not be thought of as reproducing an existing task but of introducing new ones. These have to include clear and effective mechanisms for updating and reviewing the knowledge base which are consistent with the monitoring requirements and authorities within the organization.

2. As the effects of the system will permeate throughout the organization, it is effectively impossible to draw a single boundary around the system, within which it can be evaluated. In practice this means that the value of the system has to be 'sold' to the organization rather than formally evaluated in a narrow or defined sense. In order to do this it is necessary to have a very well developed story about how the system could fit into the organization, and what benefits would accrue. Again, however, this story has to include the numerous different perspectives of interested parties.

3. The models which users have of the system are a crucial element not only for the design but also for the explanation, promotion and introduction of the system. We are also finding that the process whereby users conceptualize a problem before presenting it to a system is as significant in the interaction as the actual cognitive processes supported by the system. Yet again it is apparent that these models differ significantly across the community of users, and an appreciation of this variety is essential in designing the components of the system. One of the main failings we are finding in available analysis techniques is any real acknowledgement of the need to model the deeper conceptual processes of the user, rather than their superficial actions.

Similar requirements, of course, are already familiar to those people working on more traditional system developments – particularly in the area of decision support systems. We mention them firstly because we are finding that they are especially critical in expert systems and secondly because the expert systems literature seems to be forgetting these well established lessons. It is our evaluation that current approaches to expert systems developments are painfully inadequate for addressing these issues – largely because they are insufficiently systemic or holistic in their understanding of organization requirements. On the other hand, traditional system development methodologies tend to underestimate the added complexity of analysis which arises with KBSs – a complexity which results from trying to support the central and complex aspects of the user's task rather than the routine or clerical aspects.

We can also propose a number of requirements of any suggested approach or emerging methodology for addressing these issues. Effectively it must be able to support the identification and characterization of the following features of the organization:

- the various perspectives on the objectives of the organization and how these correspond to the activities actually being carried out within the organization;
- the uses of different knowledge items by the activities, the sources and flows of the knowledge, and the mechanisms for monitoring, validating and maintaining the knowledge;
- the organization groups and boundaries involved in the activities, including the procedures for monitoring the perceived quality of decision making and the mechanisms whereby 'authority' is exerted;
- the general attributes of the knowledge, including how explicit the knowledge is, the extent to which it is formalized within the organization, the perceived reliability and authority of the knowledge, its boundaries of relevance and significance for the decision making.

In addition, we require techniques for task analysis of individual potential users which give support in identifying and characterizing:

- the detailed processes carried out by the decision maker and the relative proportion of time and effort spent on each, the sources of information, the environment of decision making (including constraints of time, interruptions, etc), the situations in which 'problems' arise and the mechanisms for their resolution;
- the different knowledge sources which are used, for what purposes, and why; the relations between the different knowledge items and the constraints on access to specific knowledge;
- the cognitive model of the decision making, making explicit the relation between elements of the decision-making process and knowledge used; this should, in a sense, explain the previous two items.

Finally, there has to be a subsequent stage of task design concerned with the proposal of new procedures made possible by the system capabilities, including:

- the proposal of alternative, potentially appropriate support systems;

evaluation of alternatives by reference to the organization objectives and evaluation criteria;
- the definition of the allocation of tasks between user and system, the design of new tasks to improve the decision making and to maintain the new system, including requirements for monitoring and control for evolution of the system performance;
- the identification of evaluation criteria for usability, implications for job design and the work environment.

CONCLUSIONS

Before finishing we must acknowledge that it is misleading to imply that the development of these guidelines or approach are the source of our major motivation. Throughout our work we have been directed by certain fundamental principles which, we would argue, are apparent in the systems we have developed. The first of these is that computers cannot and should not attempt to replace or even replicate human decision makers. Rather we need to support people in the most comprehensive and appropriate manner possible. This may be in carrying out the 'mundane' tasks, providing helpful criticism or giving easier and more direct access to information; basically it is driven by whatever the people need. Now this is not an unusual principle to hear proposed, we are just surprised at the lack of evidence for any substantial adherence to what should be implied. Many systems fail to take account of the differences in their users and few manifest any real concern for the development of people's unique and distinctive capabilities. Obviously work in user modelling and training systems addresses these issues directly, but often, ironically, in a context which separates training and development of skills from the more general decision making. The main symptom of the failing in existing approaches is their neglect of the wider context within which people work and live. We are attempting, in contrast, to develop this wider understanding of the environment of decision making so as to develop the capabilities of decision makers into new areas of activity, rather than the perpetuation and narrowing of traditional tasks. Not only should this provide greater potential for extensive, collective impact on the organizations, crucially it provides the possibility of greater openness in the whole process of decision making.

ACKNOWLEDGEMENTS

This work was carried out as part of the 'DHSS Large Demonstrator' project, supported by the Alvey Directorate of the UK Department of Trade and Industry and the UK Science and Engineering Research Council. The project collaborators are ICL, Logica, Imperial College, London and the Universities of Lancaster, Liverpool and Surrey. The advice of other project members is gratefully acknowledged. The views expressed here are those of the authors and may not necessarily be shared by other collaborators.

REFERENCES

Adam, A.E. and Taylor, A.D. (1987). Modelling Analogical Reasoning for Legal Applications. In M. Bramer (ed.), *Research and Development in Expert Systems 111*. Cambridge University Press.
Annual Report of the Chief Adjudication Officer, HMSO 1987.
Bjorn Anderson, N. (1984). Challenge to Certainty. In Th.M.A. Belemans (ed.), *Beyond Productivity*. North-Holland.
Ogus, A.I. and Barendt, E.M. (1982). *The Law of Social Security*. Butterworths, London.
Taylor, A., Weaver, J. and Loh, J. (1987). The Local Office Analysis Report. Alvey 'DHSS Large Demonstrator' working paper.
Taylor, A.D. *et al* (1988). Local Office Demonstrator 3 Requirements Specification. Alvey 'DHSS Large Demonstrator' working paper.

Andrew Taylor, Virginia Hardy and Julie Weaver
Dept of Systems and Information Management
University of Lancaster
Lancaster, UK

Chapter 12

An Organizational Context for Expert System Design

Dan Diaper

INTRODUCTION

This chapter argues that the only criterion of success for an expert system is whether it is profitable for the organization that has purchased it. Currently most of the work on expert systems has centred on the technology involved in their actual construction. In contrast, this chapter claims that for success an expert system must be seen in the context of the purchasing client organization. To do this both the organizational structure and the personnel of both the client organization and the knowledge engineering team need to be modelled as an integral part of the design process. While the material presented here describes issues associated with expert systems, many of the principles apply equally well to the design of other information systems.

SYSTEM DESIGN

Many major software engineering projects are approached via a general method that involves the construction of prototypes of the computer system, or parts of it. Sommerville (1987), for example, has described this as the '... "waterfall" model of software development...'. He characterizes the pre-delivery design of software systems in four sequential phases: requirements analysis and definition; system and software design; implementation and unit testing; and system testing. Each phase in his waterfall model can provide feed-back to all the previous phases. From a modelling point of view, the only constraint is directional in that early phases, once changed by feed-back, can only modify later phases by modifying any intervening phases (the waterfall aspect of the model). What is not specified in Sommerville's model is the criteria that identify *which* earlier phases need modification and he suggests that the practical, real world solution to this problem is that '... after some small number of iterations, the tendency is to freeze parts of the development, such as the specification, and to continue with the later development stages.' He recognizes that such 'premature freezing may lead to systems which don't do what the user wants and which are badly structured as design problems are circumvented by tricky coding.' This 'tricky coding' strategy tends to be common in knowledge engineering where many of the practices of software engineering are not applied.

Apart from the frequent failure to follow good software engineering practices, there are some special problems associated with the design of expert systems. Cordingley (1989) has called the process of acquiring and representing human knowledge and then encoding it in an expert system as 'knowledge acquisition' and she has restricted the use of the term 'knowledge elicitation' to the early stages of this process; that is, the elicitation and explicit representation of human knowledge or expertise. It is this knowledge elicitation process that is widely recognized as 'the bottle-neck' that limits current expert system development (Hayes-Roth *et al*, 1983; Shaw and Gaines, 1986; Bainbridge, 1986;), and the problems, hardly surprisingly, are principally the psychological ones of inferring the knowledge possessed by domain experts from their verbal or non-verbal behaviours. It is probably a mistake, however, to see the problems of knowledge elicitation in isolation from the other psychological issues that must include intra-personal, inter-personal and organizational perspectives. This chapter will thus deal with the problems associated with knowledge elicitation in these broader contexts.

AN EXPERT SYSTEM DESIGN MODEL

The author, (Diaper, 1987a, 1988b, 1989) has suggested a model of the expert system design process. The model identifies a number of necessary stages, though these may in some cases be carried out in parallel, and there may be iteration between stages. The suggested stages are:

 0. Pre-project feasibility study
 1. Organizational modelling
 2. Personnel identification
 3. Knowledge elicitation
 4. Knowledge representation
 5. Knowledge encoding
 6. Direct user-interface design
 7. Prototype testing
 8. Delivery system implementation
 9. Delivery system installation
10. Delivery system evaluation

While this is a sensible and approximately chronological model for expert system design, it fails clearly to identify the different people involved, their needs and responsibilities, and the requirements of their organization. A complementary model which incorporates these stages, but organizes them with respect to the personnel who are involved with them, will be offered. The focus of this alternative model is on people's roles, as it is people's activities which will determine the organizational success of the new system and, furthermore, the individual person provides an atomic and easily identifiable unit for analysis. For convenience, this chapter will discuss people as if they possess only a single role. This is only for linguistic convenience and conceptual clarity and it is vital to recognize that many people possess a number of different roles, though there is a tendency for most people to operate in only one role at a time. For example, a domain expert, from whom knowledge may be elicited, may also be a target, direct end-user of the system. At different stages, she or he will be concerned with either the knowledge encapsulated in the system or the presentation of the expert system's output as advice, diagnoses and so forth during the development of the user interface.

The system model proposed in this chapter starts with the identification of two organizations which tend to be separate, even when employed within the same company. First, there is the client organization for which the system is to be designed, that will bear the cost of its development and will suffer the immediate consequences if the system fails. Second, there is the knowledge engineering team who are notionally responsible for all aspects of the design of the expert system yet who are employees of the client and, short of legal action, will not greatly suffer immediately if the system fails after its design. That these two organizations at even the most superficial level of analysis have such different responsibilities should make it obvious that there is a potential conflict. However, Trimble (1989) has surveyed a number of real world, commercial expert system development projects and he reports no case where successful systems have been developed where there were not basically the two, separable organizations of client and knowledge engineering team. He attributes his results to the fact that expert systems developed by enthusiasts within a client organization rarely have the backing of their senior management and it is this organizational support that is utterly crucial to the proper installation and use of a commercially viable expert system.

There are many reasons why a client organization believes, in the sense that an official policy decision is made, that it should possess expert systems. Not all of these reasons are necessarily good from the knowledge engineering team's point of view, nor for that matter, for the long-term welfare of the client organization or its personnel. It is at least helpful, however, to distinguish two different cases. First, where someone or a group, at a fairly senior level of management, within the client organization has recognized that they have a problem, even if they are unaware of the actual cause. Second, there are those cases where expert systems are seen as desirable in themselves because of the kudos of possessing the state-of-the-art technology, or because there is a general policy of possessing such technology so as to remain abreast of rival organizations. In the UK there has been a move to what is known as 'pre-competitive collaboration' between rival organizations to allow them to spread the often exorbitant costs of developing at least demonstration expert systems. However, Clare (1989) discovered that the success of such enterprises leads to such collaboration being rapidly abandoned in order to maintain commercial secrecy and market edge. Thus a client buying into expert systems on the grounds that they 'ought to' can lead to the situation of a solution (an expert system), searching for problems. The probability of the client organization's senior management, and particularly the senior accountants, being fully committed to an expert system development project in these circumstances must be low. Furthermore, without at least a recognition that there is a problem, which may or may not be solvable by the use of an expert system, it is unlikely that the knowledge engineering team will be allowed any great access to the client organization. Thus any methodology must include an examination of the client organization at an early stage.

Of course, the other route to the genesis of an expert system design project may arise from the salesmanship of the knowledge engineering team. Given the fact that the knowledge engineering team will at this point know little about their potential client, and that they are presumably committed to selling their expert system solution, then again this can lead to the less satisfactory type of project characterized above as 'solutions searching for problems'.

Thus, before even the client organization and the knowledge engineering team ever meet there are important manoeuverings that will have taken place. The expert system design project, however, might be thought to start with the first meeting between the two organizations.

DESIGNING EXPERT SYSTEMS: PART I

The first step, Stage 0 is a 'pre-project feasibility study'. This is perhaps the most important step in the whole process and one which has been generally ignored in the literature. Usually this study, perhaps too grand a title for it, is carried out between fairly senior members of the client organization and the knowledge engineering team. What too often happens is that after some initial communication, there is a meeting between the knowledge engineering team manager, the client organization's domain manager and more senior managers in the client organization. This meeting may be of relatively short duration, but the knowledge engineering team may then be expected to produce an initial costing for a project.

To expose the weakness of this crucial first step where both organizations set up their contractual obligations, it is worth examining what is actually involved in, for example, identifying the domain expert or experts within the client organization. First, it needs recognizing that expert systems cannot be built without at least one domain expert. Sharpe (1985), for example, attempted to do this in the area of Statutory Sick Pay in the United Kingdom. The rationale was that this was a small, rigidly codified area of legislation that could be simply converted into a set of rules for expert system implementation. With hindsight it is perhaps not surprising that he failed. The written word is a passive data store which is intended to be interpreted by an intelligent system (a person) and it is the implicit assumption of authors that they share with their readers a common set of knowledge which in the readers is activated, and perhaps reorganized, by the symbols of the written word (eg Diaper, 1988c; Diaper and Shelton, 1987, 1988; Bench-Capon, 1989). This is the classical philosophical distinction between signs and their significants. It is for this reason, for example, that a great deal of time, effort and other peoples' money is expended by the legal profession in the interpretation of the content of legislation so that the intention of the legislature becomes, over time, exemplified by case law. Furthermore, it is almost always the case that the knowledge engineering team members are not ideally also the domain experts.

Given that at least one domain expert is necessary, there is the problem of how to identify the expert. Modesitt (1987) suggests that the two key characteristics are that 'they solve difficult problems, and usually in a much shorter time than others' and he quotes Michie *et al* (1985) 'nice list of attributes which the author has found helpful' that experts can: '(i) apply expertise in an efficient manner, reasoning from incomplete or uncertain data; (ii) explain and justify; (iii) communicate well with other experts and acquire new knowledge; (iv) break rules and deal with exceptions; (v) determine relevance and make referrals; and (vi) degrade gracefully by becoming gradually less proficient at the boundary of their expertise.' While this may all be true, it is not clear how one could quickly recognize such an expert without doing the necessary analysis of potential experts' performance and to identify, for example, 'the boundary of their expertise'. Clearly the knowledge engineering team will have to take on trust the assurances of the client organization that they possess the necessary domain experts, who, at best, are likely to be met only briefly during the pre-project feasibility study. The client organization will often not be well-qualified to make such assurances and not all experts at a particular job will possess the right type of expertise required by the knowledge engineer. Shpilberg *et al* (1986), for example, identified four very different types of expert in their domain of corporate tax accrual and planning, and recognized that they needed to elicit different types of knowledge from these experts. Many expert systems have been built by using only a single domain expert, although it is becoming increasingly recognized that better products might be produced by the use of multiple experts (eg Shaw and Gaines, 1986; Boose, 1986). This introduces additional problems for the knowledge engineering team, such as how to resolve conflict between experts. Thus even the identification of the domain experts is non-trivial and is generally left to the non-expert, client organization at the stage which determines the scope, application and financing of the project. A further problem is that the elicitation of knowledge from domain experts is likely to be time consuming and thus expensive from the client organization's point of view. The experts are usually the very people the client organization cannot do without for any extended period. Thus there is a temptation for the client organization to restrict access to their experts or to offer personnel who are not their best experts. Both of these strategies are likely to lead to poor or failed expert systems.

Similar comments of even greater gravity can be made about the client organization's view of their own internal structure and it is very common for there to be a major mismatch between the official management structure and what actually happens within the organization. Not surprisingly, the senior managers within the client organization are far more likely to offer the knowledge engineering team the official model and in many cases be unaware of actual practice. Similarly, those who negotiate the contract with the knowledge engineering team are usually a considerable organizational distance from the direct end-users who will have to use the system. It is extremely rare that at this stage the knowledge engineering team has any access to these users and in some expert system design projects the users are not approached at all until they are required to be involved in evaluating it (eg Oliver, 1986).

Thus many of the decisions that should be the responsibility of the knowledge engineering team are in fact taken, or at least based on, the views of the senior members of the client organization who may lack the technical expertise, and usually the relevant application-related knowledge, necessary to specify the sort of expert system that they need. The weakness lies at least as much with the structure and practices of the client organization as with the knowledge engineering team and given the inertia of most large organizations it is highly likely that the problems with this approach are unsolvable. For this reason many projects identify points where the work can be terminated. Such 'bailing out', however, is obviously expensive as the client organization will have invested resources, will have no return on them, and it is basically a damage limitation exercise to prevent throwing good money after bad. The approach also leads to the knowledge engineering team providing overestimates of the likely costs of developing a system as at the stage of signing a contract there is not a well specified requirements specification. Cooper and Lybrand in the UK are one of the largest expert system developers in the financial sector yet their strategy for costing an expert system project is to take their worst estimate and add 40 per cent to it, and as Church (1988) observed, they 'still sometimes get their fingers burnt'. Church also identifies one of the most costly problems during development, that of 'creep', where the specification of the system is changed by the client organization, perhaps quite reasonably, as the developing expert system is perceived as having greater, or alternative, uses to those that were originally supposed. Such creep is extremely expensive and it may be difficult for the knowledge engineering team to charge the client organization for such modifications as the original contract and budget lacked sufficient detailed specification.

One solution might be a radically different type of contract between the knowledge engineering team and the client organization. The same problems have confronted software engineers with traditional computer applications and even today, many software development projects are delivered late and over budget. The heart of the problem is the fact that at this initial stage the responsibility and expertise are possessed by the knowledge engineering team but the information on which they have to work is supplied by those within the client organization who are not generally best placed to supply it. The members of the knowledge engineering team are, of course, looking for profitable contracts and thus may be tempted to agree with the client organization and ignore the quality of the information on which they must base their estimated costings. The client organization is similarly biased, in this case by wanting a useful, cost-effective product produced as cheaply as possible. For expert system developments where there is an inherent initial vagueness of the nature of the expertise under investigation, it might be better to consider a two-stage, linked contract. The first part of the contract would need to specify a detailed pre-project feasibility study on which the full development and costs of the system could be based. This first part would need to be profitable to the knowledge engineering team and would also need to be cheap enough so that the client organization does not feel that it must be committed to the second part because of the initial high costs incurred.

What is also needed is an effective, cheap and rapid method for carrying out this first stage feasibility study. It needs to be cheap and rapid enough so as not to deter the client organization, particularly if not all studies lead to the second contractual stage of full development. The advantages for the knowledge engineering team are that they would be responsible for gathering the information they need for costing the project and would be much better placed to identify the potential problems that are likely to arise.

220

Indeed, if carried out well, such formal first-stage evaluations could actually lead to an increase in business by suggesting a range of different and initially unanticipated expert system applications. The likelihood of project over-run, which is expensive for both the client organization and the knowledge engineering team, should be considerably reduced and the expert systems produced are more likely to be successful. The cost of delay and/or failure needs counting not only in immediate economic terms, but also in the possible change in the views of the client organizations who fund these projects and who are probably less likely to do so again.

The burning issue therefore becomes whether it is possible to develop techniques which will allow this formal, contractual first-stage, feasibility study to be carried out quickly and cheaply. Boehm (1975, 1984) suggests that it is already the case that for scientific and business systems the requirements/design costs account for an estimated 44 per cent of a system's development costs (excluding post-delivery maintenance costs). Sommerville points out that software development costs are often commercially sensitive and thus are not known and that Boehm's estimates may be inaccurate and that they are probably conservative as they will tend not to include failed systems. Partridge (1986) suggests that Boehm seriously underestimates the cost of correcting errors or omissions at the requirements stage, which Boehm suggests are a couple of orders of magnitude greater than correcting code errors. However, whereas Sommerville dismisses the possibility of '... setting out a detailed specification for software to imitate humans ...', because '... we don't understand how humans carry out tasks ...', this chapter suggests that there are appropriate techniques developed in the applied human sciences for not only understanding tasks, but also for analysing their place and importance within a client organization, and that these techniques are in fact extremely cheap by comparison to software engineering costs.

The author's work on POMESS 'a People Orientated Methodology for Expert System Specification' (Diaper, 1987a, 1988b) first specifies the types of knowledge that need to be identified and has suggested some techniques for acquiring this information. Within POMESS it is suggested that what is needed is first an independent model of the client organization based on its actual practices. The organizational model is represented as a network where the nodes correspond to the roles of the personnel and the connections model the flow of power throughout the organization. The model can be initially constructed on the basis of a variety of interview techniques varying in focus and structure (Cordingley, 1989) and can also subsequently employ indirect techniques such as those based on Kelly's construct theory (Kelly, 1955), which is already widely used as a knowledge elicitation technique. This early organizational model can be used to identify the personnel that are relevant to the expert system design project and it is suggested that three classes of personnel are identified: the domain experts; the direct end-users; and the indirect end-users. It is then possible to carry out task analysis, ideally within the real world environment of the client organization, concentrating particularly on the tasks that involve the domain experts and the potential direct and indirect end-users. Proper task analysis is a sophisticated technique requiring the employment of a skilled practitioner and involves not only systematic observation – a skilled task in its own right – but also involves quite sophisticated analytical methods. However, these analytical methods are available – for example the author's own system of TAKD, (task analysis for knowledge descriptions) (eg Johnson *et al*, 1984; Johnson, 1985; Diaper, 1988a; Diaper and Johnson, 1989).

The outcome would constitute the basis for an expert system specification that would allow some considerable confidence as to: the tasks that the proposed system would perform; an outline of the knowledge that would need to be elicited and the identification of the domain expert or experts; and an identification of who would use the system. They would also allow the prediction of the impact of the proposed system on all of the client organization's personnel and on the operations and practices of the organization itself. Furthermore, such analyses have the advantage that they may alert the knowledge engineering team to potentially catastrophic personality problems with those with whom they will have to work and allow not only the domain experts, but also all the other personnel who will use the system to be involved in the project and for them to feel that they 'own' the system. Bell and Hardiman (1989) suggest that such perceptions can be crucial to systems being accepted by their target users and ameliorate what they call the 'not invented here syndrome'.

It must be the case that a detailed, empirically-based specification of this sort would provide a much better basis on which to allow the estimation of the costs of developing an expert system. The employment of some methods such as those outlined in the early stages of POMESS would remove the problem of the mismatch between the responsibility of the knowledge engineering team and its source of information on which to base a specification. For those expert at these methods, the work can be done surprisingly quickly, and thus cheaply, and might, for example, take no more than 8–16 man weeks and probably about a minimum of 6 weeks of real time, though it might well take longer with large or ambitious expert system development projects. The advantage to the client organization is that not only will they know precisely what sort of system they are paying for, but it may also allow them to estimate just how disruptive and time consuming the production of the expert system will actually be.

However, these analyses will not result in much better cost estimates for a proposed expert system unless there is also an equivalent structure to the second, actual design stage, of the project.

DESIGNING SYSTEMS: PART II

Given a two stage contractual arrangement between the knowledge engineering team and the client organization, it is likely that one of the biggest hitches in an expert system design project will be the transition from the first, exploratory stage to the second, design stage. Contracts need to be very carefully arranged to protect the knowledge engineering team from wasted effort while still allowing sensible termination on the part of both parties. It is important that the knowledge engineering team has the option to recommend that the client organization does not need an expert system or that the possible expert system applications are not those that were first envisaged. Furthermore, the client organization's personnel may have higher expectations about both the likely success of the expert system and its delivery within time and budget. Thus the knowledge engineering team needs to be careful and realistic about what it is able to provide.

It is often claimed that one of the advantages of rapid prototyping, where a first pass, highly incomplete prototype expert system is produced very early on, is that it can convince the client organization about the utility of the proposed system, as well as quickly allowing the client organization to get a feel for what the final system may be like (eg Oliver, 1987; Trimble, 1989). Given the author's reservations about the early use of prototypes in an expert system development project (eg Diaper, 1988b) it is worth recognizing that there are alternative types of demonstration which are cheap, fast and which may be particularly suitable for demonstration to the senior management within the client organization. The simplest demonstration might involve no more than a chain of screens, drawn using a simple graphics or CAD system, which when sequenced provide the illusion that behind the screen there is a functioning expert system. Obviously such demonstrations lack flexibility but if used judiciously can provide very convincing demonstrations, particularly to those who do not want hands-on experience. In fact, such demonstrations can even be usefully presented as a series of 35mm projection slides. A slightly more sophisticated method is to use a variant of the author's 'Wizard of Oz' technique (eg Diaper, 1986; Diaper and Shelton, 1987; 1989) where a person, perhaps out of sight from those to whom the system is being demonstrated, can select screens or construct replies to user inputs. This need not be done in a misleading way but can be presented as only a demonstration of what the complete expert system will do. For the knowledge engineering team, such demonstrations may be a powerful tool to convince those within the client organization, to agree to the second design stage of the project. The disadvantage is that the knowledge engineering team may be committing themselves to a style of interface or interaction which they subsequently find not to be ideal for the expert system.

Consequences for Individuals and Organizations

Most expert system projects commence with the knowledge engineers and the identified domain experts working together to construct a prototype expert system. It is quite common for a knowledge engineer and a domain expert to sit together at the terminal of the prototype expert system and discuss its current performance as they run it. The prototype is thus used as a focusing tool to facilitate comments and criticisms from the domain expert. While this approach is widely used and has the advantage that at least a crude prototype is produced extremely quickly, there are a number of disadvantages to using it (Diaper, 1988b), such as:

1. It relies heavily on the personal skills of the knowledge engineer.
2. The direct end-users are not involved in the major part of the development project and the domain expert is asked to perform the bizarre task of guessing what non-expert users will need and want.
3. It can lead to uncontrolled, unstructured growth in the contents of the expert system as new rules or knowledge are added. This can make it difficult to modify and subsequently to maintain.
4. It is difficult to cost the approach and often the final expert system is no more than a marginally tidied version of the final prototype when a lack of time, money or both terminate the prototyping stage of the project.
5. The approach makes it difficult to identify what the system is not capable of doing and thus the completeness of the prototype is unknown. This also leads to it being difficult to know when to finish prototyping.

An alternative to a full rapid prototyping approach is to separate the first two stages of knowledge elicitation, and knowledge representation during knowledge acquisition, from the encoding stage. The advantages of this is that neither the domain expert nor the knowledge engineer become fixated too early on in the expert system and it allows a much wider range of knowledge elicitation techniques to be used. In the last few years a very wide range of techniques have been developed from the types of technique first identified from psychological theory – for example by Gammack and Young (1985) and Young and Gammack (1987) and these have been extensively tested in the field (see Cordingley, 1989, for a review of the techniques), and in the laboratory (eg Burton and Shadbolt, 1987, 1988; Burton et al, 1987; Gammack, 1987). A further advantage is that the knowledge to be encoded is more completely represented before encoding it in the prototype expert system. This can provide a much greater scope for structuring the knowledge in alternative ways before committing it to the expert system. The ideal of Johnson's (1987, 1989) mediating representations is that these could be virtually complete before any encoding needed to be done and would always stand in a one-to-one correspondence to the content of the expert system. However, as yet mediating representations of sufficient power and flexibility do not exist. There are very few software tools available to aid knowledge elicitation because the main problems are psychological. In contrast, many software tools such as KEATS (Motta *et al*, 1986), ETS and AQUINAS (Boose and Bradshaw, 1987a, 1987b) have been developed to aid knowledge representation and particularly knowledge encoding. However, these tools still require the intervention and the application of human intelligence in the encoding process and are likely to continue to do so in the absence of adequate mediating representations. In fact, the criticism of systems such as KEATS is that they are really no more than a sophisticated combination of a hypertext system and linked graphical editor which solve none of the theoretical problems of either elicitation or encoding and, moreover, they may have disadvantages over paper-based systems in that they may force particular types of representational forms on to the knowledge engineer and so bias the approaches adopted to knowledge elicitation. There are, of course, additional problems with the use of multiple domain experts. No software tools can resolve these problems although some may help to identify the problems of conflict between experts (Shaw and Gaines, 1986; Boose, 1986).

Perhaps the major problem with knowledge acquisition is how to involve the direct end-users, and also all the other people within the client organization (the indirect users) who will be influenced by the final installation of the expert system. Bell and Hardiman (1989) report and predict catastrophe for expert systems when the users are not involved but they also recognize that their involvement is difficult for many reasons. In fact, they tend to no longer use the term 'user', which they see as prejudicial when contrasted with 'expert', and prefer some other term such as 'client' (ie clients are the people who will use the final system). Neither the client organization's management, nor the users, may perceive the users as 'experts' and Bell and Hardiman report that in training simulations of knowledge elicitation, the person taking on the role of the user appears to undergo a personality change and to become 'ever so humble'.

The worst case in knowledge elicitation is for domain experts to simulate users. By being expert, they are probably the least qualified people to understand the problems which the real users of the expert system will face. This is self-evident once one accepts that expertise is not the simple accretion of quantities of knowledge but involves qualitative changes in the structure of what the expert knows. The exception to this is, of course, the case where the domain expert is also the only intended direct end-user. The use of previous cases can be valuable but is not ideal, particularly if originally solved by the domain expert as there is a potential conflict between the domain expert's memory of the case and the current resolving of the case, and there are problems even when only the outcome is known to the domain expert. In such instances the domain expert is likely to provide what are *post hoc* justifications for decisions rather than provide insights into how decisions were reached prior to reaching the solution. This is a general problem with the use of verbal behaviour (eg Bainbridge, 1986; Diaper, 1987b) and is merely exaggerated in the use of case histories previously dealt with by the domain expert. Furthermore, and crucially, the use of case histories still generally only involves the users at a distance and many of the rich, complex problems that they had at the time will not be reported in the case history.

A much more satisfactory, but also more expensive, approach is to involve direct end-users and domain experts simultaneously during knowledge elicitation. It is difficult for a single knowledge engineer and a team of two or more are better able to cope with managing and recording such sessions. This use of end-users is not restricted to cases where a prototype is available and the role of the end-user is to identify the problems with the user interface. However, these multiple personnel elicitation sessions will naturally tend to be task based and there will still need to be sessions with the domain expert alone where non-task type elicitation techniques are employed.

Ideally the current real tasks of the direct end-users would be used during knowledge elicitation, though in the real world, these are usually neither of sufficient frequency nor conveniently available when everyone is available for an elicitation session. Alternatives may involve case histories, preferably novel ones for all concerned or representative tasks which can be constructed. One of the uses of doing a relatively extensive task analysis prior to such elicitation sessions is that it can guide the design of such representative tasks so that it is known that they cover both the typical cases and also the exceptional ones (ie the range of tasks used for designing the expert system is known to be complete, provided the task analyses were themselves demonstrably exhaustive). Of course, ideally, the indirect users would also be involved during such sessions but, in practice, this is almost impossible to organize and is, from the client organization's point of view, usually prohibitively expensive. There is also a further problem with involving the direct end-users in that they may acquire additional expertise during these sessions and thus no longer be representative users. Thus if possible it is desirable to use a range of direct end-users relatively infrequently. Such a strategy also has the advantage of sampling the direct end-user population more thoroughly.

Once sufficient knowledge has been elicited, a prototype system can be built. This is probably best done as a two-stage exercise separating out the encoding of the expert system from the design of its interface. The advantage of this separation lies in the possibility of de-confounding examples of where the expert system fails owing to inadequacies in the knowledge base and inference engine from those that arise because of the style of inputs or outputs. Extensive evaluations are needed to test the logical properties of the expert system for completeness, consistency, redundancy and conflict, and the usability of the system also needs testing. Great care needs to be taken when modifying the expert system so that modifications are not made in an *ad hoc* manner. New example cases will need to be run through the system and again the prior task analyses can guide the construction of these test cases. In fact, particular care needs to be taken on the example tasks used for the evaluation of the prototype as it is essential that, at least by this stage, the indirect users are also considered and preferably actively involved in these evaluations so that they can approve, and also feel involved in, the expert system's development. The organizational model previously developed can be invaluable here and at least part of the evaluation should consider how the system will be installed and how it will require changes to be made to the structure and practices of the client organization itself and to the tasks of the direct and indirect users.

It often appears as if all the effort and responsibility for the major development of the expert system lies with the knowledge engineering team. This is not, however, the case as the team needs the active support and co-operation of the client organization in nearly every stage of the prototype's development (the exception being during the encoding of the expert system). The knowledge engineering team need access to the records of the organization and these may contain commercially sensitive information. They may also contain embarrassing information with respect to the past competence of the client organization and its personnel. Thus the client organization may be reluctant to release what may be the most informative records and the knowledge engineering team must possess a considerable degree of tact when dealing with such cases. The knowledge engineering team will also need access to the current tasks and operations of the client organizations and these too are likely to be sensitive. Perhaps the major expense to the client organization is the disruption that is likely to be caused to their current operations by the loss, even for limited periods of time, of their expensive and valuable domain expert or experts. Clare (1989), for example, describes an expert system development project to aid dealers on the New York stock exchange and, because of the nature of the market and the expense of disrupting dealing, he was restricted to a single day with each domain expert. Thus, if a successful expert system is to be developed then the client organization must be a willing partner in the enterprise. It is tempting to suggest that the knowledge engineering team would be better off withdrawing from projects where such support from their clients is not forthcoming.

EXPERT SYSTEM DELIVERY

Expert System Installation

Having developed and evaluated the prototype expert system it is now nearly ready for installation within the client organization. Prior to installation the prototype may need to be ported into a different hardware system. While this is a common procedure in software development, it still needs to be carried out with care so as not to corrupt either the system or to lose some of the properties such as response speed, necessary file storage capacity etc, which were an integral part of the evaluated prototype. Where such modifications are needed then the prototype can provide a bench-mark against which the final delivery expert system can be tested. Occasionally, particularly where there are necessary changes to the interface, further evaluations may be needed using the direct end-users.

There is a great temptation for the knowledge engineering team to deliver their software and hardware accompanied by some sort of manual, take their money, and leave the rest up to the client organization. This may be one of the major reasons why many delivered expert systems end up unused in the client organization. The more responsible knowledge engineering teams will install the expert system, provide comprehensive documentation about both the hardware and the software – particularly documentation on the contents and architecture of the expert system – and also provide some training for the client organization's personnel. The knowledge engineering team need to consider providing different documentation and training to the different personnel as many indirect end-users will need training on the utility and limitations of the system, whereas perhaps only the direct end-users will need training about specific aspects of running the expert system itself. The client organization's technical staff may require a very differen. type of training from other personnel. Where a single expert system has been designed to support more than one class of task, then different training may also be required for these different task types, which may, of course, interact with who receives what training.

While supply of the above is admirable, it can be argued that it is still not enough and there are still other tasks that the knowledge engineering team should undertake. Firstly, the introduction of an expert system into the client organization will inevitably lead to changes in the organization and to the tasks undertaken by its personnel. Considering the simplest case first, the domain expert or experts whose knowledge has been encoded in the expert system, will suffer a change in the nature of their work. There appears to be no tendency for expert systems to make domain experts redundant, but rather that they free the expert from dealing with routine tasks. This is hardly surprising given the limitations and domain specificity of all current expert systems. While some expert systems have been developed where the domain experts are also the direct end-users, such systems are in a minority and it is more common for an expert system to be used by those who, while perhaps being knowledgeable about the domain, are not the real domain experts from whom the knowledge was extracted. Even in the former case, the expert system will still change the domain experts' tasks.

Where expert systems have been designed to distribute expertise within an organization, then the consequences can be very considerable. The domain expert is likely to be retained, if at all possible, to handle cases beyond the scope of the expert system and thus may enjoy a more interesting job. The direct end-users would have a greater amount of responsibility. While it is often suggested that this will make the direct end-users' jobs more interesting, it is also likely to increase their stress. An expert system cannot be held responsible for its output and it cannot be punished, sacked or prosecuted. Furthermore, the knowledge engineering team are unlikely to be prosecutable for negligence if they have done their job thoroughly. Thus it is the direct end-users who are most likely to be placed at risk with the introduction of an expert system. Moreover, some of these direct end-users may be neither emotionally nor intellectually able to cope with the additional responsibilities thrust upon them. This is in addition to any stress caused if this is the first time they have been required to deal with computer equipment. In the long term, this may have disastrous consequences for the client organization. Apart from losing staff, such users may avoid using the system, or use it so inefficiently that the earlier, pre-expert system state was actually more efficient.

A further personnel problem can arise with the indirect users working within the domain. One major possibility with expert systems that are used by those of a relatively junior status is that it is their immediate superiors whose jobs are at risk. The increased efficiency, or responsibility, of the direct end-users may simply squeeze out those who previously supervised the work of the juniors. In a similar area of automation, Wells (1987) suggested that this has happened in the case of design office supervisors once CAD systems are installed. The distribution of expertise at junior levels may in effect be flattening the management pyramid so that the routine problems and decisions can be handled by the junior, direct end-users and those problems that cannot be handled by the expert system are those that would anyway have been dealt with by the domain expert in the pre-expert system organization. These indirect users can rarely be demoted to being direct end-users, and at the very least, it is questionable if they can survive unless they are prepared to be flexible and to accept considerable changes in their job descriptions. However, given the narrow, domain limitations of expert systems, there is probably, in most cases, an altered, supervisory role for such indirect users provided that they have a good understanding of the system. The potential increased responsibility and stress on junior direct end-users may in part be solved by restructuring the middle management role so as to place responsibility with these indirect end-users. To do so, it is crucial that these personnel understand not only what the expert system can do, but also what its limitations are and be able to recognize at an early stage those problems that are outside of the domain of the expert system.

There may also be problems with the client organization's existing computer staff if they have not been involved in the development project and their roles have not been considered. In fact, there is often a resistance to the distribution of any locally intelligent systems from such personnel who have previously been responsible for central computing facilities. Thus, where the expert system does not run on their mainframe, they may be reluctant to deal with what are often trivial problems associated with even the hardware of local expert systems. It is possible that a perfectly well-designed expert system could fail simply because it is unsupported and appears to the users to be less reliable than is really the case. In everyday office automation, the computer cognoscenti should not underestimate the ignorance of quite sophisticated users of software who are unable to do simple things like backing up disks and purging them. Thus the expert system needs the support of the technical staff, even when it appears they have only a very minor role to play.

Finally, there can be problems with an expert system if the terminals are not conveniently located, or in the case of shared terminals, that one has to wait to use them. Wyatt and Emerson (Chapter 4) for example, report the case of their expert system ACORN which is used by their hospital's casualty department admissions staff. The problem was that initially the expert system was located close, but '... out of sight of the main casualty area ...' and nursing staff were reluctant to leave, even briefly, their main area of operation.

All of these types of problem should be addressed by the knowledge engineering team. What is required at this stage is a proposed management structure for the installation of the expert system and a detailed installation plan. In many cases installation of an expert system will probably be in two stages, the first being a transitional stage during installation and the second, the final state once installation is completed. What is rarely provided and perhaps what should be the most important aspect of training, is not how to use the system, but training for all the personnel in how their jobs will change. Clearly this is only possible if it can be predicted in advance and is thus utterly dependent on an understanding of the organization's pre-expert system practices.

Post-Delivery Evaluation

It also needs recognizing that however good the organizational and personnel models actually are, there are likely to be some unanticipated problems with introducing a technology that has far reaching effects on the whole client organization. Potentially it takes only one or a small number of staff who, for some reason, dislike the new system and the changes it has caused, to influence other personnel with their negative opinions. A planned, post-delivery evaluation may nip these problems in the bud and thus save, what is an expensive system, from failing to be successful. Only the knowledge engineering team has the essential skills and the relevant information to tackle such an evaluation and to be able to offer what are often cheap and easy corrective measures. If the knowledge engineering team waits for the client organization to recognize that they have a problem then it may already be too late to save the system at all, or the solutions may be very expensive.

Maintenance and Modification

In most expert system applications, there will be a need to change the expert system as the world in which it operates changes. Boose, at a workshop in 1987, suggested the notion of software decay and meant by this, not that the software changed over time, but that by failing to change (ie by not being maintained) it became increasingly less useful and relevant to the environment and tasks it once successfully supported. As Schatz *et al* (1987) point out '... a knowledge base almost always requires updating and modification, expert systems developers could increasingly spend more time modifying current systems rather than developing new ones.' In software engineering, Sommerville states that '... for most large, long-life systems maintenance costs normally exceed development costs by factors which range from two to four ... Indeed, Boehm (1975) quotes a pathological case where the development costs of an avionics system were $30 per instruction and the maintenance costs were $4000 per instruction.' However, whereas Sommerville claims that, in general, software maintenance costs are independent of the design method employed, this is not entirely accepted by the author in the case of expert systems. The temptation to encode the prototype expert system piecemeal and to add new rules when necessary during knowledge acquisition, leads to unstructured knowledge bases where knowledge can be scattered over many rules. Thus a trivial change such as modifying an interest rate or a tax rate may involve not a single modification to the rule base but many modifications, all of which will need to be found. The spaghetti-like properties (Johnson, 1989) such systems can acquire can make them essentially unmodifiable in that it is cheaper to rebuild the system almost from scratch.

Schatz *et al*, who specifically address the issue of long-term expert system maintenance, state that '... a system that is successfully maintained may lend itself to further corporate commitment because the system continues to be a valuable asset. This creates a cycle that keeps up the level of interest and may create opportunities for building additional systems.'

THE ADDITIONAL COSTS FOR SUCCESS

The issues discussed in the previous section all need to be considered at the beginning of a project when the total costs are projected and, in a two-stage, linked contract by the end of the first, evaluative part of the contract. Commerce and industry do not, in general, have a good record of coping with these sorts of issues and it is certainly true that far more effort has gone into the technology of designing expert systems than into the problems associated with their installation and long-term use in the real world. While the knowledge engineering team cannot afford to cost themselves out of work, it is neither in their interests, nor that of their clients, for expert systems to be well designed and then to fail. There are many reasons why an expert system development project may fail, or at least not fulfil its potential. The general position presented in this chapter is that while a great deal of effort and ingenuity has gone into building the hard technology side of the expert systems business, little attention has been paid to what are probably the cheap and crucial organizational and human aspects that may make or break a system. The problems are not special to expert systems: computer science and software engineering have a long history of bias to the technological aspects and have generally ignored, and still in many instances continue to ignore, the real purpose of computer systems.

A successful system can ultimately only be judged by its use in the real world. To be useful any computer system must firstly support the real requirements of its purchasing organization. Recent history suggests that this has frequently not happened and that computers have, in some cases, actually resulted in greater expense and reduced efficiency compared to the pre-computerized state of affairs. Many of these costs may not be visible as they are hidden in other operating costs, or they may be incurred by the organization's customers and only become apparent by a gradual loss of business, which may not be attributed to the new computer system. However, Catt (1973) lists numerous examples of expensive disasters directly caused by the introduction of new computer systems.

For success at the organizational level, it is essential that the system is used and liked by the organization's personnel. While direct end-users might be forced to use a system, it is unlikely that under such conditions the system will ever be a great success and it certainly will not perform to its maximum possible potential. It has also been suggested in this chapter that it is not only the direct end-users of an expert system who must be considered and catered for, but also all the other personnel within the organization who, while not using the system, will have their jobs affected by its introduction.

So far there have been very few commercially successful expert systems and very little reporting or analysis of why this has been the case. This chapter suggests that some balance must lie with the nature of the expectations of the client organizations and their general failure to take seriously, if at all, their very considerable responsibilities within expert system development projects. The knowledge engineers must at least share the blame as they have acquiesced to this view. This view may be extremely short sighted as this chapter argues that they are almost bound to fail in the long term if they do not have the full and active support of their client organizations and all the relevant personnel. This chapter argues that the solution is not in more, increasingly expensive technology, but in finally getting around to addressing the really difficult issues that involve real people and the organizations they work for.

REFERENCES

Bainbridge, L. (1986). Asking questions and Accessing Knowledge. *Future Computing Systems*, **1**, 143–50.

Bell, J. and Hardiman, B. (1989). The Third Role – The Naturalistic Knowledge Engineer. In *Knowledge Elicitation: Principles, Techniques and Applications*, Diaper D.(ed.), 47–86. Ellis Horwood, Chichester.

Bench-Capon, T. (1989). People Interact Through Computers, Not With Them. *Interacting with Computers*, **1**, 1, 31–38.

Boehm, B. (1975). The High Cost of Software. In *Practical Strategies for Developing Large Software Systems*, Horowitz, E. (ed.). Addison-Wesley.

Boehm, B. (1984). Verifying and Validating Software Requirements and Design Specifications. *IEEE Software*, 75–88.

Boose, J. (1986). Rapid Acquisition and Combination of Knowledge from Multiple Experts in the Same Domain. *Future Computing Systems*, **1**, 191–216.

Boose, J. and Bradshaw, J. (1987a). AQUINAS: A Knowledge Acquisition Workbench for Building Knowledge-Based Systems. In *Proceedings of the First European Workshop on Knowledge Acquisition for Knowledge-Based Systems*, Reading University, Addis, T., Boose, J. and Gaines, B.(eds).

Boose, J. and Bradshaw, (1987b). Expertise Transfer and Complex Problems: Using AQUINAS as a Knowledge Acquisition Workbench for Knowledge-Based Systems. *International Journal of Man-Machine Studies*, **26**, 3–28.

Burton, M., Shadbolt, N., Hedgecock, A. and Rugg, G. (1987). A Formal

Evaluation of Knowledge Elicitation Techniques for Expert Systems: Domain 1. In *Proceedings of the First European Workshop on Knowledge Acquisition for Knowledge-Based Systems*, Addis, T., Boose, J. and Gaines, B. (eds).

Burton, M. and Shadbolt, N (1987). A Formal Evaluation of Knowledge Elicitation Techniques for Expert Systems: Domain 1. In *Proceedings of a SERC Workshop on Knowledge Acquisition for Engineering Applications*, Pavelin, C. and Wilson, M. (eds), 20–8. Rutherford Appleton Laboratory, RAL-87-055.

Burton, M. and Shadbolt, N. (1988). *Characteristics of the Experts in Knowledge Elicitation*. Unpublished paper given at the BCS HCI/Expert Systems Northern Group.

Catt, I. (1973). *Computer Worship*. Pitman.

Church, C. (1988). Time, Budgets and Contracts . . . Knowledge Acquisition in the Commercial Context. Unpublished paper given at the BCS HCI/Expert Systems Northern Group.

Clare, J. (1989). Knowledge Elicitation for Financial Dealers. In *Knowledge Elicitation: Principles, Techniques and Applications*, Diaper D. (ed.), 235–246. Ellis Horwood, Chichester.

Cordingley, E. (1989). Review of Knowledge Elicitation Techniques. In *Knowledge Elicitation: Principles, Techniques and Applications*. Diaper D. (ed.), 87–175. Ellis Horwood, Chichester.

Diaper, D. (1986). Identifying the Knowledge Requirements of an Expert System's Natural Language Processing Interface. In *People and Computers: Designing for Usability*, Harrison, M. and Monk, A. (eds), 263–80. Cambridge University Press, Cambridge.

Diaper, D. (1987a). POMESS: A People-Orientated Methodology for Expert System Specification. In *Proceedings of the First European Workshop on Knowledge Acquisition for Knowledge Based Systems*, Addis, T., Boose, J. and Gaines, B. (eds).

Diaper, D. (1987b). Designing Systems for People: Beyond User Centred Design. In *Software Engineering, Proceedings of the Share European Association (SEAS) Anniversary Meeting*, 283–302.

Diaper, D. (1988a). Task Analysis for Knowledge Descriptions: Building a Task Descriptive Hierarchy. In *Contemporary Ergonomics 1988*, Megaw, E. (ed.), 118–24. Taylor and Francis, London.

Diaper, D. (1988b). The Promise of POMESS (a People-Orientated Methodology for Expert System Specification). In *Proceedings of Joint Ergonomics Society/ICL Conference on Human and Organizational Issues of Expert Systems*, Stratford Upon Avon, May 1988.

Diaper, D. (1988c). Natural Language Communication with Computers: Theory, Needs and Practice. In *Proceedings of the Conference on KBS in Government '88*, Duffin, P. (ed.), 19–44. Blenheim Online.

Diaper, D. (1989). Designing Expert Systems: From Dan to Beersheba. In *Knowledge Elicitation: Principles, Techniques and Applications*, Diaper D. (ed.), 15–46. Ellis Horwood, Chichester.

Diaper, D. and Shelton, T. (1987). Natural Language Requirements for Expert System Naive Users. In *Recent Developments and Applications of Natural Language Understanding*. 113–24. UNICOM Seminars Ltd.

Diaper, D. and Shelton, T. (1989). Dialogues with the Tin Man: Computing a Natural Language Grammar for Expert System Naive Users. In *Natural Language Understanding: Recent Developments and Applications of Natural Language Understanding*, Peckham, J. (ed.). Kogan Page, London.

Diaper, D. and Johnson, P. (1989). Task Analysis for Knowledge Descriptions: Theory and Application in Training. In *Cognitive Ergonomics*, Long, J. and Whitefield. A. (eds), 191–224. Cambridge University Press, Cambridge.

Gammack, J. (1987). Modelling Expert Knowledge using Cognitively Compatible Structures. In *Third International Expert Systems Conference*, 191–200. Learned Information, Oxford.

Gammack, J. and Young, R. (1985). Psychological Techniques for Eliciting Expert Knowledge. In *Research and Development in Expert Systems*, Bramer, M. (ed.) 105–12. Cambridge University Press, Cambridge.

Hayes-Roth, F., Waterman, D. and Lenat, D. (eds) (1983). *Building Expert Systems*. Addison-Wesley, Massachusetts.

Johnson, N. (1987). Mediating Representations in Knowledge Elicitation. In *Proceedings of the First European Workshop on Knowledge Acquisition for Knowledge-Based Systems*, Addis, T., Boose, J. and Gaines, B. (eds).

Johnson, N. (1989). Knowledge Representations in Knowledge Elicitation. In *Knowledge Elicitation: Principles, Techniques and Applications*, Diaper D. (ed.), 172–94. Ellis Horwood, Chichester.

Johnson, P. (1985). Towards a Task Model of Messaging: An example of the Application of TAKD to User Interface Design. In *People and Computers: Designing the Interface*, Johnson, P. and Cook, S. (eds), 46–62. Cambridge University Press, Cambridge.

Johnson, P., Diaper, D and Long, J. (1984). Tasks, Skills and Knowledge: Task Analysis for Knowledge-Based Descriptions. In *Interact'84 – First IFIP Conference on Human-Computer Interaction*, Shackel, B. (ed.), **1**, 23–7. Elsevier, North-Holland.

Kelly, G. (1955). *The Psychology of Personal Constructs*. Norton, New York.

Michie, D., Michaelson, R. and Boulenger, A. (1985). The Technology of Expert Systems. *Byte*, April.

Modesitt, K. (1987). Experts: Human and Otherwise. In *Third International Expert Systems Conference*, 333–42. Learned Information, Oxford.

Motta, E., Eisenstadt, M., West, M., Pitman, K. and Evertsz, R. (1986). *KEATS: The Knowledge Engineer's Assistant. Human Cognition Research*

Laboratory, Open University, technical report 20.

Oliver, A. (1986). Control of Rapid Prototyping in Expert Systems Development. In *Second International Expert Systems Conference*, 247–52. Learned Information, Oxford.

Oliver, A. (1987). How to make Rapid Prototyping Effective when Developing Expert Systems. In *Third International Expert Systems Conference*, 271–6. Learned Information, Oxford.

Partridge, D. (1986). *Artificial Intelligence: Applications to the Future of Software Engineering*. Ellis Horwood, Chichester.

Schatz, H., Strahs, R. and Campbell, L. (1987). EXPERTAX: The Issue of Long-Term Maintenance. In *Third International Expert Systems Conference*, 291–300. Learned Information, Oxford.

Sharpe, W. (1985). Logic Programming for the Law. In *Research and Development in Expert Systems*, Bramer, M. (ed.), 217–28. Cambridge University Press, Cambridge.

Shaw, M. and Gaines, B. (1986). Interactive Elicitation of Knowledge from Experts. *Future Computing Systems*, **1**, 151–90.

Shpilberg, D., Graham, L. and Schatz, H. (1986). Expertax: An Expert System for Corporate Tax Planning. In *Second International Expert Systems Conference*, 99–124. Learned Information, Oxford.

Sommerville, I. (1987). Software Engineering: Perspectives and Directions. In *Software Engineering, Proceedings of the Share European Association (SEAS) Anniversary Meeting*, 1–16.

Trimble, G. (1989). Knowledge Elicitation: Some of the Practical Issues. In *Knowledge Elicitation: Principles, Techniques and Applications*, Diaper D. (ed.), 221–34. Ellis Horwood.

Wells, C. (1987). The Design Supervisor – A changing role with CAD? Institute of Mechanical Engineers, technical report C369/87, 27-35.

Young, R. and Gammack, J. (1987). Role of Psychological Techniques and Intermediate Representations in Knowledge Elicitation. In *Proceedings of the First European Workshop on Knowledge Acquisition for Knowledge-Based Systems*, Addis, T., Boose, J. and Gaines, B. (eds).

Dr Dan Diaper
Department of Computer Science
University of Liverpool
PO Box 147
Liverpool L69 3BX, UK

Chapter 13

Responsibility Issues in Intelligent Decision Support Systems

Erik Hollnagel

AI AND DECISION MAKING

The introduction of information technology – in public administration, industrial production, business, communication, and in private life – has brought dramatic changes to our working and living environments. The effect has been particularly pronounced in the many areas where computers and people work together – in the so-called man-machine systems. Here the technological developments, such as the introduction of computers and knowledge processing systems (also known as artificial intelligence – AI – or expert systems), have been very rapid and the changes have consequently been significant.

The new information technology can, however, not simply be plugged into, or added to, the organization. Technology is never value-neutral, but always leads to a social change whether or not this has been anticipated or intended (Rochlin, 1986). The way the work is carried out, roles are distributed, and functions depend upon each other, together constitute an equilibrium. The introduction of a new 'machine' will necessarily affect one or the other, hence force the system into a different state of equilibrium. Since the social structure is more adaptive and flexible than the technical, a social change is usually the result. Modern information technology, which in itself represents a technological revolution, has caused a fundamental change in the way knowledge processing functions – such as decision making, planning, etc – can be implemented in a system or an organization. In hindsight this is not very surprising, although it would have been difficult to predict exactly.

One essential aspect of knowledge processing systems is whether they provide an amplification of the knowledge processing functions in the system (and in particular of the cognitive functions of the decision maker), or rather a restructuring of them (Pea, 1985). While the restructuring is obvious and inevitable – simply because the way in which organizational roles and functions change as a result of introducing the new technology – it should not be overlooked that one consequence of the restructuring is a necessary change in efficiency. New information technology leads to a changed balance among the various steps in the decision-making process and to changes in task allocation and responsibility. In most cases this change provides an increase in efficiency (because that is the explicit purpose), hence a *de facto* amplification of the knowledge processing functions.

One advantage of knowledge processing systems is that it becomes possible to utilize better the potential of the decision maker by delegating trivial and routine tasks to the machines. The parts of decision making that mainly involve manipulation of data and information, as well as the frequently recurring decision problems, can be automated in whole or in part. This produces fundamental changes in how the organization works, hence requiring a substantial amount of adaptation, often approaching the limits of the organization's capacity and often leading to the detriment of other functions. It is obviously of great value to be able to foresee the changes that are required, to plan and compensate for possible detrimental effects.

THE DEVELOPMENT OF COMPUTER APPLICATIONS

One can distinguish between three major steps in how computers have been introduced into practical, rather than scientific, applications. Originally, computers were used for data processing as giant electronic calculating machines. Here their processing power was essential. The main attraction was their ability to carry out complex and lengthy calculations rapidly and reliably and to produce an output from a given input with, hitherto incredible, speed. The impact of computers has always been greatest where they could most easily be applied (which did not always agree with where it made sense to use them). Computers as data processors were, consequently, mostly used where numeric data were abundant – ie in technical or engineering environments (process industries, the military, in science, etc).

The next step was to use computers as information processing and information storage systems. Here their power to store and retrieve data and information was in the foreground. Computers as information processors extended their use to new fields where facts played an important role and where their capacity as super-fast calculators was only a secondary concern, eg in information sciences, libraries, record keeping, statistics, etc. The main attraction was the ability to store and retrieve huge amounts of information rapidly and flexibly – and also gradually to combine it, ie to enhance processing by using data other than that explicitly provided by the input.

The third, and so far the last, step is to use computers as knowledge processing systems. Here the emphasis is on knowledge, ie relations between facts rather than the facts themselves, and on the rules and principles by which these relations can be expressed and changed. The main emphasis is on the computer's power of reasoning, be it ever so humble. This ability extends the application of computers beyond previously known limits. The rapid development – since the mid-1970s – of artificial intelligence and expert systems has, naturally enough, been applied mostly where the need was most easily seen, which mainly were the existing areas of computer application where information processing systems had reached the limits of their abilities. It must, however, be foreseen that the use of knowledge processing systems will spread to many other areas, eg administration, finance, commerce, and communication as well as discrete manufacturing, planning, control, etc.

COMPUTERIZATION AS AUTOMATION

The trends in the development of computer applications is quite analogous to the general characteristics of industrial automation. Here automation seems to be directed at two classes of task. One class consists of the relatively simple tasks which involve routine and repetitive action, eg mechanical assembly. These are well described and can easily be improved by replacing the human with a machine. The other class consists of the relatively complex tasks where human capability is known to be limited, eg tracking a target. In both cases automation is desired because it is believed to be cost-effective and it is normally introduced when it is technologically possible. Together these classes gradually grow to cover the middle range of tasks, leaving the very simple and very complex tasks to the human user. The reasons are, however, different. The simple tasks are left because it is not worth the effort to automate them. The complex tasks are left because they are too difficult to be automated. And although the middle range, where automation is possible, may grow at either end, it will never cover the whole range of tasks.

The use of computers appears to follow a similar trend and this is, perhaps, even more obvious in the case of AI or knowledge-based systems (KBSs). Computers as data processors and as information processors have taken over many of the human functions in the class of simple tasks. This has, however, mostly been considered an advantage since humans are relatively bad at simple data and information processing, to say nothing of reliable storage and retrieval or reproduction of facts. Humans, rather, excel in combining facts in novel ways. Furthermore, the basic data processing tasks were generally considered tedious and computers were seen as a relief.

The introduction of AI has significantly increased the range of complex tasks that can be automated, thus beginning to affect the other end of the tasks spectrum as well. Computers as knowledge processors bring totally new perspectives to the application of information technology. Although fears about the invasion of intelligent machines into all realms of life are unwarranted, the fact remains that computers as KBSs will penetrate many areas where they hitherto have been considered either irrelevant or of only marginal use and interest.

The repetition of this trend is partly caused by the 'blind' application of computers as a replacement of the technological automation. In other words, computer applications are introduced from the bottom-up rather than from the top down, ie based on ease and possibility rather than on a serious analysis of goals and requirements. This may be why we in many cases see the same reactions to the introduction of computer applications as we have seen to automation. Perhaps a closer study of recent industrial history could prevent us from making the same mistakes again!

THE NEED FOR DECISION SUPPORT

A specific application of KBSs which has already started, and which will continue to grow, is in decision support systems. Decision making constitutes a significant part of the work that is left to humans, partly due to the increasing automation. The need for support stems from the fact that human beings on the whole are bad decision makers, at least if judged from the view of decision theory. A closer look at existing man-machine systems reveals that designers normally have a very optimistic view of humans as decision makers. They are generally considered:

- to be nearly rational;
- to go through the decision in a logical sequence of steps;
- to search for all relevant information;
- to examine all relevant decision alternatives;
- to make an objective decision;
- to choose the best alternative and act accordingly; and
- to follow standardized, authorized methods.

This, at least, is what a decision maker should be able to do in order to fit into most existing system designs. Put differently, if decision makers do not meet these criteria many systems will fail to function satisfactorily outside a narrow band of normal conditions. On the other hand, the general experience from the empirical study of decision making (Rasmussen, Duncan and Leplat, 1987) suggests that decision makers rather should be considered:

- to be mostly non-rational and driven by habit;
- to take short-cuts in decision making whenever possible;
- to follow established routines 'blindly';
- to limit their search for information to familiar areas;
- to use the first acceptable alternative they find;
- to revoke their initial choice only if questioned or challenged;
- to be highly subjective in their decision criteria;
- to use their own (idiosyncratic) methods; and
- to perform worse under stress.

Neither this pessimistic nor the previous optimistic view are completely correct. But the discrepancy between them clearly indicates that some kind of decision support may be needed. There have, accordingly, been many attempts to develop and apply decision support systems, particularly to cases where time is critical or where the consequences of an incorrect decision can be very serious. This has been done with limited success for computers as data processors and as information processors. The appearance of computers as knowledge processors makes the scope for developing decision support systems much larger, but also extends the range of possible applications. The possibility of creating joint man-machine systems, where the machine has some kind of intelligence, inevitably brings up the problem of responsibility for the decisions that are made.

Decision making can take place on three main levels, ie operational, tactical and strategic. The degree of responsibility differs between these levels, at least for the person involved. Quite often there is little responsibility on the operational and tactical levels where users are simply carrying out orders or instructions from the system, but much more so on the strategic level. Strategic decision making in a sense sets out the limits and criteria that are used on the other levels. The responsibility on the tactical and operational levels will mostly be in terms of precision and reliability because the reasons for the decisions are derived from the strategic level. But on the strategic level it is not possible to refer to a higher instance. The determination of responsibility therefore becomes more important and the discussion about responsibility will naturally focus on decisions on the strategic level. Also, rather than looking at the technical problems in designing, implementing and using intelligent decision support systems the following sections will consider some of the consequences of introducing such systems in more and more applications.

THE DILUTION OF RESPONSIBILITY

The purpose of an intelligent decision support system is to enhance the quality of information for the decision maker. This is basically done by selecting or producing the right information (determining *what*), presenting the information in the right way (determining *how*), and presenting the information at the right time (determining *when*).

In decision making, responsibility can both refer to who can be held responsible in legal terms and who is responsible in terms of having knowledge of what the decision was about (the conditions, the alternatives, the consequences). As the decision support systems become more intelligent through the use of knowledge processing, the problem of responsibility in decision making becomes more important. The solution to this problem depends very much on how the intelligent decision support system is applied in the task. The general attitude is that an intelligent decision support system should be a tool rather than a prosthesis for the decision maker, ie it should assist him rather than replace him (Woods, 1986). If the intelligent decision support system is a prosthesis then, clearly, the responsibility has, in fact, been taken away from the decision maker, at least for that particular task. If, on the other hand, the intelligent decision support system is introduced as a tool, the decision maker has the final responsibility for the decision. In process control terms, it is the decision maker who closes the loop.

This is, however, partly an illusion. In every industrial process there are, for instance, large parts which have become automated so all the time decisions are made on a low level without involving the user – and often even without informing him about it either. This has happened because the complexity of the processes and the multitude of tasks involved make it virtually impossible for an unaided human to control them. In other cases where computers are extensively used – medicine, data analysis, finance, administration – the same development can be expected, if it has not already taken place. The general trend in the application of computers and information technology is that routine tasks are taken over by the computers, just as in technological automation in general. As the power of computers grow and the range of tasks moves from information processing to knowledge processing, using expert systems and artificial intelligence technology, new tasks become routine and are taken over by the computers, now often referred to as knowledge-based systems. The immediate benefit is that it relieves the decision maker of many trivial tasks that are better, and more reliably, done by a machine anyway. But the disadvantage is that the decision maker gradually is left out of the loop. This creates practical problems, eg in providing an adequate interface between human and machine, in terms of staying 'tuned' to the process, as well as in principal problems of the locus of responsibility for system performance.

SYSTEM ADAPTABILITY

The discussion of the responsibility of decision making must take into account the adaptability of computers vis-a-vis the systems where they are introduced. This can be interpreted in two different ways. At present, computers only have a limited adaptability, but the organizations that use them are highly flexible. Accordingly, the introduction of a computer system in a decision support role will lead to organizational changes. Since organizations – as well as individuals – continuously try to optimize their performance, the designed or specified role of the decision support system will not remain stable for long. The organization will quickly try to use the capacity of the decision support system to the full, ie adapt itself to the new functionality. But even though the actual role may change, the formal role may remain the same, ie the altered state of affairs may not be fully recognized. This is particularly important with regard to the locus of responsibility.

The other type of adaptability is that where the computer is adaptable. Although this is not yet the case on a commercial scale, there are no reasons why it will not happen since the conceptual background is well established, eg in control theory (adaptive regulators) and cybernetics. We may thus foresee a fourth stage in the development of computers, going from knowledge processing systems to knowing or cognitive systems (compare this to Hollnagel and Woods, 1983). These would be characterized by organizing their behaviour in relation to goals, and by having knowledge about themselves vis-a-vis the environment and task, including the co-actors or participants. Such systems would not follow a fixed distribution of responsibility, but would adapt to the current demands, user ability and situational criteria (eg time, resources). This would, accordingly, require special considerations during design, assuming that the overall goal still is to maintain the decision maker as the locus of responsibility. In a sense, the problems described below (explanation, information presentation, etc) are even more crucial at this stage – unless one chooses the other alternative and relinquishes control to the more able machine. This, however, poses ethical problems.

MAINTAINING ACCESS TO INFORMATION

Assuming that the decision maker should maintain control and remain responsible, one must consider how this is possible. In principle, it can mean either that the decision maker makes all the decisions or that he agrees with the decision the computer suggests (or even makes).

If the decision maker makes all the decisions, he must have access to all the data and be able to control and verify the processing done by the computers – whether as data processing, information processing, or knowledge processing. In practically all systems which require interactive decision making (industrial processes, administration, transport, commerce, communication, etc), computers are needed to collect, pre-process, and store measurements and data. Even in information processing database systems the facts are what the computer stores and presents rather than the 'real-world' facts. As we have seen, this inevitably means that some low-level decisions are made automatically. The information that reaches the decision maker will thus always be mediated, ie it has been transformed in some way, hence differs from the raw measurements and data. Put differently, the very limits of human cognition – in terms of capacity and speed – require data processing and information processing. Thus, in order to overcome these limits we are forced to give up some of the control of the situation, and therefore some of the responsibility. There are thus no cases where the decision maker makes all the decisions.

The problem of responsibility, therefore, becomes the problem of understanding correctly the information and knowledge that describe the situation. This points to a possible dilemma between information presentation by computers and decision making. It is well known from the behavioural sciences, particularly the study of problem solving, that the way a problem or case is presented may heavily influence the way it is understood, hence the way decisions are made. This can easily be exemplified from the psychology of reasoning (Wason and Johnson-Laird, 1972), social psychology and the study of attitudes, information, as well as propaganda and mass communication (in a benign sense). For intelligent decision support systems the crucial problem therefore becomes how the information presentation influences the decision, even in the cases where the intelligent decision support system is used purely as a tool.

The central issue is one of relinquishing control in a trade-off between speed and efficiency. One place where this becomes particularly important is in decision making that must be exercised quickly, in dynamic environments with rapid transients or fluctuations, eg crisis management, electronic fund transfer and dealing, and process control. Here it is clearly crucial that the presented information is easy to understand (at a glance) and that it relates clearly to the problems faced by the decision maker. When this is not the case, it often leads to errors or accidents which may have serious consequences. In the summer of 1988 the attack by the USS Vincennes on Iran Air 655 was the most prominent example, but I am sure that there will be no shortage of similar cases in the future.

One main problem therefore is how the filtering and processing of data (data, information, knowledge) and the following representation can be controlled either so that nothing essential is lost or so that we know what is lost, hence are able to retrieve and verify it when the need arises. This is closely tied to the problem of explanations in expert systems and the calculation of the cost-efficiency trade-off that must be included in any extended search for information.

THE NEED FOR INPUT

A different, and in a sense the opposite, view on the access to information is how input is provided to the intelligent decision support system. An intelligent decision support system is normally thought of as a system that provides guidance and advice to the decision maker, ie mostly a system that produces output. The role of input to the system is, however, just as important. In many cases one can expect the intelligent decision support system to ask for information that it needs but does not have. The design of this particular type of dialogue is crucial for the functioning of the system. In order to get the right information, it must formulate its requests precisely, possibly even explain in greater detail what is needed and why (compare this to the following section). It may, however, still need some kind of interpretation of the input, possibly triggering a dialogue sequence. It must also form the requests such that they do not lead to a deterioration of the situation, eg by burdening the decision maker with additional tasks, or by making him uncertain about what is going on, effectively disrupting his trust in the intelligent decision support system. On the whole, the more complex a system is, the stricter are the demands regarding the precision of the input.

User-friendliness often refers only to the way the system represents its output to the user. There is, however, another side to user-friendliness which often is either misunderstood or neglected. Many AI and expert systems claim to have a (pseudo) natural language interface which allows the user to interact with the system in a natural way. This, however, generally means that the mutual understanding – which is the foundation for a natural dialogue – is based on the user's ability to comply with the restrictions on the system's capabilities of understanding. The decision maker thus becomes responsible in a double sense. He is responsible for the decision, but also for providing information to the system which can be understood by it. If he is unable to do so, the system may either give an incorrect answer or be unable to function at all.

THE ROLE OF EXPLANATIONS

If the decision maker lets the intelligent decision support system make some of the decisions (and he often has no choice in the matter), he must be able to get an explanation from the intelligent decision support system that he can understand, in order to agree or disagree with the intelligent decision support system. The role of explanations has received considerable attention in the development of expert systems. The solution has, however, generally been simply to repeat the reasoning done by the system, eg by tracing back from the conclusion to the premises. This solution has probably been adopted because the reasoning of the system in itself is based on the expert's explanations as extracted through knowledge elicitation. It is, however, often grossly insufficient partly because the formalized reasoning of an expert not necessarily constitutes an explanation, and partly because the explanation a decision maker needs at any given time must relate to the current situation rather than to general reasoning rules. Quite apart from that, the explanation mechanisms built into expert systems have mostly been for the purpose of debugging and validation, rather than to support a general user. The main problem is how the computer's knowledge processing and reasoning can be rendered to the decision maker so that he understands and trusts the results, and how the decision maker intentionally can delegate responsibility to the machine without running the risk of being abandoned in the sense of being left with the responsibility without really knowing why the decision was made.

For systems that actually produce advice and recommendations for the decision maker, the explanations given are vital, both for understanding them and for trusting them (Muir, 1987). The decision maker is in many cases given the option of vetoing the recommendations of the intelligent decision support system. This option is, however, illusory if he does not understand what the options entail and why they have been given. The paradox, however, is that artificial reasoning is used (in the intelligent decision support system) to compensate for shortcomings in the human reasoning. It is therefore a little strange that the human reasoning of the decision maker should be able to understand the reasoning of the machine. If that is really the case, why not abandon the machine completely? The answer, of course, is that there are concerns of speed and reliability, and that understanding something is different from inventing it (the passive versus active dimension).

A particular effect of increasing trust is the loss of competence. It is often pointed out that highly automated systems such as one may find in the process industry, may lead to a loss of competence of the people who operate them. If the system always handles the most frequently occurring situations, the operators will gradually forget their own skills. Thus, when they are required to step in they are unable to do so (Reason, 1987). Another possible effect of that is the deterioration in competence assessment, ie the assessment of one's own competence to handle a situation. It can be argued that the ability to maintain actual control of a system depends on the ability to predict accurately how it is going to develop and whether one is able to handle (control) the situation (Hollnagel, 1987a). In terms of decision making, taking responsibility requires that one is able to make the decision. If, therefore, the decision maker becomes used to following the advice of the system (possibly because he is unable to understand it but also unwilling to challenge it), he will gradually become less able to make the decision himself. More and more of the responsibility is thereby taken over by the system, even beyond what the designer had in mind. The danger is that it happens gradually and unnoticeably. Not only does the decision maker slowly become unable to make the decision, but he is also unaware of it and may therefore maintain an illusion of competence, hence responsibility. If anticipated, this may be countered by the system design.

POSSIBLE SOLUTIONS

Even this short discussion of the main problems makes it clear that one cannot dodge the responsibility issue in intelligent decision support system design. The really radical solution *not* to delegate any responsibility to intelligent decision support systems and computers is not possible in practice. A computerized support system must make some decisions of its own. We are already so dependent on computers making decisions on a low level, that we would be unable to function without them. In every intelligent decision support system the designer – and, consequently, the computer – decides on, for example, information reduction and presentation. This is required to make the decision maker's task easier, but it also takes some of the decisions away from him. Sheridan has proposed a scale of autonomy in human-computer interaction (Sheridan, 1982). On the lowest level the computer simply carries out the orders given by the human. On the highest level the computer performs in an autonomous way, and further decides whether or not the user should be told. Where we are on that scale depends on the level of decision making. On the operational and tactical levels the position may be rather high, ie the computer dominates the decision making. On the strategic level the position may be somewhat lower, but still increasing. The problem is thus not whether we are going to move to higher levels, but rather how we can avoid the negative consequences of doing so.

   Although there are no easy solutions, it is possible to suggest several different ways in which the problem can be handled. First of all, the responsibility issue must be treated seriously in the design of the system. This can, for instance, be accomplished by using a systematic task analysis that focuses on cognitive (knowledge intensive) tasks, which are the ones where decision making, hence issues of responsibility, occurs (Woods and Hollnagel, 1987). Such a cognitive task analysis can produce a functional decomposition of the tasks which clearly relates goals and requirements, thereby also delineating where the responsibility lies.

Another possibility, which is not excluded by the cognitive task analysis, is to improve the transparency of the system, thereby making it easier for the decision maker to understand what is taking place. One way of doing this is to provide better and more detailed explanations, but transparency may also be increased by a number of different techniques which address fundamental aspects of human-computer interaction (Hollnagel, 1987b).

A third possibility is to endow the intelligent decision support system with a rudimentary form of self-appreciation. If the intelligent decision support system *de facto* carries part of the responsibility it should also have the means to realize this. The simplest way of doing this is to have the system employ a set of second order rules (often referred to as meta-rules) by which the conclusions and advice can be evaluated before they are presented to the decision maker. The intelligent decision support system should be given a set of higher order criteria – 'ethical principles' to match its reasoning capacity – which can be applied to the outcome of its knowledge processing. This would effectively define a band of responsibility within which the system could function. Depending on the nature of the tasks and the experience with the system, the width of the band could be adjusted as required.

This, of course, assumes that the output can be evaluated (in effect, quantified) in a reasonable way. One might envisage something analogous to the three laws of robotics (Asimov, 1983), which are:

- A robot may not injure a human being or, through inaction, allow a human being to come to harm.
- A robot must obey the orders given it by human beings except where such orders would conflict with the First Law.
- A robot must protect its own existence as long as such protection does not conflict with the First or the Second Law.

For an intelligent decision support system one should, perhaps, rest with a single law (or rule) which could state that an intelligent decision support system must not present a recommendation or advice which conflicts with the main functional criteria for the task domain, except when explicitly authorized to do so. An example could be to avoid recommendations that incur a cost beyond a certain limit, a time span outside a certain range, a release of energy or material beyond the given limits, etc. There are, in fact, many cases where such guiding principles for permissible actions exist and it should be possible – although not necessarily trivial – to include them in intelligent decision support systems.

Finally, one could err on the side of conservatism, by having all intelligent decision support systems display the warning: 'The Government has determined that following the recommendations produced by this system may endanger your safety and wealth', although experiences from other domains seem to indicate that this may not be very effective.

REFERENCES

Asimov, I. (1983). *The Complete Robot*. Grafton Books, London.

Hollnagel, E. (1987a). *Competence, prediction and planning*. Paper presented at the First European Meeting in Cognitive Science Approaches to Process Control, Marcoussis (France), October 19–20.

Hollnagel, E. (1987b). Cognitive models, cognitive tasks, and information retrieval. In I. Wormell (ed.), *Knowledge Engineering – Expert Systems and Information Retrieval*. Taylor Graham, London.

Hollnagel, E. and Woods, D.D. (1983). Cognitive systems engineering: New wine in new bottles. *International Journal of Man-Machine Studies*, **18**, 583–600.

Muir, B. (1987). Trust between humans and machines. *International Journal of Man-Machine Studies*, **27**, 527–41.

Pea, R.D. (1985). Beyond amplification: Using the computer to reorganize mental functioning. *Educational Psychologist*, **20(4)**, 167–82.

Rasmussen, J., Duncan, K. and Leplat, J. (1987) (eds). *New Technology and Human Error*. John Wiley & Sons, London.

Reason, J. (1987). Cognitive aids in process environments: Prostheses or tools? *International Journal of Man-Machine Studies*, **27**, 463–70.

Rochlin, G. I. (1986). High-reliability organizations and technical change: Some ethical problems and dilemmas. *IEEE Technology and Society Magazine*, September, **3-9**.

Sheridan, T.B. (1982). Supervisory control: Problems, theory and experiment for application to human-computer interaction in undersea remote systems. MIT technical report, Cambridge, Massachusetts.

Wason, P. C. and Johnson-Laird, P. N. (1972). Psychology of Reasoning. Structure and Content. B. T. Batsford, Ltd, London.

Woods, D.D. (1986). Paradigms for intelligent decision support. In E. Hollnagel, G. Mancini and D.D. Woods (eds), *Intelligent Decision Support in Process Environments*. Springer-Verlag, Heidelberg.

Woods, D.D. and Hollnagel, E. (1987). Mapping cognitive demands in complex problem-solving worlds. *International Journal of Man-Machine Studies*, **26**, 257–75.

Erik Hollnagel
Computer Resources International
Birkerol
Denmark

Chapter 14

The Way Forward

Dianne Berry and Anna Hart

This book has clearly demonstrated that the success of an expert system cannot be measured in terms of technical excellence alone. Solutions, however impressive, are only useful if they match the problems for which they were intended. In quality assurance, quality is defined as 'fitness for the intended purpose'. In the case of expert systems the intended purpose is frequently difficult to describe with any precision, especially in the early stages of project development. The definition of what a system is for often emerges as prototypes are seen and evaluated. This does not mean that criteria for quality should not be drawn up at the start of a project, but it does mean that these criteria may have to be revised.

For expert systems, 'understanding the problem' is complicated. It requires a consideration of human, social and organizational issues, as well as technical ones. Unfortunately, many technical people are relatively unfamiliar with the social science and psychology literatures and many non-technical people find technical jargon confusing and off-putting. Neverthe-less, ideas and theories from many different disciplines need to be considered if expert systems are to prove useful.

The chapters in this book have described various approaches to the human issues associated with expert systems. Clearly, there is still much work to be done. Some issues have only been briefly addressed in the preceding chapters, while others have been totally neglected. Part of the reason for this is that expert systems are still relatively new and there has been little opportunity to study many of their long-term effects. It is likely that some issues will arise in the future which cannot be predicted. It is possible, however, to identify a number of issues that are already beginning to cause concern. In order to provoke thought, discussion and further research, the following topics have been identified as being of importance.

INTEGRATION OF EXPERT SYSTEMS WITH OTHER COMPUTER SYSTEMS

A systemic analysis of an organization is unlikely to result in clearly defined sub-systems which can be mapped on to particular types of computer system. In many situations expert systems are of limited use in isolation from other computer systems. For example, a knowledge-based medical-diagnosis system may benefit from being linked to a more conventional medical-records system. In software engineering interoperability is an index of system quality and this is now recognized as being important for expert systems. Problems can arise due to incompatibility of languages, interfaces and operating systems, but these are starting to be resolved.

In many domains tasks are becoming increasingly computerized and automated and we now see examples of computer systems being controlled by other computer systems. In the area of process control, for example, expert systems are being designed to have a supervisory role, monitoring and interpreting data from computer control systems. This does not necessarily mean that operators will have less complexity to handle. Rather, the introduction of expert systems and decision aids may simply change the nature of the complexity. The difficulty of taking information in from hundreds of individual screens has been replaced with the difficulty of knowing which particular displays to call up at which time.

Increasing computerization also makes it difficult for operators to retain sufficient knowledge of the control situation so that they can intervene when necessary. If operators' mental models are based on a few high-level concepts then intervention may become difficult or even impossible. It has been suggested that the current intermediate level of automation is not practical. The argument is that we should either have total automation or no automation. The question of whether or not the human operator should remain within the control loop is clearly controversial. A good account of the issues is given in Hollnagel, Mancini and Woods (1988) and in Goodstein, Andersen and Olsen (1988).

Even within a single task people may use a variety of different reasoning methods. Heuristic methods do not necessarily remove the need for procedural and numerical methods but may be used in conjunction with them. Expert-system techniques are part of a collection of methods available to the system designer who, given a problem, sets about building a computer system. Work still needs to be done, however, on deciding how best to allocate the different methods of machine reasoning to different real world tasks.

EXPLANATION

A frequently cited advantage of expert systems is that they not only solve problems and recommend advice, but that they can also provide explanations of the reasoning processes employed. It has been argued that trust in a system is determined not only by the quality of its results, but also by a clear description of how they were derived. Although many researchers and practitioners would see explanation as being an essential aspect of expert systems, in practice many users are tending to ignore explanation options. Slatter, Nomura and Lunn (1988) describe an example of this in relation to an expert system for bid estimation in a manufacturing industry. They found that users not only criticized the particular mode of explanation employed by the system, but also queried the general utility of having an explanation facility at all. Similarly Hart and Wyatt (in press) report that nurses consulting ACORN made very little use of the explanation facilities.

Why then are explanation facilities not proving useful? A good explanation facility should be helpful at several levels. At the least it should help knowledge engineers to test and debug a system during development. More importantly, it should assure a sophisticated user that the system's knowledge and reasoning processes are appropriate, and it should instruct the naive user about the knowledge in the system. In other circumstances it could inform users about alternative courses of action, with their associated costs and benefits. One problem is that many of the early rule-trace-based explanation facilities only fulfilled the first of these roles. Although useful during system development, they rarely provided answers to the types of question that users actually wanted to ask.

Some advances have been made due to research on topics such as analysis of human–human consultations (Kidd, 1985); the implementation of different question and answer types (Hughes, 1987; Swartout, 1986); the importance of the timing of explanations (Berry and Broadbent, 1987); and the benefit of graphical as opposed to textual explanation (Dodson, 1986). Problems still remain, however, some of which stem from the use, or misuse, of the term explanation. A number of people have tended to use the term in a very loose way, to cover almost any request for further information. Users might, for example, have a need for further instruction, more data, feedback, explication of terms, or justification of the reasoning methods used or advice given. Clearly a different form of information is needed in each case: grouping them all together under the heading 'explanation' is not helpful. The 'right' information must be presented in the right way at the right time. Similarly, in recent years we have seen a demand to make systems more opaque or transparent. Although many people believe that the answer lies in the provision of explanation, it seems clear that this in itself will not be sufficient. Again it is necessary to determine what information needs to be made explicit and how this might best be presented to the user.

EVALUATION

Evaluation is crucial for improving design and performance and should pervade all stages of the system-building process. Moreover, such evaluations should not only be carried out by the system designers and domain experts but also by the intended users of a system. Evaluation by users can help to determine the utility of a system: whether it produces meaningful results, the extent of its capabilities, its ease of interaction, the intelligibility and credibility of its results, its efficiency speed and reliability.

Evaluation should be carried out in a rigorous and controlled way and should not cease when a system is released for use. However, very few existing expert systems have undergone formal field testing. A possible exception is the medical domain where some decision aids have been evaluated. For example, ANEMIA, an expert system for the management of anaemic cases, was assessed by five independent medical experts. They judged the system's reasoning and advice in comparison with that supplied by human experts without knowing which was which. Clearly this type of evaluation procedure can only look at the 'correctness' of the knowledge base. Other trials need to be carried out to assess the usability of the system.

One reason why the medical profession might be ahead in terms of running field trials is that many practitioners are already familiar with such trials for drugs. Wyatt (1987), in fact, draws an analogy between the development of an expert system and that of a drug. He states that neither can be tested thoroughly before release and each has risks associated with its use and its non-use. The methodology for drugs is already established. Once a prototype drug has been developed it must be tested on animals and on human volunteers. If it passes these tests it must then undergo a properly designed clinical trial, and only after this is passed can the drug be granted a product licence. Even after release it will be subjected to post-marketing surveillance. Wyatt recommends that a similar procedure be adopted for expert systems and he is carrying out such a procedure for ACORN (Chapter 4).

When constructing a field trial it is essential to bear in mind what is being investigated. The trial should be designed to ensure that the effects of interest are measured and can be attributed to the use of the system rather than to some confounding factor. It is necessary to decide on the nature and number of users and on the length of the trial. In order to assess the effectiveness of the system one should have a control group which is similar in all respects except that the expert system is not actually used. The judgements about decisions should be carried out by peer review and not by people who have a vested interest in showing that the system is good. These evaluators should be unaware whether or not they are assessing the advice from a computer, so care must be taken over the way in which information is presented.

A final note of warning is that one should be careful to ensure that any observed change is a result of the introduction of the system. There are some well-known confounding effects such as the Hawthorne effect and the

Checklist effect. In the former case, performance may improve simply because something new has been introduced and performance is being monitored. The improvement is not actually due to the specific nature of the change. The Checklist effect is where an improvement in performance is due to the effects of better data collection rather than to the use of the system itself. Practical guides to evaluation can be found in Ravden and Johnson (1989) and Clegg *et al* (1988).

RESEARCH METHODS

Applied research is notoriously difficult. In most situations one has to search for a compromise between control and realism. Wickens (1984) proposes five different types of research procedure:

1. observation in the real world;
2. field studies of fully developed systems;
3. simulation;
4. laboratory experiments;
5. mathematical modelling.

He states that whereas the flexibility of modification and degree of generalizability to other systems increases from 1 to 5, the degree of validity of conclusions decreases from 1 to 5.

Laboratory experiments have the advantage that it is possible to look specifically at the effects of one or two variables keeping other factors constant. Experimental 'subjects' can be randomly assigned to particular conditions. Given sufficient precision and control one can be highly confident that any changes observed are due to the specific variables manipulated. The major disadvantage is that in order to ensure control it is usually necessary to make problems far less complex than in everyday life. For example, a particular aspect of a system might be selected and examined in detail. The problem then becomes one of 'scaling up'. It is difficult to have confidence that the same results will hold in the real situation. Similarly, it may be difficult to feed the results back into the design process.

Towards the other extreme are formal field studies and observation in the real world. In these cases it is difficult to exert control over particular variables and to have confidence that observed changes are due to specific factors. Even where it is possible to exert some control, variables cannot be manipulated directly as in laboratory experiments. Moreover, subjects generally cannot be randomly assigned to conditions. Rather, subjects are observed in the conditions in which they naturally fall.

Clearly we are characterizing two ends of a continuum here. It is possible to design field studies so that partial manipulation of the variables is attained. Similarly it is possible to design laboratory experiments that are far more complex and extensive than those typically carried out (for example, by looking at the effects of several variables and their interactions, rather than just one variable, and testing subjects for tens of hours rather than just for one hour). It is also the case, however, that these different types of research procedure are likely to be useful at different stages of the system-development process. Mathematical modelling and laboratory experiments have a role early in system development whereas formal field trials clearly come at a later stage.

A comprehensive introduction to experimental and non-experimental designs is given by Spector (1981). Summarized accounts can also be found in Robson (1973) and Monk (1984).

EXPERT SYSTEMS AND THE LAW

The legal profession has been slow to take account of information-technology issues. This is exemplified by the fact that the relevance of copyright law for software was not discussed until the 1980s. Nevertheless, it is important that system developers and their clients are aware of the possible legal implications of the use of expert-system technology.

The first concern is legal rights. Where conventional methods are used to produce a system it is likely that the laws for conventional software will apply. If the system is essentially different (in some way which will require definition), it may not be regarded as software, and existing laws, such as those for copyright, may not hold. There may also be disputes over ownership rights with regard to both the expert's knowledge and that which is embodied in an expert system. There is sometimes a debate over whether knowledge and ideas belong to the individual or to the company. The situation is even more complicated when a system has some component of machine learning. After some time such systems can behave in ways that have never been validated by anyone.

The other major concern is legal liability; in recent years people have become increasingly concerned about this. If a decision is made based on advice from an expert system, who is legally responsible? Is it the expert on whose knowledge the system was based, the knowledge engineer, the software company, or the user? Many systems now carry disclaimers, but the issue is far from clear cut. One could envisage a situation whereby a user might be negligent one day for having consulted a system and taken its advice, and negligent the next for *not* having consulted the same system. The legal profession has not yet come up with answers to these questions. Much of its time has been spent debating definitions of expert systems, rather than over rules for liability and responsibility. While legal liability might not cover all aspects of responsibility, it seems clear that a legal debate about the nature and role of expert-system technology is long overdue.

There is a difference between legal liability and professional responsibility. Hence, there is a need for professional codes of practice in this area. The fact that legal issues are still to be resolved, cannot absolve people from professional or ethical responsibility. Although the law may be undecided, some agent nevertheless has to take responsibility. It has been noted that some existing systems have not been put into regular use because no-one 'dared' to authorize their use.

REPLACING HUMAN EXPERTS

Expert systems were originally conceived of as a means of replacing expertise, or of making it more widely available. More recently, it has become apparent that there is far more to being a human expert than can easily be encompassed in a computer system. In many domains an expert's knowledge is the result of years of practical experience and hence some aspects of it tend to be implicit in nature. As Berry (1987) points out, if people learn to perform tasks so that important aspects of their knowledge are implicit in nature, then knowledge engineers will not be able to extract this knowledge and represent it in a meaningful way in a computer system.

Typically, human experts display creativity, highly developed analytical skills, good interpersonal skills and common sense. It has thus been suggested that expert systems should carry out the knowledge-intensive, unimaginative aspects of tasks, leaving the human user free to carry out the more challenging and interesting aspects. In the area of design, for example, the non-creative elements could be allocated to the machine and the creative elements to the human. As Cooley (1987) points out, however, the design activity cannot be separated in this arbitrary way into two disconnected elements. The process by which the creative and non-creative elements are normally united in design is an ill-defined and ill-researched area. He suggests that the sequential basis on which the elements interact is of extreme importance. For example, designers might need experience of the non-creative aspects in order for their creativity to emerge. A further problem is that the computer can carry out the non-creative elements at an incredible rate. As the designer attempts to keep abreast of this and cope with the creative elements, the stress upon him or her might become very severe.

Some researchers are more optimistic about the notion of joint cognitive systems (Rector *et al*, 1985; Woods, 1986; Stenton, 1987; Slatter *et al*, 1988). Woods, for example, has suggested that rather than designing systems to simulate those aspects of reasoning at which human experts are highly competent, a more effective way to employ AI technology would be in supporting those aspects of reasoning at which humans are weak as a result of their built-in cognitive limitations. Examples of such weaknesses in human reasoning include failing to take account of negative evidence, difficulty in thinking through the consequences of complex interactions and weaknesses in counterfactual reasoning.

DESKILLING AND THE EFFECTS ON KNOWLEDGE

Given that so few systems have been in regular use for a long period of time, there is little objective data about their long-term effects. Repeated use of an expert system is almost certain to change the ways in which users tackle problems. One would hope that any change would be beneficial and that systems would have some educational value. As Young (1984) states, increasing a user's understanding of a domain should be considered a primary rather than secondary role of an expert system. He suggests that one measure of success of a consultation with an advisory system is that the user should not have to come back and ask the same questions again the next time a similar problem arises.

Many people worry, however, that expert systems may actually have detrimental effects. It has been suggested that extensive use of a system may lead to an over-reliance on it. Similar concerns have been voiced about the use of calculators. It is often stated that people who rely on calculators lose the ability to perform approximate arithmetic, to verify answers or to notice obvious mistakes. The skills that are required for effective computation using a calculator are different from those for hand calculations. There is a demand for a higher level of conceptualization and the ability to appreciate the capabilities and restrictions of the machine and to evaluate the results.

Nevertheless, calculators do allow more and more complex computations to be carried out in less time. It is not unusual for formal representations to facilitate more complex tasks. For example, the invention of a formal musical notation enabled the creation of highly complex multi-part musical symphonies. Similarly, mathematicians invent notations for their concepts and these forms of notation enable complex theorems to be formulated.

Formal notations can also have limiting effects however. Sinding-Larsen (1988) has studied folk musicians in Norway and has observed a change in the nature of music as a result of the invention of musical notation. He points out that it became very difficult to retain the types of music which could not be represented using the notation. The definition of proper music thus became that which was possible with the notation. Sinding-Larsen draws analogies between this and the effects that expert systems might have on machine-representable versus non-representable knowledge. This implies that knowledge that can be represented in a computer system might in time acquire a different status from that which cannot.

Clearly, expert systems can have far-reaching effects. The challange is to make effective use of the technology for the benefit of individuals, organizations and society. This requires a better understanding of the types of problems that we are trying to solve. The onus is on us, not on machines, and to this end the chapters in this book have drawn attention to many of the important issues that require further consideration.

REFERENCES

Berry, D.C. (1987). The Problem of Implicit Knowledge. *Expert Systems: The International Journal of Knowledge Engineering.* v.4. 144–51.

Berry, D.C. and Broadbent, D.E. (1987). Explanation and Verbalization in a Computer Assisted Search Task. *Quarterly Journal of Experimental Psychology*, 39A. 585–609.

Clegg, C., Warr, P., Green, T., Monk, A., Kemp, N., Allison, G. and Lansdale, M. (1988). *People and Computers: How to evaluate your company's new technology.* Ellis Horwood, Chichester.

Cooley, M. (1987). Creativity, skill and human-centred systems. In B. Goranzon and I. Josefson (eds), *Knowledge, Skill and Artificial Intelligence.* Springer Verlag, London.

Dodson, D.C. (1986). Explanation Explanation....A Brief Sketch. *Proceedings of Alvey IKBS Theme Workshop on Explanation.* University of Surrey. March 1986.

Goodstein, L.P., Andersen, H.B. and Olsen, S.E. (eds) (1988). *Tasks, Errors and Mental Models.* Taylor and Francis, London.

Hart, A. and Wyatt, J. (in press). Connectionist Models in Medicine: An investigation of their potential. *Proceedings of Artificial Intelligence in Medicine*, AIME89. Springer Verlag.

Hollnagel, E., Mancini, G. and Woods, D.D. (eds) (1988). *Cognitive Engineering in Complex Dynamic Worlds.* Academic Press, London.

Hughes, S. (1987). Question Classification in Rule Based Systems. In M. Bramer (ed.), *Research and Development in Expert Systems* III. Cambridge University Press.

Kidd, A. (1985). The Consultative Role of an Expert System. In P. Johnson and S. Cook (eds), *People and Computers: Designing the Interface.* Cambridge University Press.

Monk, A. (1984). How and When to Collect Behavioural Data. In A. Monk (ed.), *Fundamentals of Human Computer Interaction.* Academic Press, London.

Quaglini, S., Stefanelli, M., Barosi, G. and Berzuini, A. (1988). A performance evaluation of the expert system ANEMIA. *Computers in Biomedical Research.* v. 21, 307–323.

Ravden, S. and Johnson, G. (1989). *Evaluating Usability of the Human-Computer Interface.* Ellis Horwood, Chichester.

Rector, A., Newton, P.D. and Marsden, P. (1985). What kind of system does an expert need? In P. Johnson and S. Cook (eds), *People and Computers: Designing the Interface.* Cambridge University Press.

Robson, C. (1973). *Experiment, Design and Statistics in Psychology.* Penguin, Harmondsworth.

Sinding-Larsen, H. (1988). Notation and Music. In H. Sinding-Larsen (ed.), *Artificial Intelligence and Language.* Tano, Oslo.

Slatter, P., Nomura, T. and Lunn, S. (1988). A representation for manufacturing sequencing knowledge to support co-operative problem solving. In *Proceedings of Joint Ergonomics Society/ICL Conference on Human and Organizational Issues of Expert Systems.* Stratford Upon Avon, May 1988.

Spector, P. (1981). *Research Designs.* Sage Publications, London. (Series/ Number 07-023).

Stenton, S.P. (1987). Designing a co-operative interface to an expert system. In *Proceedings of Third International Expert Systems Conference. Learned Information.* Oxford.

Swartout, W. (1986). Knowledge Needed for Expert Systems Explanation. *Future Computing Systems*, v.1, 91–114.

Wickens, C. (1984). *Engineering Psychology and Human Performance.* Merrill, Columbus, Ohio.

Woods, D.D. (1986). Cognitive Technologies: The design of joint human-machine cognitive systems. *AI Magazine*, Winter (6), 86–92.

Wyatt, J. (1987). The evaluation of clinical decision support systems: A discussion of the methodology used in the ACORN project. *Lecture Notes in Medical Informatics*, v.33, 15–24. Springer-Verlag.

Young, R. (1984). Human Interface aspects of Expert Systems. In J. Fox (ed.), *Infotech State of the Art Report on Expert Systems.* Infotech, Pergamon.

Index

Note: KBS (Knowledge Based System) is used throughout the index to represent all types of 'expert system'.

35.00